• NATIONAL ARCHIVES OF INDIA •
Archives in India Historical Reprints

NARRATIVE OF A JOURNEY
OVERLAND FROM ENGLAND

By The
CONTINENT OF EUROPE,
EGYPT, AND THE RED SEA.

to
INDIA

• NATIONAL ARCHIVES OF INDIA •
Archives in India Historical Reprints

NARRATIVE OF A JOURNEY OVERLAND FROM ENGLAND

By The
CONTINENT OF EUROPE, EGYPT, AND THE RED SEA.

to
INDIA

Including

A RESIDENCE THERE, AND VOYAGE HOME, IN THE YEARS 1825, 1826, 1827, and 1828

MRS. COLONEL ELWOOD

IN TWO VOLUMES
VOLUME ONE

ISBN : 978-93-5324-377-7 (Set)
ISBN : 978-93-5324-378-4 Vol. 1 (HB)
First Published, London, 1830
Published, 2020
Published by

Facsimile Publisher
12 Pragati Market
Ashok Vihar, Ph-2
Delhi-110052
E-mail: books@facsimilepublisher.com
Printed at: G. Print Process, Delhi.

• **National Archives of India** •
Archibes in India Historical Reprints

**Narrative of a Journey
Overland from England**

**By The
Continent of Europe,
Egypt, and The Red Sea.**

**to
India**

Mrs. Colonel Elwood

NARRATIVE

OF A

JOURNEY OVERLAND FROM ENGLAND;

BY THE

CONTINENT OF EUROPE,

EGYPT, AND THE RED SEA,

TO

INDIA;

INCLUDING

A RESIDENCE THERE, AND VOYAGE HOME,

IN THE YEARS 1825, 26, 27, AND 28.

BY MRS. COLONEL ELWOOD.

IN TWO VOLUMES.

VOL. I.

LONDON:
HENRY COLBURN AND RICHARD BENTLEY,
NEW BURLINGTON STREET.
1830.

PREFACE.

In submitting the following letters to the public, the writer is acting upon the suggestions of those on whose judgment she has a firmer reliance than on her own, and who are of opinion, that they may possibly be deemed not wholly uninteresting at this peculiar time, when India, and the over-land communication with that country, are topics of such general conversation.

She begs also to state, that in so doing, she is likewise complying with the wishes of several friends, who have frequently expressed themselves desirous of being informed of the particulars of her journey to, and residence in India.

She fears that some may deem her presumptuous, in thus offering observations to the public, which were made upon the spot, frequently under the disadvantageous circumstances of exposure to Siroccos and Camseens—whilst travelling in a Takhtrouan or Palanquin—sailing in Cangias, Dows, and Pattemars, and living in Tents, Caravanseras, and Durrumsallahs,—all which were originally written in a journal kept merely for her own private amusement, and in their present form were addressed to a near and very dear relation. But, since she can safely affirm that she has given a true and faithful description of what she saw and felt, in the very peculiar circumstances in which she occasionally found herself, and in the singular countries which it was her fate to visit, and since, if she may judge from her own feelings, women naturally take a lively interest in what concerns their own sex, she flatters herself, that the following account of the adventures of the first and only female who has hitherto ventured over-land from England to India, may at least prove not wholly unacceptable to the fair part of the reading community. She likewise hopes, that it is not impossible some future over-land traveller may derive benefit from her experience, which has already enabled her to give hints, and to furnish suggestions and information, that have been found useful by parties proceeding to and returning from India.

CONTENTS

OF

THE FIRST VOLUME.

ERRATA.

VOL. I.

Page		for		read	
2	*for*	Tachtrouan	*read*	Takhtrouan
128	—	Patiensa	—	Pazienzia
260	—	Agermens	—	Agrémens
349	—	Jovett	—	Jowett
350	—	Attargut	—	Attargul
368	—	tops	—	topes

VOL. II.

Page		for		read	
19	*for*	poortruy	*read*	poortrays
65	—	Styavratar	—	Styavrata
73	—	Imam	—	Imaun
73	—	Maji	—	Magi
180	—	Raoka	—	Rao ka
197. 199. 200 } 201. 208. 208, }	—	Jahrejah	—	Jharejah
246	—	presents	—	present
247	—	Note. Buhootacha	—	Buhoot acha
251	—	See	—	Sie
277	—	Hulwud	—	Hulwaod
315	—	Vivants	—	Vivans
322	—	Sinbad	—	Sindbad

LIST OF ENGRAVINGS.

VOL. I.

VOL. II.

JOURNEY

OVERLAND FROM

ENGLAND TO INDIA.

LETTER I.

Departure from England.—Paris.—Fontainbleau.—Dijon.—
The Jura.—Beautiful view near Vattay.—Geneva.

MY DEAR SISTER.

SINCE you wish me to give you an account
of our Journey from England to India, and of
our residence in the latter country, I shall have
much pleasure in complying with your request ;
for even in this erratic age, when every one
talks familiarly of

> " The Alps and Apennines,
> The Pyrenean, and the river Po,"

I believe I may safely say, that I am the only
Lady who ever travelled thither overland, by
this, or perhaps by any other route ; and probably mine was the first Journal ever kept by

an Englishwoman in the Desert of the Thebais, and on the shores of the Red Sea. Instead of the Popes and Cardinals who grace the Diaries of other migratory damsels, you will meet with Agas and Cacheffs, and hear of Pashas and Rajahs ; and for the ceremonies of the Holy Week, you will have the initiatory rites of the Mahometan Hadje, the Mohurrum, and the Hindoo Hoolie. You must ascend the Pyramids, and descend into Joseph's well, penetrate into the tomb of King Sesostris, and explore the caves of Elephanta. You will be exposed to Camseens and Siroccos; to Monsoons and Tropical heats ; you will sail in Egyptian Cangias, Arab Dows, and Indian Pattemars ; travel in a Tacktrouan and Palanquin; take up your abode in Tents, Caravanseras, and Durrumsallahs ; hear of places seldom or perhaps never before visited by any of our countrywomen ; and I shall have the pleasure of introducing you to a Turkish Divan at Djidda, an Arab Haram at Hodeida, a Jahrejah's Zenana at Bhooj, and a Bramin's Pinjrapole at Broach. Have you the courage to accompany me ? *Allons donc.*

When we first started our idea of travelling to India by the way of Egypt, our project was treated as visionary by several, and numbers considered it as impracticable *for a Lady*. Some kind friends sought to deter us by magnifying

the dangers of the expedition, and others recommended "a comfortable China ship" in preference; but though we were fully aware this
was a route hitherto but little frequented even
by gentlemen, and that *no* lady had ever attempted the *outward* overland journey to Bombay, we were not to be deterred by imaginary
difficulties. We resolved, at least, to *try* whether our plan were feasible, and we found in
the variety of the interesting countries through
which we passed, sufficient amply to compen-
sate for the fatigue and inconveniences we encountered on our journey.

Our chief embarrassment was, the difficulty
and the uncertainty of obtaining a passage
down the Red Sea, which obstacle does not
exist on the route homewards, as ships not unfrequently sail at once from Bombay to Cosseir.
However, as we heard from the family of
Lieutenant-General the Honourable Sir Charles
Colville, that he intended to return from India to England through Egypt, and that he
would leave Bombay in November, we determined to proceed quickly to Cosseir, in order
to take advantage of his ship, and as we did
not take into consideration the Sirocco, the
storms, and the pirates of the Mediterranean,
we calculated we might reach that place easily
by Christmas.

On the 6th of October, 1825, we left Windmill Hill for New Susans, at East Bourne, which latter place we quitted on the 8th, and proceeded along the coast to Dover, our first day's journey on our route to India!

Washington Irving asks, " Who can tell, when he sets forth to wander, whither he may be driven by the uncertain currents of existence, or whether it may ever be his lot to re-visit the scenes of his childhood?" This idea, independent of parting with one's family and friends, would necessarily sadden the heart; but I will not trouble you with an account of my feelings at leaving my native land; and as you must be well acquainted with Paris and the road thither, I will spare you any description of the country, which at this time was rich in all the varied hues of autumn ;

" Dusk and dun, of every hue, from wan declining green
To sooty dark ;"

and merely observe, that we crossed to Calais on the 9th, and sleeping at Montreuil sur Mèr and Granvilliers, we reached the gay metropolis of France on the evening of the 12th. There is no occasion to trouble you with an account of the Tuileries, the Louvre, the Hotel des Invalides, and all the other lions, with which you are as much at home as myself; and therefore we will proceed at once to Fontainbleau.

With the palace there we were certainly much
gratified ; but we were far more interested in
one small room, simply and unostentatiously
furnished, than with all the other splendid and
magnificent suites of apartments through which
we passed. On a table there, as simple in its
structure as remarkable for the deed performed
on it, Napoleon signed his abdication, and on
it may still be seen the marks of the pen-knife,
which in the perturbed state of an agitated
mind, he hastily dashed on its surface. The
scenery of the forest of Fontainbleau was wooded
and pretty, and after passing Sens, we followed
the windings of the Yonne, upon whose broad
and peaceful bosom several barges were sailing,
and whose graceful meanderings through a fertile country added much to its beauty.

On the 17th we slept at Auxerre, the ancient
Autisiodorum, and on the three successive
nights at Rouvray ; at Dijon, the former capital of Burgundy, and the birth-place of Bos-
suet, Buffon, and Crebillon, which, with its two
fine spires, of St. Benigne, 375 feet, and St.
Jean, 300 feet high, stands in a fertile plain,
enriched with vineyards ; and at Poligny, situated at the immediate base of the Jura, in
whose neighbourhood the vines began to disappear, and were replaced by trees and brush-
wood. On the 21st we commenced to ascend

these mountains by a steep but excellent road,
the sides of which were prettily fringed with
shrubs, and we soon passed a magnificent defile,
beautifully wooded with beech and fir trees,
where the dark and sombre hues of the latter,
powdered with a slight shower of snow, presented a pleasing and striking contrast to those
of the former, at this time rich in every autumnal tint. We passed a fine cascade at
Dombief, and we continued among fine Alpine
scenery, till a rapid descent brought us upon
Morêt, a pretty little town, standing close to a
brawling stream denominated Le Bief de la
Chaille, and upon the river Bienne, which flowing through a narrow valley, inclosed by perpendicular rocks of prodigious height, scarcely
leaves room for two rows of houses and the
street that separates them. In this secluded
spot, buried apparently in one of the deepest
dells of the Alpine regions, we spent the night;
and on the following morning we ascended
a very high mountain, occasionally passing
through immense forests of fir, which were
literally bending under the weight of the snow
with which they were covered, whilst our road
continued along fearfully steep precipices,
where not the slightest parapet intervened
between us and destruction. Above frowned
awfully stupendous rocks, and over the per-

pendicular cliffs we beheld a beautiful and a fertile valley smiling beneath. At times, emerging from the deepest solitudes, might be seen parties of smugglers stealing cautiously along in search of an illicit and unlawful gain, daring and encountering dangers, the which but to think of quite horrified the imagination.

After passing Vattay, a sudden turn of the road brought us upon one of the most magnificent views that can be conceived. We were among the wintry snows and cloud-capped hills of the Jura, and the lovely Lake of Geneva, with the luxuriant and beautiful Pays de Vaud, burst suddenly upon our enraptured sight; whilst beyond towered the majestic Alps of the Valais, and the stupendous mountains and glaciers of Savoy. It was one of the loveliest and finest scenes we ever beheld, and the bare recollection, in itself, amply compensates for the fatigues and troubles of travelling. We then began rapidly to descend, and we soon left the stormy regions of the summits of the Jura for the well-wooded scenery and fertile pasturage at the base; and after passing Voltaire's villa at Ferney, we quickly reached the cheerful and well-cultivated environs of Geneva, the scenery of which lake is at once sublime and beautiful, and is interesting to the poet and the man of taste from its associations with departed genius. " Voltaire, Rousseau, our Gibbon, and De Staël," and that immortal poet, who erst-while sung his illustrious predecessors, and who loved to sail upon its bosom, and seek for " Mont Blanc, the ' Monarch of Mountains,' " as reflected in its glassy wave, have all resided upon its banks, and their dwellings, and the places described and immortalized by them, are now eagerly sought for, and pointed out to the traveller in these magnificent and romantic regions.

LETTER II.

Aix aux Bains.—Chamberi.—Valley of La Maurienne.—Lans le Bourg.—Passage of Mont Cenis.—Susa.—Valley of the Doria Reparia.—Turin.

A brilliant sun illuminated and animated the landscape as we left Geneva, though a bitterly cold blast blew from the snow-capped mountains and icy glaciers in its vicinity. We passed over a succession of well-cultivated and pastoral-looking hills and dales, till we reached Aix aux Bains, whose warm and sulphurous waters were known to the Romans, and are still in high repute. Chamberi, the capital of Savoy, is a pretty little town, situated in a rich and fertile plain, watered by the rivulets

Leisse and Albano. The heights in the immediate neighbourhood are covered with vineyards, pasturage, and forests of fir. Lady Mary Wortley Montague and Rousseau both spent some time here, and we never saw any place which appeared better calculated for an agreeable residence. At Mont Melian we had a noble view of the Alps: Mont Blanc was, however, so coy, that he seldom vouchsafed to unveil his majestic head. We here saw one of the unfortunate ideots, so common in these mountainous regions. He was sitting basking in the sun, at the door of a cottage, yet, though we were positively shocked at his appearance, he had a happy and contented air, and seemed much pleased at our putting a piece of money into his hand, turning it over and over, and playing with it as with a toy.

The military road commences at Aiguebelle, and we then entered the wild and desolate tract of country called La Maurienne; a narrow valley, which gradually contracts, whilst the awful and stupendous Alps approach so near as barely to leave room for the road, and for the river Arc, a noisy, rapid, and brawling stream, which is a tributary to the Isère. St. Jean de Maurienne, where we slept, is the capital of these cheerless regions, and it really seems like an outpost to the stronghold where Winter maintains an everlasting reign, amongst snowy mountains and icy glaciers. Amidst this desolation, however, we occasionally came upon some exquisite little *morceaux* of scenery, beautiful and picturesque as can be conceived, and like the oases in the desert, doubly interesting from the contrast they presented with all around. The dark fir, the yellow birch, the red beech, with their autumnal tints and rich foliage, formed a delightful refreshment to the eye that had just rested on the rude and rugged Alps of the background.

After passing Modano the road became one sheet of ice; the mountains were whitened with eternal snows, and where their precipitous sides prevented it from remaining, dark and barren rocks abruptly burst to view. Innumerable waterfalls and cascades, often arrested and fast bound in mid-air, presented themselves, whilst the river ran brawling by with impetuous fury. We kept gradually ascending, and the air became piercingly cold, till at the head of a long, gloomy, and dreary valley, we at last reached Lans le Bourg, situated at the base of Mont Cenis, which was frowning several thousand feet aloft in the air. As we gazed on the snow-capped mountain, shining in dazzling splendour beneath the radiant light of the moon, we could but exclaim,

" And yet e'en here
Does winter in a lovely dress appear."

Mont Cenis, over whose summit, 11,977 feet
high, Pompey the Great is said to have attempted a passage, from his days to those of
Napoleon, was only to be crossed on mules, or
in *chaises à porteurs.* In 1811, in the space of
five months, the Imperial energy of the latter,
aided by the talents of Fabbroni, caused a road
to be cut by three thousand workmen, by which
the heaviest carriages may now pass at every
season of the year; and the most delicate invalid, the most nervous lady, may be safely
transported from the valley of the Arc to that
of the Doria Reparia.

After crossing a handsome wooden bridge, we
began slowly to ascend the mountain with six
horses, passing through forests of fir and larch
covered with snow, and by several Refuges,
twenty-six in number, which have been erected
for the safety and accommodation of the unfortunate traveller who might be storm-bound
or benighted on these wintry wastes. The
road gradually wound up the side; and on
reaching the top, as if to congratulate us
that we were about to leave the churlish regions of the north for the more genial climate
of Italy, the sun in full splendour suddenly
burst from behind dense clouds, disclosing to

view a wintry scene of the most brilliant magnificence. 6027 feet above the level of the sea,
and surrounded by a parapet of frowning
mountains 9260 feet high, upon the bosom of
the plain of San Nicolo, where was scattered
the little hamlet of Les Tavernelles, sparkled
a beautiful little lake, said to be unfathom-
able. Bright confusion reigned around, and
a dazzling waste of snow fatigued the eye,
whilst every shrub glittered with icicles, and
every pointed thorn and blade of grass seemed
as if it were wrought in glass.

The Hospice, founded by Charlemagne, was
restored by Napoleon, to whom travellers cannot feel too much obliged for having, like Hannibal, melted the Alps, by making good roads,
and providing excellent accommodations, in
places formerly the retreat of wolves and bears.

The scenery on the Piedmontese side of
Mont Cenis is, perhaps, even superior to that
on the Savoyard. Stupendous rocks, rugged
precipices, headlong torrents and noble cascades,
are seen in every direction, till the fertile little
valley of Cenis, with the villages of Novalezza
and Velano, are discovered smiling some thousand feet below.

After passing Molarêt, near which an ava-
lanche often falls, we took leave of these regions of eternal frost and snow, and soon came

upon chesnut trees in all their autumnal
glories; vines hanging in tangled festoons from
tree to tree, and olives lightly waving in the air,
alternately displaying a deep green or a silvery
hue, as the chance breeze, carelessly kissing the
leaves, turned them to the eye of the beholder.

In six hours and a half from Lans le Bourg,
we crossed Mont Cenis, and reached Susa on
the opposite side, which, from its frontier situation, is not unaptly termed " the key of Italy,
and the gate of war." Its ancient name was
Segusium, which was built by Augustus,
when he wished to keep open a route into
Dauphiné. Tradition relates that it was by
this route Hercules passed to subdue Gaul, and
by the self-same that Hannibal came to conquer Italy. The valley of the Doria Reparia,
rich and fertile in mulberry trees, and vines
" married to their consort elms," is surrounded
by lofty mountains, whose sides are clothed
with verdure, and where may be seen, nestling
on high, churches and convents in the most
romantic situations. The softness of the scenery, the brilliancy of the sun, the serenity
of the Italian sky, formed a striking and delightful contrast to the frost-bound valley of
La Maurienne, and to the brawling river Arc,
the desolate regions we were traversing on the
yesterday. A noble road, perfectly straight,

and planted on both sides with trees, conducted us to Turin, which we entered by the magnificent Strada della Dora Grossa, three thousand feet long; and we soon reached the superb Piazza del Castello, which is esteemed one of the largest and handsomest in Europe, and which was at this time illuminated by the splendid light of the full moon, in these happy regions scarcely inferior to the wintry sunshine of northern climes. As we refreshed ourselves by a blazing fire, we thought ourselves fortunate in having traversed Mont Cenis before the season was farther advanced, and we congratulated ourselves at being at L'Hotêl de l'Univers at Turin, rather than at L'Hotêl Royal at Lans le Bourg.

LETTER III.

Turin.—Duomo.—Capella della Santissima Sindone.—Palaces. — Museum. — Alexandria. — Marengo. — Genoa.—Beautiful Scenery.—Massa.—Lucca.—Pisa.

TURIN may boast of very high antiquity, if it were founded, as tradition relates, by Phædon, the brother of Osiris, who, 1529 years before Christ, brought an Egyptian colony thither, and constructed a city at the confluence of the Po and the Doria, upon which he bestowed a name significant of the God Apis. In his selection of a spot he certainly displayed much taste, for the situation is most beautiful. It stands on a fertile plain, bounded by gently swelling hills, with a majestic line of snowy mountains in the background, whose ice-covered summits towering aloft, cleave the air like embattled pinnacles. From one particular spot in the Piazza del Castello, several streets diverge as from a common centre, each terminating in a vista of the most magnificent and beautiful scenery. The Duomo, which is dedicated to John the Baptist, was founded by Agilas, and was repaired in 1498. Behind the high altar is the Chapel of La Santissima Sindone, which being wholly composed of black marble, has a somewhat lugubrious and funereal appearance; its cupola, by Guarini, which is formed of arches interlacing each other, has, perhaps, rather a singular than a pleasing effect. In the Museum of the University are several statues, which the French, in their days of spoliation, considered worthy of being carried off, in order to their being installed in the Louvre. There is also the celebrated Isiac tablet, which was discovered in Mantua.* The interior of the King's Palace, in

* This valuable relic of ancient art, on the plunder of

the Piazza del Castello, is gorgeous beyond conception, and contains some good pictures. Its exterior presents a striking contrast to the ancient domicile of the Dukes of Savoy, which stands in the centre of the same square. Among the modern buildings with which it is surrounded, the latter edifice certainly looks out of its place, and, moreover, the majestic and venerable appearance of the frowning old fabric is much injured by the fine Corinthian front, which in the time of Lewis XIV. was patched on in very bad taste by Christina.

Leaving Turin, we crossed the Po by a magnificent bridge, and proceeded along a noble road to Asti, once celebrated for its hundred towers, and famous for being the birth-place of Alfieri. Alexandria stands on the Tanaro, in the fertile plain of Lombardy, abounding in corn-fields,

Rome by the army of Charles the Fifth, about the year 1527, became the property of a common artificer, and was sold by him to Cardinal Bembo, by whose name it has since been frequently distinguished. At the death of that Cardinal, the Table of Isis came into the possession of the Duke of Mantua, in whose family it was preserved as an inestimable rarity till the palace of Mantua was plundered of its immense treasure of curiosities by the Imperial General, in 1630, after which it was for some time lost to the world. This curious tablet exhibits at one view, under various human and bestial figures, the deities adored in Egypt, but is supposed by the learned to allude particularly to the mystic rites of Isis and Osiris.

mulberry-trees, and vineyards. Not far from thence is Marengo, where the battle took place, June 14, 1800, when Napoleon headed the French in person ; but there is nothing now to mark where contending armies fought and bled : even the column that was erected where Desaix fell is no more to be seen. After Voltaggio, instead of crossing the summit of the Bocchetta, we penetrated through the romantic defile of the Val di Scrivia, and soon after the Mediterranean burst upon our view, and the well cultivated environs of Genoa. The road runs along the banks of the mountain-stream Polcevera, which, though by nature originally merely bare and rugged rocks, by the hand of art are now studded with magnificent villas, and the whole ravine is richly planted and ornamented with orange and lemon groves, olives, vineyards, and cypresses, whilst that graceful tree the flat-topped pine greets the eye in every direction, and beautifully diversifies the view. A sudden turn of the road brought us upon Genoa, *la superba*, which, like a city of enchantment, raised by the potent wand of a magician, burst most unexpectedly upon our astonished sight in all its beauty and magnificence. Springing immediately from the bosom of the vasty deep, were marble palaces and superb edifices gradually rising up the base of the hill,

whilst immediately behind rose the lofty alti-
tude of the Alps, frowning in awful grandeur,
and forming an apparently inaccessible barrier.
It was a striking spectacle, and so like a fairy
scene, that we could have almost expected to
have seen it vanish into empty air. The whole
was lighted up with the rich blaze of an Italian
setting sun. The palaces and churches of
Genoa are richly and even gorgeously ornamented, but we were most struck with the
Church of Carignano, which, situated on the
swell of a hill, is connected with the neighbouring one by a bridge thrown boldly over
the deep ravine that separates them ; and looking down, we were surprised to behold a regular
street in the hollow dell below. This is an
interesting monument of the affection of a
Genoese husband, who built it to save his lady
fair the fatigue of daily ascending and descending the steep declivity when she went to mass.
Oh those days of conjugal gallantry ! when
will Europe produce such another hero ?

The immediate neighbourhood of Genoa is
absolutely studded with palaces and villas,
agreeably diversified with olives and cypresses,
groves of chesnut-trees and vineyards. Thanks
to a kicking horse, we were here nearly precipitated into the Mediterranean ; however, we
escaped without any farther damage than the

being constrained to submit to very inferior
accommodations at Recco ; but perhaps we had
no business to complain, for royalty had recently put up with the same, as our host informed us with harmless vanity and ostenta-
tion, that " the Kings of Sardinia and of Naples, but a short time before, had breakfasted
in the very room we were dining in !" When
we again set forth, we were much amused at
his addressing us with great *naïveté* and *bonhommie*, and telling us he hoped we should
often call to mind and think of " Il Grande
Reale Albergo di Recco, and the host and
hostess, Monsieur and Madame Lavoir." We
were off before sun-rise, and, dimly appearing
through the gray twilight, we passed some of
the most romantic scenery imaginable—swelling hills, clothed with the richest foliage, and
glens tapestried down to the water's edge,
thrown into deep shade, whilst young-eyed
Day advancing, every moment revealed some
new beauty, and produced a fresh exclamation
of delight. The road from thence to Borghetto
was very bad, but the views were magnificent.
Sometimes we beheld the blue waters of the
Mediterranean resting in calm tranquillity in
numerous creeks and inlets, whilst round the
bold headlands of the coast the bright waves
petulantly played, sparkling in the morning

sun, and sportively reflecting back the beau-
teous scenes around. Convents might be seen
nestling high in the bosom of the mountains,
or partially revealing themselves among the
deep recesses of thick groves of chesnuts and
lightly waving olives. The rocks were fringed
with myrtle and arbutus ; rich clumps of vi-
vidly green orange trees flourished around ;
the vines hung in tangled festoons, Indian figs
and aloes grew in luxuriance, and the spiral
cypress contrasted itself with the beautiful flat-
topped pine. At times we ascended lofty
mountains of marble, and looked over a magnificent horizon of sea ; then, descending to
the shore, we found ourselves amid vineyards
and plantations of mulberries. We slept at
Borghetto, and on the following day we passed
Spezià, prettily placed at the head of a deep
gulf, Sarzana and Laventia, from which last port
the Carrara marble is embarked for the different countries of Europe. We then crossed a
well-cultivated country to Massa, which is
agreeably situated at the foot of the Apennines, and o'er-topped by a huge castle. We
were here much amused with the *naïveté* of
a stout-looking girl, who asked for charity,
"that she might get a husband." Now as no
one would be cruel enough to disappoint a
demoiselle of " *un bon parti*," we willingly

contributed our mite to the furtherance of the views of this would-be slave of the ring.

A fertile plain covered with olive-trees, and vines flinging themselves fantastically and coquettishly from tree to tree, and often suspended in tangled festoons across the road, led to Pietra Santa, in whose neighbourhood we began to see the noxious marshes that produce such prejudicial effects. Lucca, *la industriosa*, is nearly enclosed by the Apennines, and stands in a vale, irrigated by the river Serchio, which is so well, and so minutely cultivated, that it looks like one large productive garden. The ramparts have a singular appearance, from being planted with forest-trees, which make it look like a fortified wood ; and the town has a Flemish, rather than an Italian appearance. The cathedral, built about 1070, is a fine gothic edifice. Its façade of marble is composed of arches interlacing each other, and it contains the tombs of Adalbert the Rich ; the progenitor, according to Muratori, of the House of Este, and of the Countess Matilda, the champion of the Church, and the guardian and instructress of " il fanciullo Rinaldo." At length the Apennines opening and receding to some distance, disclosed to view the immense plains in the neighbourhood of Pisa, which, with its famous leaning tower, appeared in the horizon, though this peculiarity was not very perceptible till we were in its immediate neighbourhood. Indeed, several of the other edifices are also very considerably out of the perpendicular, which some attribute to an earthquake, others to a great fire, and others again say, that from some unknown cause, the ground, and consequently the foundations, have given way. An air of solitude and of desolation reigns in the vicinity of this city, which appears as if it still were suffering from the effects of its ancient wars with its rival Florence; but, however, though shorn of its pristine grandeur, it still retains an imposing appearance, and offers much to interest and to amuse the traveller.

LETTER IV.

Pisa — Its origin.— Duomo.— Battistereo.— Campanile. — Campo Santo.—Curious frescos.—Fire in the Hotel.— Road to Florence.

TRADITION assigns to Pisa an Arcadian origin, and tells us it was founded by the inhabitants of its namesake in Elis; others, who wish to give it a still higher antiquity, trace it back to Pelops, the son of Tantalus. It figured in the wars of the Guelphs and Ghibellines,

and in 1509 it passed under the yoke of the
Medicis; since which period, with its freedom
have also expired its grandeur and population.
In the days of its glory it rendered considerable assistance to the Crusaders, and its conquering fleet, the terror of the Saracens and
the African corsairs, wrested from them Sardinia, Palermo, Carthage, and delivered Alexandria from its besiegers. The decidedly
Oriental style that pervades the architecture
of its highly ornamented edifices, bespeaks its
early connexion with the East; and, indeed,
the curious little church of Santa Maria della
Spina so exactly resembled some of the buildings we subsequently saw in Arabia, that we
might easily have fancied, like the migratory
house of Loretto, that it had flown hither
from thence through the air. In an insulated
corner of the city stands the Duomo, the
Battistereo, the Campanile, and the Campo
Santo, forming, perhaps, a group unparalleled
in beauty, and deriving additional interest
from their secluded position, and from the
awful silence and sanctified quietude that prevail in their sacred precincts. The exterior of
the Duomo is not particularly striking, but its
interior presents a noble gothic structure, rich
in marble columns and fine pictures. The
Battistereo, a fine rotunda, resembles an ancient

temple, and contains a font so exquisitely carved, that it looks like fairy-work, and a fine marble pulpit, the *chef-d'œuvre* of Nicolo Pisano. The singularly graceful Campanile, with its eight light and airy galleries of arches, is so peculiarly elegant, that, with Matthews, we thought it might well bring leaning towers into fashion throughout Christendom. But the glory of Pisa is its unique and beautiful Campo Santo. The holy earth, brought from Mount Calvary by Archbishop Ubaldo Lanfranco, is enclosed in a rectangular building, surrounded by arched cloisters, richly ornamented with exquisite gothic or arabesque tracery. This is the cemetery of more than six hundred illustrious families, whose monuments appear on the walls and pavement : and here I would recommend all those who are too much in love with the pomps and vanities of this wicked world, to take a solitary ramble, to " consociate with their sister worm," " and mingle with the dead." I do assure you, it would prove more beneficial than a thousand sermons, though, like myself, I fear, in returning to the crowd, even the Campo Santo of Pisa would be forgotten.

The tomb of the Countess Beatrice, the mother of the Countess Matilda, is an ancient sarcophagus, covered with bassi relievi. The walls

of the edifice are painted by the early masters,
Giotto, Buffelmacco, Ghirlandajo, and others.
Among these interesting frescos which are sadly
defaced by time, the most striking are the Tri-
umphs of Death and the Last Judgment, by
Andrea Orcagna, and the Infernal Regions, by
his brother Bernardo.   In the first, a group of
gay cavaliers is represented as gazing at a
hideous spectacle of mortality, three bodies in
different stages of decomposition.   The departure of the soul from the body is quaintly
expressed by small figures issuing from the
mouth, as the dying men breathe their last
sigh ; whilst, in the true Parsee style, good and
bad angels are watching to seize them, and one
spirit is nearly torn asunder in mid air by the
contending parties.   Demons are depicted as
pointing and hissing at the expiring persons in
a most contemptuous manner ; whilst Sin is
personified by the serpent crawling everywhere,
and defiling every place with its filthy slime.
The execution of this allegory is, perhaps, not
equal to the boldness of the original idea, but
still there is a vigour of conception in this,
and in many of the other productions of the
early masters, often superior to the polish and
refinement of later artists.   Indeed, to the
lover of the beaux arts, Pisa is highly interesting as the cradle where they were nur-

tured and cultivated in their infant state, and
from whence they subsequently emanated, to
arise to such glorious perfection at Florence
and Rome. Giunto Pisano preceded even
Cimabue and Giotto, who may be denominated
the patriarchs of painting. The art of sculpture was revived by Nicolo Pisano, and his
sons Giovanni and Andrea; and of their skill
in architecture, the unrivalled Campo Santo still
affords an exquisite specimen.

About midnight our slumbers were disturbed by dismal shrieks, and cries of "*al
fuoco, al fuoco!*" and we beheld from our window the whole street illuminated by a 'lurid
light, and all the neighbourhood on the *qui
vive*. To our anxious enquiries of a venerable
priest, who was gazing from his casement at
the fire, as to whether the fire were in our
neighbourhood, we obtained a calm and composed " Sicuro." " Was it in the street?"
" Sicuro." " In our hotel?" " Sicuro." Sig-
nore Sicuro was right; the fire *was* in the
hotel, and all was terror and confusion. It had
originated in the flame of a lamp communi-
cating with a musquito-net, and but for the
gallantry of some Greeks, who fortunately
were in the house, and who, hearing female
shrieks, in the true Conrad style rushed to the

assistance of the inhabitants of the apartment where the fire originated, and at their own personal risk extinguished it, the albergo might have been burnt to the ground. It appeared to be our fate to fall in with fires, for we had but a short time before been present at one of a similar description at Lausanne ; and whilst horror-struck we were gazing at the awful conflagration which threatened to consume the cathedral, and perhaps the city, I shall not easily forget a waiter, who on being told, in answer to his enquiry where some one was, " *Il est parti ;*" with looks of consternation and dismay, lifted up his hands and eyes, and ejaculated, " *Mon Dieu ! et—il—n'a—pas—payé !*"

On the following morning we proceeded along the banks of the Arno to Florence. The country is level and fertile, abounding in wheat and vegetables, olives, vines, and mulberries, but its beauty is spoilt by the minute subdivisions and the hideous stone walls, that often totally obscure the view. We saw San Miniato at a distance, from whence the Buonaparte family is said to have derived its origin ; and we passed some considerable potteries, where were earthen jars of such immense size, that they reminded us of the exploits of Morgiana's

friends " the forty thieves." At the doors of
the cottages were peasant-girls plaiting the
Leghorn straw ; a comely race, with little black
beaver hats, ornamented with tremendous
plumes of ostrich feathers, on their heads, and
their persons decorated with a prodigious quantity of rings, necklaces, ear-rings, &c. We
soon after reached the gates of Firenza, *la
bella*, and in this beautiful city we took up
our abode for the night.

LETTER V.

Florence.—Piazza del Gran Duca.—Gallery.—Palazzo Pitti.
—Churches of San Lorenzo and of Santa Croce.—Duomo.
—Battistereo.—Campanile.—Museum.

FLORENCE, the Etrurian Athens, the capital of Tuscany, possesses in an eminent degree
that nameless charm, that indescribable fasci-
nation, which is derived from the associations
connected with departed genius. Her churches
are consecrated to the imagination by the ashes
of the mighty dead which they contain, whilst
her swelling domes and splendid palaces, can-
vass that glows and marble that breathes, show
what mind has done, what mind may do. She
is rich in reminiscences of the middle ages, and

" Not a stone
In the broad pavement, but to him who has
An eye and ear for th' inanimate world,
Tells of past ages."

Surrounded by a majestic range of hills, she stands in a fertile plain, on the banks of the poetical Arno, whose clear and placid waters add considerably to the beauty of her situation. If the beaux arts originated at Pisa, they were matured and perfected here ; and if liberty languished, learning and science flourished under the patronage of the Medicis. But we must proceed to the far-famed Gallery, where, if you will accompany us, you will see some superb specimens of their taste and munificence. In the way thither you pass through the Piazza del Gran Duca, where, under the fine Loggia of Andrea Orcagna, are the Perseus of Benvenuto Cellini, the Judith of Donatello, and the Rape of the Sabine, by Giovanni di Bologna. Also, an equestrian statue of Cosmo I. by the same master ; Neptune, by Ammannato ; and in front of the Palazzo Vecchio, the colossal David of Buonarotti, and the Hercules of Bandinelli. There are some curious frescos by Vasari, representing many of the principal events that took place during the republican times ; and you may see several portraits of the Medicis, if you feel interested in their

fortunes, and are disposed to pay a visit to the
interior of the palace, whose tower, by Arnolfo
di Lapo, is esteemed a masterpiece of architecture.   Close by, is the Loggia degl' Uffizii,
erected by Cosmo I. from the designs of Vasari,
from whence you enter the Gallery, after ascending a very fatiguing staircase.   In a ves-
tibule are several busts of the Medicis, placed
there as if to welcome the traveller to this
splendid and magnificent collection of the
works of art ; but they have but little power
to detain, for every one hastens to pay their
homage to " the statue that enchants the
world ;" probably the most exquisite personification of perhaps the sweetest idea that ever
floated across a poetical imagination ;

> " The loveliest dream
> That ever left the sky on the deep soul to beam."

In an elegant octagon paved with marble,
and encrusted with mother-of-pearl, stands, as
in a temple, filling the air around with beauty,
the celebrated Venus de' Medici.   She has such
indescribable modesty and dignity, such con-
summate grace, that every other statue looks
clumsy by her side.   The Apollino is the only
one worthy of her, and he and the Venus really
seem made for each other ; but what business
have the Knife-grinder, the Wrestlers, or even

the Faun, in the presence of the charming Queen of Love and Beauty? If, after seeing her, you can admire any other sculpture, you will perhaps be pleased with the Genius of Death, with the Mercury of Giovanni di Bologna, who, standing on a Zephyr, appears ready to soar aloft into the air, and with the sweet figure of Psyche, who seems gazing regretfully after her Cupid, who has vanished from her enamoured sight. The Hall of Niobe is a most elegant apartment, but the pathos of the story is totally spoilt by the tasteless arrangement of the statues, which, instead of forming one interesting group, are placed round the room like so much furniture. Among the most striking pictures are two Holy Families; La Fornarina and St. John, by Raphael; an exquisite Virgin and Child, by Correggio; the Venuses of Titian; a Virgin by Guido, and by that magician of painters, Guercino, a Sibyl, and Endymion. In Eastern climes, this last picture has frequently been recalled to my memory, where the silvery crescent of the moon may often be seen sinking towards the earth as here depicted. These are all in the Tribune; but in the other cabinets, or *studioli*, are the famous Medusa of Leonardo da Vinci, the sight of which alarmed his father, and filled him with horror and dread; a sweet Magdalen, by Carlo Dolce; a magnificent pic-

ture of our Saviour delivering the Souls in
Purgatory, by Baroccio; Madame de Sevigné
and the Countess Grignan, by Mignard; and
with all "the hair-brain sentimental traces" of
a poet, Alfieri, and "sua Donna," the Countess
of Albany. Besides these, are two rooms full
of the portraits of painters, and a cabinet of
gems rich in agates, chrysolites, and topazes,
statues of amber, and columns of alabaster,
recalling the Arabian Nights to the memory.

If not fatigued with this enumeration, will
you proceed onwards to the Palace Pitti, and
see the Venus of Canova, who stands in an
elegant apartment, hung with pier-glasses.
Like the bashful Musidora, she seems shrinking
from every gaze, and casts a timid, fearfully
modest look around, as if wishing to hide
herself from the garish eye of day. There are
also some magnificent pictures here. The
sweet, the incomparable Madonna della Seggiola,
by Raphael; Bentivoglio, by Vandyke; St.
Mark, by Frà Bartolomeo; Catiline's Con-
spiracy, by Salvator Rosa; and that sternly
impressive one, by Buonarotti, of the Fates.

The exterior of many of the churches in
Florence presents a strange contrast to their
highly ornamented interior. Some, San Lorenzo for instance, resemble old barns, and the
traveller is quite surprised to see the profusion

of marbles and gorgeous decorations within.
This church was built by Juliana, and consecrated in A. D. 392. It was rebuilt by Brunellesco, in 1425, and in it may be seen in a
few minutes the whole history of the family of
the Medicis. Under a marble slab sleeps " Cos-
mus Medicis, Decreto Publico, Pater Patriæ."
A porphyry tomb, by Verrecchio, encloses the
remains of his sons Pietro and Giovanni, and
Lorenzo the Magnificent reposes with his brother in one of bronze. Giuliano, the brother
of Leo X. has immortality bestowed on him in
a monument by Michael Angelo Buonarotti,
whose Day and Night produced the following
lines :—

"" La notte che tu vedi, in si dolce atto
  Dormire, fu da un Angelo scolpita
  In questi sassi ; e perche dorme, ha vita.
  Desta la, se no l' credi, e parleratti.

To which he answered :

"" Grata m'è, e il suono, e più l'esser da sasso
  Mentre che il danno, e la vergogna dura
  Non veder, non sentir, m' è gran ventura
  Pero non mi desta.—Deh, parla basso."

The monument of Lorenzo Duke of Urbino,
the father of Catherine de Medicis, is opposite,
and ornamented with the unfinished statues of
Dawn and Twilight. The Duke himself sits
above in such deep abstraction, that he may

serve as a personification of " Thought," by
which appellation the figure is known. The
superb Chapel of the Medicis, an octagon literally encrusted with precious stones and with
the most valuable marbles, is a splendid instance of the short-sightedness of man. It was
begun by Ferdinand I. in 1604, and is not yet
finished, though the family is now all but ex-
tinct. Their mortal remains are deposited in
a subterranean vault, awaiting the time when
their splendid mausoleum shall be completed,
as they are *then* to be placed in it. The Medicis
line is past ; the present dynasty may also be
annihilated ere that period arrives, and who
will think of the merchant Dukes ?

Far more pleasure is derived from a visit to
Santa Croce ; " the centre of pilgrimage, the
Mecca of Italy ;" built by Arnolfo di Lapo, in
1294, and subsequently repaired by Vasari.
There is an indescribable charm about its precincts ; a holy calm, a poetic gloom, that seem
to raise and exalt the mind above " this dim
spot which men call earth."

> " Here repose
> Angelo's, Alfieri's bones, and his
> The starry Galileo, with his woes ;
> Here Machiavelli's earth returned from whence it rose."

The imagination is engrossed not only with
those that sleep around, but also with those

that have celebrated their illustrious predecessors; we admire their admiration, and as Byron mourned for Corinna, for her "whose eloquence was poured over these illustrious ashes, and whose voice is now as mute as those she sung;" so must we lament that master-spirit of the age, and find no words so fit as his strains to describe our feelings for Italy and himself.

The Duomo is a fine structure; its cupola, by Brunellesco, if not equal to that of St. Peter's, was its prototype and predecessor. It inspired Michael Angelo, who desired to be buried where it might be seen from his tomb. This cathedral ranks amongst the finest in Europe for magnitude, grandeur, and boldness. It was begun by Arnolfo, in 1294, and completed in 1445. The light and airy Campanile, encrusted with black and white marble, was so much admired by Charles V. that he declared it should be kept in a case, and only shown on holidays. The bronze gates of the Battistereo, by Ghiberti, were deemed by Michael Angelo worthy to be those of Paradise. It is an octangular building, and on the mosaic pavement is the following inscription, which reads backwards and forwards the same:

"En giro torte, Sol ciclos et rotor igne."

The churches of Santa Maria Nuova, which Buonarotti termed " his spouse," of S S. Annunziata, San Spirito, Del Carmine, and several others, deserve a visit if you have time; and in the Museum is a horribly fine collection of anatomical subjects in wax; but those must have strong nerves, who could view them without shuddering and turning away with disgust; and there are some representations of the plague, so painfully distressing, that it is scarcely possible to refrain from tears whilst viewing them. But we must no longer linger at Florence, attractive and lovely as she is; we must onwards on our journey. *Il faut marcher.*

LETTER VI.

Sienna.—Duomo.—Piazza Publico.—Radicofani.—Montefiascone.—Campagna di Roma.—Entrance of Rome.

WE left fair Florence with regret, and proceeded along a very fine country, passing Casciano and. Tavernelle, to Poggibonsi, where, in the Royal palace, " that old den, high up among the trees," two of the Medicis, Isabella the daughter, and Eleanor of Castile the niece and daughter-in-law, of Cosmo I. were murdered by their respective husbands. Night closed in, and we had some unpleasant floundering in and out of ditches, before we reached Sienna, the capital of the once fruitful and populous, now deserted and pestiferous Maremma. It is pleasantly situated on an eminence among hills; the air is fine, and the language spoken here is considered the purest in Italy. The Cathedral, a fine gothic edifice, with a highly ornamented exterior, was begun about 1284, by Giovanni Pisani, and finished in 1333, by Agostino and Agnolo, Siennese architects. The pavement is covered with curious mosaics, and the nave is ornamented with the busts of several Popes, the predecessors of Alexander III.; and report says our countrywoman, the damsel Pope Joan, once held her place among these worthies, though she now no longer retains her station there. The Piazza Publica is in the singular shape of a shell, or rather of a fan; and in the Palazzo Publico are some curious old frescos, of the school of Giotto, representing the manners and costumes of the day, and several events in the life of Alexander III., who was born here, as were also Pius II. Pius III. and Paul V. and St. Catherine. From Sienna our road passed over barren, dreary, and apparently interminable hills, and we had the pleasure of encountering so violent a tempest, that we literally expected to have the carriage blown

over. At a distance we saw Mont Alcino and
Monte Pulciano, famous for its wine, " *che
d' ogni vino è il Rè*." At Buon Convento, the
Emperor Henry VII. was poisoned by a Do-
minican monk, whilst taking the Sacrament;
and near San Quirico are the Baths of
St. Philip, where excellent casts are taken,
which are formed by its waters, when precipitated upon moulds of medals, depositing a fine
calcareous tufo. We at last reached Radicofani, situated 2470 feet above the level of the
Mediterranean, where, in an inconceivably wild
and desolate spot, stands an albergo, which was
formerly a hunting-seat of one of the Grand
Dukes of Florence, and which, from its rambling and forlorn appearance, seems admirably
adapted for the abode and lurking-place of banditti, and for the scene of the adventures of the
heroine of a romance. The tempest howled
without; the wind whistled through the immense saloons, and mournfully sighed through
the dark passages; the rain beat furiously against
the windows, and in addition to all this, our
chimney smoked! We, however, escaped without being either robbed or murdered, and descending the mountain, we soon entered the
dominions of the Papal See; where, our *lasciar
passare* not being arrived, we underwent the
ceremony of having our baggage plumbed at

the Douâne. Acqua Pendente is romantically
situated near water, and among hanging rocks
fringed with wood. In the neighbourhood of
San Lorenzo Nuovo, the tufo rocks are curiously perforated with caverns. Close to the road
is a curious basaltic rock, with regular prisma-
tic columns, hexagonal and flattened at both
ends; and we saw several trees, partly burnt
down, and still remaining in a charred state,
which was the determined and energetic method the French took to clear the country of
banditti, who formerly made this part their
resort, but who, it is said, still find a refuge
and a nestling-place in the ruins of San Lorenzo Vecchio. Marble columns strewed on
the ground, and other magnificent remains of
antiquity, bespeak the modern but insignifi-
cant town of Bolsena, once the ancient Volsi-
nium, to have been formerly a place of importance; and on the bosom of its lake are
two small islands, Besendina and Martona,
which, according to tradition, floated in the
time of Pliny. On the latter, Amalasintha,
Queen of the Goths, was strangled by the command of her husband; but notwithstanding
this bloody story, I could not help exclaiming,

" Oh, had we those bright little isles of our own!"

when we looked down on them from the

commanding heights of Montefiascone. It was at this place that a jovial German prelate lost his life, in consequence of drinking too largely of the delicious Muschat wine made here ; and his domestic, who generally preceded him, and marked " Est, est," in those places where the liquor was good, inscribed on his tomb,

" Est, est,"
" Propter nimium est, est,
Dominus meus mortuus est."

We crossed an extensive plain to Viterbo, the chief town of the patrimony of St. Peter, which stands at the base of Mount Cimino ; and here, in the old cathedral, is a fine chapel, dedicated to St. Valentine, the patron saint, I presume, of all the would-be wits of the 14th of February, and the stone on which he suffered martyrdom is still preserved and exhibited. After traversing the beautifully wooded scenery of Mount Cimino, we came upon the enchanting little Lake of Vico, three miles in circumference, and which, though once said to have been the crater of a volcano, now exhibits a scene of exquisite loveliness. Ronciglione, a dark sombre-looking town, built of tufo, looks up a pretty little valley, watered by the Tereia ; and soon after passing Monterosi, we came to—

" Where Campagna's plain forsaken lies
 A weary waste expanding to the skies."

It has a wild and desolate appearance, as if
neither foot of man or beast had passed
through it for years ; but the very solitude has
something sublime in it, and more suited to
the present widowed state of Rome, where
she sits " the Niobe of nations," than palaces
and triumphal arches.   There is but one Rome
in the world, and the peculiarity of the approach strikes the imagination far more forcibly
than the ordinary purlieus of a city ; one or
two ruined towers are alone to be seen, in which
" the fox looks out of the window, and the
thistle shakes its lonely head ;" yet the soil
teems with luxuriancy, and the very weeds
have a singular fertility, rankness, and grandeur
in their appearance, and seem as if caressing the
soil which was formerly the scene of so many
noble and illustrious transactions.   As Madame
de Staël elegantly observes, a land which has
witnessed so much glory, would be ashamed
now of being *useful*.   Like the awful stillness
that precedes a storm, so does the solitari-
ness and desolation around prepare the mind
for—Rome.

After passing the lonely post-houses of La
Storta and Baccano, a turn in the road brought
us upon " the Eternal City."   Her columns,

obelisks, swelling domes and palaces, burst
upon us; every spot was classic ground, and we
crossed the celebrated Tiber by the Ponte
Molle, in whose neighbourhood Constantine
beheld his famous vision of the miraculous apparition of the luminous cross in the air, and
where he subsequently defeated Maxentius,
which event produced the conversion of the
Emperor, and caused Christianity to become
the religion of the Roman empire and of the
civilized world.

The entrance to Rome is very striking. On
one side stands the Chiesa di Santa Maria del
Popolo, erected on the site of the family burial-place of Domitian; on the other is the
Custom-house. In the front is the Egyptian
Obelisk, the first ever seen at Rome, the workmanship of Senneserteus, or Psammuthis, the
son of Necho, who flourished 522 years before
the Christian æra, and whose name is inscribed
among the hieroglyphics. It was brought from
Heliopolis by Augustus, who placed it as the
gnomon of a dial in the Circus Maximus; and
its subsequent erection in its present position,
by Sextus V. was not accomplished till after
years of preparation, and till after all the wits
of all the men of science in Europe had been
consulted and employed in effecting the wished-
for object. From this, as from a common cen-

tre, branch off, like the radii of a circle, the Corso, leading to the Capitol, the Strada del Babbuino, and the Strada di Ripetta, with the twin churches at the place from whence they diverge. Every nation seems to have sent a deputy here to commemorate itself. The Capitol recalls the glories of Ancient, the churches remind us of the splendour of Modern Rome : the Pincian Hill, with its prettinesses and neatnesses, is characteristic of the French ; whilst the cosmopolite Englishman may be seen wandering every where, unrestrained by Swiss guards and Austrian troops.

LETTER VII.

Rome.—Coliseum.—Capitol. —St. Peter's.—The Vatican.— The Pantheon. — Fine Paintings and Sculpture in the Palaces and Churches.—Ancient Christians.—Fountains. —Obelisks.

I SHOULD not envy the feelings of that person who could, without a quickened pulse and beating heart, first mount the Capitol, or view the Forum. Though now, as in the days of Æneas and the good king Evander, cattle again low in places which once resounded with the eloquence of Cicero ; yet there does the

genius of Ancient Rome still seem to preside,
and every spot in the vicinity abounds with
interesting reminiscences. The majestic Coliseum,

> " Which in its public days unpeopled Rome,
> And held, uncrowded, nations in its womb,"

still stands, though in ruins, a noble specimen
of the magnificent ideas of the Romans. It
was erected by Vespasian, on the site of the
fish-ponds of Nero, and was so termed from a
colossal statue of the latter Emperor, one hundred and twenty feet high, in the character
of Apollo, which was placed there by Titus.
Gladiatorial shows were exhibited in this amphitheatre till the year 404, when an eastern
monk, Almachius, or Telemachus, rushing into
the area to endeavour to separate the combatants, was slain in consequence by the orders
of the Prætor Alypius. He was, however, subsequently canonized, and these inhuman shows
were abolished by Honorius. The building was
standing nearly perfect when visited by Saxon
pilgrims, who connected its fate with that of
Rome, and Rome with that of the world ; but
the edifice spared by barbarians, and by the
hand of time, was dismantled and ruined, to
erect palaces at a comparatively recent period,
by modern Goths and Vandals.

On the Palatine Mount, which, in the early

ages of the Roman empire, constituted both
its cradle and its boundary, whilst, in its days
of grandeur, its limits were found too confined
for the golden house of Nero, now nought
remains of its gorgeous splendour, but fragments of columns strewn about in all di-
rections, choked up vaults, and subterranean frescos; and at this period " The spider
spreads the veil in the palace of the Cæsars,
and the owl stands sentinel " on the Imperial
Mount.

In its neighbourhood are the Triumphal
Arches of Titus, Constantine, and Severus, with
many elegant columns, the graceful vestiges of
fallen fanes and forsaken temples.

Ascending the tower of the Capitol, a most
interesting panoramic view presents itself from
thence of the ancient and modern hills which
give Rome so picturesque an appearance. The
Palatine, now one shapeless mass of ruins ; the
Aventine, where Hercules slew the robber
Cacus in his cavern ; the Esquiline, where
dwelt that patron of learning, Mæcenas, and the
poets Horace, Tibullus, and Propertius ; the
Cælian, Quirinal, and Viminal Hills, with the
Janiculum, Vatican, and Pincian, and the
modern and artificial Monti Testaceo and Citorio. Intermingled with swelling domes appear
obelisks cleaving the air like pillars of fire ; the

lofty Columns of Trajan and of Marcus Aurelius, and the mighty masses of the stupendous remains of the Thermæ of Titus, Caracalla, and Diocletian. In the court below, which is enclosed by the Museum and the Palaces of the Senators and the Conservatori, is the spirited equestrian statue of Marcus Aurelius, with which Michael Angelo was so struck, that when he first beheld it, he involuntarily exclaimed, " cammina!" Entering the Museum, is Marforio, formerly the witty respondent of the caustic and sarcastic Pasquin, whose statue still retains its station in the vicinity of the Palazzo Braschi ; and in the galleries are the Dying Gladiator, the exquisitely beautiful Cupid and Psyche, Cupid bending his bow, the shrivelled Hecuba, smiling Innocence with a dove, and the brazen Wolf, " the thunder-stricken nurse of Rome." There is also a fine collection of pictures, and an interesting assemblage of the busts of the illustrious dead ; the magnificent idea of Canova, who thus paid a superb tribute to departed genius of all nations, by proposing to the Pope the installing them after death in the Capitol.

I must not allow you to quit the Capitol without introducing you into the Mamertine dungeons, where St. Peter and St. Paul were imprisoned; and to the Academy of St. Luke, where is a splendid picture of that Apostle by Raphael, beaming with genius and inspiration; and as you are a craniologist, or phrenologist, you may exercise your skill upon his skull, which is here shown, and you can point out for the benefit of the uninitiated and unlearned, what peculiar bump or organ gave rise to the glorious performances of that unrivalled painter. The Tarpeian Rock is in this immediate neighbourhood, but its ancient height is so diminished, that it no longer wears a formidable appearance. Not far from thence is the spot where Romulus and Remus were exposed, also the Arch of Janus, and the Cloaca Maxima, the wonderful, and almost the only remains of regal Rome, which magnificent sewer was constructed by Tarquinius Priscus. Into this a small limpid stream discharges itself, which tradition reports to be the Lake of Juturna, where Castor and Pollux watered their horses after the battle at the Lucus Regillus.

In the way to St. Peter's you cross the bridge and pass the Castle of San Angelo, which is so called from the angel of bronze at the top, and which was built by Adrian for his own mausoleum, though now converted into a prison for malefactors. Two majestic porticos sweep around, and form a noble approach to perhaps the grandest building in the world. Between fountains that unceasingly play, stands the Obelisk of Nuncoreus, the son of Sesostris, which was brought to Rome from Heliopolis by Caligula, and erected in its present situation by Sextus V. The talents of Corinne alone could do justice to St. Peter's; for in its immensity, its sublimity, and its beauty, it so far transcends all other edifices, that I feel that no description of mine could convey any adequate idea of its magnificence. The walls, that glow with the richest marbles, the swelling dome, the noble statues, the fine pictures, the richly ornamented altars, positively overwhelm the senses; whilst the even temperature of the atmosphere, the lamps always burning, the swells of music that occasionally fall upon the ear, the fragrant incense wafted around, give the impression that it is an edifice of enchantment, and, as you wander about, you half expect to wake, and to find it is a delightful dream. In this temple, " worthiest of God, the holy and the true," processions of religious orders are constantly seen worshipping at the different shrines; the monk and the friar silently stealing through the distance; the pilgrim, " with cockle-shell and sandal shoon," kissing with the warmest devotion the foot of St. Peter; and the penitent humbly kneeling at the confessional, and pouring out his sorrows and his sins to his unseen spiritual director; all of which considerably add to the effect of the *tout ensemble*.

In the Vatican are the celebrated frescos of Raphael, in the Loggia and the Camere which bear his name: the latter are four rooms literally covered with the finest paintings in the world. The Sala di Constantine records the deeds of Constantine—the miraculous apparition of the cross to him, previous to his battle with Maxentius, in A.D. 312;—the battle itself;—his baptism, and his donation of the patrimony of the Church. In the next apartment, La Sala di Eliodoro, are the Angels appearing to Heliodorus in the Temple; the Miracle of Bolsena; Saint Peter and Saint Paul arresting the progress of Attila, and the Angel delivering Saint Peter out of prison. La Sala della Scuola di Atene, contains that fine picture, in which Raphael has introduced himself conversing with his master Perugino; the Cardinal Virtues; Mount Parnassus, and the Dispute of the Holy Sacrament. The fourth, or Sala del' Incendio, contains the dreadful fire of Rome in the time of Leo IV.; his victory over the Saracens at Ostia; the Coronation of Charle-

magne, by Leo III., and the same Prelate
clearing himself of the crimes laid to his charge.
These frescos, as well as those in the Loggia,
which consist of Scripture subjects, are much
injured by time, as well as by the barbarity of
the soldiers of the Duke of Burgundy, who
used these apartments as barracks at the sack-
ing of Rome in the time of Charles V.; but
enough still remains to show they are invaluable and inimitable.   In the Sistine Chapel is
the celebrated Last Judgment of Michael Angelo, and some superb Sibyls and Prophets by
the same master.   In the apartments above are
some of the finest easel paintings in existence —
the Transfiguration by Raphael; the Madonna di
Foligno and the Communion of Saint Jerome
by Domenichino.   After these you will scarcely
vouchsafe a glance on the other pictures, magnificent as they are, and would be in any other
collection ; but as a loyal subject, you must pay
your homage to our Monarch George IV.
whose portrait, by Sir Thomas Lawrence, is
installed in the Vatican.   It is a curious situation for the first Protestant Monarch in the
world, but it is a high compliment to the
talents of the artist, that his performance was
deemed worthy of being placed in the same
collection with the *chef-d'œuvres* of Raphael.
The cicerone informed us the Pope was some-

what surprised to find he had a thousand guineas to pay for this picture, as this modern Mæcenas intended it should have been presented to him.

After traversing an almost interminable corridor, a flight of steps leads to a cabinet in the Museo Pio Clementino, where is the celebrated Belvedere Torso; and passing onwards to a court surrounded by a portico, with an elegant little temple in each angle, in one of them you will find "the god of life, of poesy, and light," the superb, the magnificent, the incomparably elegant Apollo!—the Perseus of Canova, the Belvedere Antinous, or Meleager, and the far-famed Laocoon occupy the other vestibules. The Muses, in the hall that bears their name, are very fine, and one of them is inspiration itself, and seems just writing down,

"Thoughts that breathe, and words that burn."

The long geographical gallery terminates in the chambers hung with tapestry, after the designs of Raphael, seven of whose Cartoons, which were painted for this express purpose, are now in England. Our Saviour issuing from the Tomb is incomparable! This was a mere *passeggiato* through the Vatican, for we were too much limited for time to bestow more than a glance *en passant* on many objects, which merited as many days as we had minutes to spare for observation.

As we returned to our hotel, we stopped to view the magnificent Pantheon, which was erected by Agrippa, and repaired by Severus and Caracalla. The bronze with which the ceiling was originally cased was taken away by Urbin VIII. to make the baldachino of Saint Peter's, and the cannon of Saint Angelo, and of him it was said in consequence—" Quod non fecerunt Barbari Romæ, fecit Barberini." It is probably the most perfect specimen remaining of an ancient temple, and it is not easy to describe the grand, the imposing effect of this majestic edifice.

If the traveller have time to bestow upon the exquisite paintings in the numerous private collections, he will be much pleased with those in the Borghese, Corsini, and Doria Palaces; with Guido's celebrated fresco of the Dawn of Day, which is truly embodied poetry, and which may be seen in the Casino Rospigliosi; and also with those in the Farnesina, where are the Galatea of Raphael, and the beautiful fable of Cupid and Psyche, which is painted on the ceiling from his designs, together with the famous Black head of Michael Angelo in an adjoining room. The innumerable churches also deserve attention; the walls and pavements glow with the richest marble, and their ceilings are often painted by the first masters. Highly ornamented chapels, splendid altars, and magnificent altar-pieces, exquisitely carved shrines, fine mosaics, noble frescos, stately baldequins, and superb monuments, are to be found in many and in most, besides several beautiful pictures and choice specimens of sculpture. The statues of our Saviour and of Moses, by Michael Angelo Buonarotti, are to be seen in the churches of Santa Maria sopra Minerva, and San Pietro in Vincoli; that of Jonah, from the designs of Raphael, in the Chiesa di Santa Maria del Popolo; whilst the Archangel Michael, by Guido, in the church of the Capuchins is termed "the Apollo of painting."

Besides its classical attractions, Rome is consecrated to the Christian traveller, from having been the scene of the labours and of the sufferings of several of the Holy Apostles. St. Peter was crucified on the spot where the sacristy bearing his name now stands: St. John was cast into a cauldron of boiling oil near the Lateran; and St. Paul, " who dwelt here two whole years in his own hired house, and received all that came to him," was beheaded *alle tre Fontane.* Many of the early Christians sought refuge during the bloody persecutions of the Roman emperors in the gloomy defiles and recesses

of the Catacombs ; and surely nothing, even in
the most heroic period of the annals of Rome,
can compete with the wonderful magnanimity,
the fortitude, and pious resignation with which
these holy men endured tortures worse than
death, and resigned " the pomps and vanities
of this wicked world," with all that makes life
dear, for the sake of their religion.   Ah, why
have such touching, such interesting, such affecting incidents, been deprived of their instruct-
ive pathos by the monstrous inventions and
absurdities superadded by the monks ?—But
I am growing serious, and you have yet to admire the fountains of Rome, which, with their
noble cascades and copious streams, give such
an air of originality to the city.   The Fontana
Paolina, di Trevi, di Termini, with those in the
Piazza Navona, and the Piazza Barberini, are
truly magnificent, whilst the agreeable sound
of the murmurs of their waters, falling on the
ambient air, soothes and delights the listening ear.

Besides the Obelisk in the Piazza del Popolo,
and that in front of St. Peter's, there are two
small ones, which once, it is thought, stood
before the Temple of Isis and Serapis, and
are now erected, one in front of the Pantheon,
and the other, elevated on an elephant, before
the Church of Santa Maria sopra Minerva.

That which now ornaments the fountain of the Piazza Navona, was found in the Circus of Caracalla, and one on the Pincian Hill in the Circus of Sallust. The obelisk, which is on Mount Citorio, is attributed to Sesostris, or his son, whose names are both inscribed upon the surface. That in front of Santa Maria Maggiore, between the equestrian statues of Castor and Pollux, of red granite, forty-three feet high, without the pedestal, was brought to Rome by Claudius, and was originally placed at the entrance of the mausoleum of Augustus. There is another, in the grounds of the Villa Mattei, and one still lies prone on the ground, in one of the courts of the Palace of the Vatican.

LETTER VIII.

Departure from Rome. — Albano. — Velletri. — Pontine Marshes. — Terracina. — Fondi. — Capua. — Aversa.

On the 15th of November, we again set forth on our journey, and proceeded along the Via Felice, over the Esquiline, Viminal, and Cælian Hills, passing the magnificent Basilica of Santa Maria Maggiore, and San Giovanni in Laterano; which latter

is termed the Mother Church of Rome. In
its neighbourhood are the Baptistery of Constantine, which is a fine octagonal building,
containing an immense font: the Triclinium of
St. Leo, and the Holy Staircase, up which, for
the remission of sins, thereby supposed to be
obtained, the superstitious pilgrims work their
way upon their knees. The twenty-seven steps
of which it consists, are supposed to have been
brought from the Palace of Pilate, and to be
the identical ones up which our Saviour was
carried. Near here stands the Obelisk of Rameses, the son of Heron, who flourished fifteen
hundred years before Christ, and which originally stood in the Temple of the Sun at
Heliopolis, from whence it was transported to
Rome by Constantine II. and was subsequently
erected in its present situation by Sextus V.
It is esteemed one of the largest here, being
115 feet high, and nine in diameter. Upon
each of its four sides, inscribed in hieroglyphics, appears the name of Mesphres, who
was, according to Manetho the fifth king of
the eighteenth dynasty of Egyptian monarchs,
and who flourished seventeen hundred years
before Christ.

After passing the Porta San Giovanni, we
left Rome, and again entered upon the dreary
and desolate Campagna, across which, in every
direction, sweep the majestic remains of immense

aqueducts. The Tomb of Ascanius stands at the entrance of Albano. A learned antiquary might possibly say it is wrong thus to call it, but as it is better to have too much, rather than little faith, upon such disputed points, I am perfectly contented to *believe* that the son of Æneas lies there interred; for who would wish to have so pleasing an illusion destroyed?

" Where ignorance is bliss, 'tis folly to be wise."

On leaving the town, we passed either the tomb of the Curiatii, or of Pompey the Great. Delightful uncertainty!

Whilst rambling about the environs of Velletri, where we slept that night, we were accosted by a person with something of the air of *un vieux militaire*, who put several questions to us concerning the state of parties at Rome, and the health of the Pope. He then volunteered to us several particulars of the robbers who infest these regions, informing us that Gasperoni, their captain, at this time prisoner in the castle of St. Angelo, had followed his profession for thirty years, and in his day had taken several English ladies and a German Colonel prisoners. Our communicative friend seemed so perfectly *au fait* with the movements of the banditti, and with their deeds of prowess, that though here presented himself to be only a gentleman of Cori, come forth to

take an evening promenade, yet on his request-
ing us to ascend an eminence, in order that he
might point out his house to us, we began to
think we were not over prudent in thus trusting ourselves to a stranger, as we might possibly be performing the counterpart to the adventure of Allermanno Principesso Popkins,
which is described in Washington Irving's
Tales of a Traveller. It had long been dusk;
the shades of night were closing in; suspended
over the battlements of the gateway, a bandit's
head grinned horribly at us; however, I was
not doomed to become the rival of the Princi-
pessine Popkins; our *incognito* walked quietly
off, and we returned to our hotel in inglorious
safety. Comfortless enough it was, and sufficiently large for half a dozen robberies and
murders; but fortunately the inn at Velletri
produced nothing to compete with the deeds
narrated to have taken place at that of Terracina.

We started early on the following morning,
and day began to dawn as we descended upon
Cisterna, where the scenery was enriched with
fine ilex trees scattered about in solitary grandeur, and with some beautiful hedges of myrtle! At Torre tre Ponti, where is an inscription to Pius VI. we crossed the Astura, and
entered upon the famous, or rather *in*famous

Pontine Marshes, through which runs a noble road, twenty-five miles long, perfectly straight, and one continued avenue of trees: it passes between canals or ditches, which are lined with sentry-boxes and watch-houses, where the poor sickly sentinels, whose looks bespoke the insalubrity of the air, were evidently sacrificing their lives to insure the safety of those of others. These marshes are watered by the Ufens and Amasenus, and are bounded on the north by Mount Albano, glittering with tumuli, towns, and cities, whilst to the east the Volscian Mountains sweep from thence towards the south, forming a vast semicircle, and immense forests on the west spread towards the sea. A fine, but coarse and rank vegetation everywhere prevailed, and herds of buffaloes were to be seen grazing on the rich pastures. At first there was something very striking in this magnificent road over desert marshes, but its monotony fatigued, and we were both rejoiced when we came to its termination.

We at length reached Terracina, the ancient Anxur; a poor place in itself, but commanding magnificent views of Mount Circéllo, and of the Bay of Naples. The sea here washes the base of some huge rocks which overhang the town in a most romantic manner, and which are picturesquely variegated with the richest

tints of yellow and red.   The summits are
crowned by the Temple of Jupiter Anxur, or
the Palace of Theodoric.   This was the scene
of Oswald and Corinne's evening walk, when
the latter, dismayed with a cloud passing over
the moon, interpreted it to be an evil omen,
presaging future woe and misery.   The Cathedral contains a mosaic pavement, and a
baldequin, supported by four beautiful marble
columns, from the temple of Apollo; also a
curiously twisted pillar; and in the portico is
a large marble cenotaph.

Our inn, "*the* inn at Terracina," was situated
under an impending rock, apparently " nodding
to its fall," and close to the sea ; but though
the *gran sala* was fully occupied, we saw no
" melting, bewitching Venetian," no " French
painter" to narrate bandit stories, and " no stiff
and stately Englishman."   So, there being little
appearance of adventures, good, bad, or indif-
ferent, we ordered our dinner in our own apartment, and retired to rest, lulled by the dashing
of the waves.

> " E non udite ancora come risuona
>   Il rauco ed alto fremito marino ?"

At Torre dei Confini we entered the Neapolitan dominions, and after passing a pestiferous lake, not far from which is a cavern

where Sejanus saved the life of Tiberius, we reached Fondi, a wretchedly poor place, which, like Troy of old, was ruined by the beauty of a woman. In 1534, Barbarossa, attracted by the fame of the charms of the lovely Julia Gonzago, the wife of Victor Colonna, made a descent upon the town, in order to gain possession of her; but the lady having no taste for the seclusion of the seraglio of the Grand Signior, for which she was destined, made her escape to the mountains *en chemise,* and the barbarian wreaked his vengeance for the disappointment upon the town, which has never recovered from the effects of his rage.

Mola di Gaëta is o'ertopped by the Torre di Orlando, formerly the mausoleum of Minutius Plancus, the founder of Lyons. In this neighbourhood is the cenotaph of Cicero, who was murdered near here; and in the garden of the albergo di Cicerone are the interesting remains of his Villa Formianum. Not far from hence, Marius attempted, though unsuccessfully, to conceal himself from his enemies; and the ruins of an aqueduct, majestically sweeping across a plain, and of a theatre, induce antiquaries to fix the site of Minternum in their vicinity. We crossed the Garigliano, the ancient Liris, by a bridge of boats, and continued along the Via Appia to San Agatha, passing over a plain

covered with olive-trees and vines, flinging their
fantastic branches, ornamented with red and
yellow autumnal foliage, in tangled festoons
from tree to tree, as on the plains of Lombardy.   Fig-trees and pomegranates were
growing wild in the hedges; myrtles bloomed
around; groves of oranges and limes, and immense aloes and Indian figs appeared in luxuriant abundance, whilst occasional palm-trees gave
a southern aspect to the scenery.   Capua, on
the Volturno, at this period presents none of
the attractions and luxuries which enervated
the army of Hannibal; but even in this men-
dicant country, the importunity of the beggars
at this place transcended every thing we had
hitherto met with, and we were absolutely
scolded into parting with a few carlini.   Is it
not melancholy, that where Nature has done so
much, man will do so little?   That, where she
has poured her choicest gifts, the population
should be so degraded?   That,

" Where the flowers ever blossom, the beams ever shine,
  All but the spirit of man is divine?"

At Aversa, King Andrew, the husband of the
beautiful Queen Joan, was strangled; but with
that lovely, that sweetly innocent countenance,
as pourtrayed by Raphael, in the Louvre, it
would be difficult to believe she could have
been privy to his assassination.   If she were

a murderess, no faith can be placed in physiognomy. We soon after reached Naples, and after passing a large Foundling-hospital, and driving along the famous Strada di Toledo, we took up our abode in an hotel which commanded a magnificent view of the Bay, in which were two English men-of-war at anchor.

LETTER IX.

Naples —Chiesa dei Certosini.—Fine view from thence.—Castle of St. Elmo.—Villa Reale.—Grotto of Pausilippo.—Virgil's tomb.—Museo Borbonico.—Pompeii.—Portici.

" *Vedi Napoli e poi mori*," says the Italian proverb; and probably there is no place in the world better worth visiting, ere one takes one's leave of this terrestrial sphere. It is a spot richly teeming with classical and poetical reminiscences; and it has, from time immemorial, been the favourite retreat of the great and the wise, of the philosopher and the man of pleasure.

Tradition relates that it was founded by an Argonaut, thirteen hundred years before the Christian æra, and afterwards peopled and enriched by Greeks from Rhodes, Athens, and Chalcis. Its ancient name of Parthenope was

bestowed on it by the Phœnicians, in consequence of its charming situation; or, as some
say, it is derived from one of the Syrens who
was interred here; and Neapolis was the appellation bestowed upon it after it had been destroyed and rebuilt in obedience to an oracle,
by the people of Palæopolis, a neighbouring
town, which is said to have been founded
by Hercules. Neapolis and Palæopolis were
subsequently united by Augustus; and in the
territories of Naples are still extant many Greek
customs, and the manners, and even language,
still retain many traces of their former Grecian
connexions.

From the Belvedere, in the garden Dei Certosini, may be seen one of the finest views in
the world; indeed, one near Constantinople is
the only one which is, I believe, acknowledged
to be superior. From thence you look over a
magnificent extent of country. The Campagna, teeming with luxuriance, and bounded
only by the distant range of Apennines, and
the graceful declivities of Mount Vesuvius;
the beautiful Bay, studded with isles, and the
line of coast, with bold headlands, stretching
from the promontory of Pausilippo to that of
Sorrento; whilst beneath is seen the flat-roofed
city of Naples, with its palaces and churches,
and the pretty oval-shaped Castel del' Uovo,

situated where formerly stood one of the villas of Lucullus.

The *ci-devant* Convent dei Certosini, by the strange changes and chances of this mutable world, is now converted into a hospital for invalid soldiers. What different sounds must at this time re-echo through its walls, which erst-while heard only the sounds of prayer and repentance, when inhabited by the silent, austere, and self-denying Carthusians!

The Church is highly ornamented with precious marbles, lapis lazuli, and fine paintings. In the Tesoro is the *chef-d'œuvre* of Spagnoletto—a dead Christ, with the Virgin, the Magdalene, and St. John, for which Lord Bristol offered some thousand piastres. In the Sacristy is a picture of our Saviour carried up the Holy Staircase, by Massino and Viviani, which has a fine effect. The ceilings were painted by Luca Giordano and the Chevalier d'Arpino; the pavements are dazzlingly beautiful, and the cloisters are very fine, as is the Campo Santo: St. Bruno and St. Januarius appear the *heroes* of the place. The frowning but picturesque old castle of St. Elmo, which is necessarily passed in returning from the Convent dei Certosini, overlooks, and commands the city, and was founded by the Nor-

mans, though subsequently strengthened by
Louis XII. and Charles V.

The Villa Reale is a most delightful public
promenade, adorned with noble plantations, and
washed by the Mediterranean, the murmurs of
whose waves intermingle agreeably with the
sighing of the wind among the trees, and with
the music which frequently plays here.   In
the centre is the celebrated Toro Farnese, which
originally came from Rhodes, representing Am-
phion and Zethus tying Dirce to the horns of
a wild bull; the subject is too ferocious to be
pleasing.   It was at this time in contemplation
to remove it to the Museum, with a view to its
better preservation.   Near here, in the Capella
dei Crocelli, sleeps the classical Eustace; the
inscription on his monument, which was erected by his sister, mentions his having been cut
off by a fever, and concludes thus,

" Care, vale ! Patriæ manet, æternumque manebit
  Te genuisse decus, non tumulasse decor."

After passing the extensive suburb of La
Mergellina, and the promontory of Pausilippo,
covered with the ruins of Norman palaces, in
which the sea-fowl builds her nest, and the
poor lazaretto finds a dwelling-place, where the
ill-starred Queen Joan, perhaps, once held her
state, a noble road, commanding a magnificent

view, gradually winds up the hill, till it almost
meets that of Pozzuoli. As we returned, we
visited the Grotto of Pausilippo; with lights,
which only serve to render darkness visible, it
strikes the imagination most forcibly. There
is something inexpressibly grand and sublime
in the gloom, and the sudden transition from
the glare and bustle of Naples to the darksome
cavern, and the re-emerging, on the opposite
side, to the cheerful light of day, reminded us
of the valley of death, through which we must
all pass, let us humbly hope to a joyful resurrection. Overhanging the entrance of the
Grotto, is the tomb of Virgil, situated in a most
sequestered and romantic spot, to which we
ascended by a toilsome path, and which seems
like the retreat which the Mantuan swain
would himself have selected, when he wished
to sing the charms of " formosam Amaryllida."
An oblong building, with small cavities on the
sides, apparently intended for the reception of
cinerary urns, contains, or rather did contain,
the mortal remains of the great Latin poet;
at present, nought is to be seen, but the names
of all the world written and carved all about.
The laurel planted by Petrarch has totally disappeared; but over the vaulted roof, an ilex,
which romantically grows from an adjoining
rock, caressingly flings its branches, as if wish-

ing to guard the hallowed spot where Tityrus
was interred, from the scorching beams of the
summer sun.   But for the cicerones, this would
be quite the place to lose oneself in poetic reveries : but, oh ! those guides ! they ruin all
the feelings of the sublime and beautiful !   The
inscription on the tomb is,

> " Qui Ceneres ? Tumuli hæc vestigia conditur
> Ille hoc qui cecinit Pascua, raru, duces olim.
>   Can : Reg : MDLIIII."

From a rustic kind of seat, where there is an
inscription in French, purporting that " Here,
where the shepherd lies, friends should draw
the silken bands of love still tighter," may be
seen a magnificent view of Naples,—its bay,—
and Mount Vesuvius.   By the common people, Virgil is, or was considered to have been
a great magician ; and a bronze horse, which
went by his name, was superstitiously revered
by them, and believed capable of curing all disorders, till the zeal of some bishop caused it to
be destroyed.   The head, however, still may be
seen in the Museo Borbonico, whither we will
now direct our steps.

In this collection are several noble statues ;
the Hercules of Glycon, and the famous Flora,
both of which were found in the Baths of
Caracalla.   The latter is a most gigantic dam-

sel ; *if* a beauty, there is no denying she is a *great* one ; but ladies of pigmy stature must hope Matthews was in the right, when he observed that colossal proportions in a female are seldom pleasing. There are plenty of Venuses; the Venus Callipyga of Praxiteles, and the Venus Genetrix, between whom Adonis very properly has taken his station ; also the Venus Accovicciata, and the Marine Venus : Atlas, bearing a globe ; Antinous, beautifully graceful and effeminate *à l'ordinaire*, and a most majestic statue of Aristides, which is life itself. We were also much pleased with several females, and with some equestrian statues of the Balbus family. In the apartments containing the paintings are some fine models, in cork, of the ruins of Pompeii and the Temples at Pæstum ; also a succession of pictures from the earliest time, when the painter, determined to make his picture valuable, was more lavish of gold than of colour. Here are the original sketch of the Last Judgment, by Michael Angelo Buonarotti, which is in the Sistine Chapel at Rome ; Leo X. between the Cardinals Bembo and Passerino, a Holy Family, and a Fencing Master, by the divine Raphael ; Domenichino's Gouvernante, a portrait of Columbus, and a Child, attended by a Guardian Angel ; Danaë, by Titian,—but I will not trou-

ble you with a dry enumeration of names;
I dare say you will take my word for there
being some fine performances by Correggio,
Leonarde da Vinci, Annibal Caracci, Guercino,
Claude Lorraine, Vernêt, and the usual painters
of eminence to be found in all collections.

Limited as we were for time, we contrived
to spare one day for Pompeii. We crossed the
river Sebeto by the Ponte Maddalena, where
is a statue of the patron saint of Naples, St.
Januarius, stationed there as if to protect the
city from the fury of Mount Vesuvius. Our
road passed through the Palace of Portici,
Resina, Torre del Greco, Torre del Annunziata, till we came upon sheets of lava, and
beds of ashes, which, though interspersed with
gardens, showed our vicinity to the volcano.
But of Pompeii not a vestige was to be seen, till
the coachman, after driving some time between
high banks of cinders, suddenly drew up at
a rustic farm-yard sort of gate, and exclaimed,
ere we were aware that we were in its neighbourhood, " Ecco Pompeii !"

A few instants brought us into the Comic
and Tragic Theatres, both paved with marble,
and in perfect repair. Near these, in a large
court, stands the diminutive Temple of Isis,
to which Johnson's observations concerning
ancient temples may very well apply, for this

might, with its fellow temples, very easily
" play at leap-frog in St. Paul's," and half a
dozen such might run about there very safely,
without the slightest danger of incommoding
each other. Behind the high altar, still remains a covered closet or secret recess, where,
in times of yore, the priests were wont to conceal themselves when they delivered oracles to
the people, and from whence at this moment
issued one, promising me a favourable voyage
up the Nile and down the Red Sea. The
guide, who was considerably amused at the
trick my *compagnon de voyage* played me,
on his emerging from his hiding-place, exclaimed, " Oh those priests! they were sad
' Birbanti ;' " thus unconsciously uttering a severe sarcasm on the deceits and artifices, of a
similar nature, which are said to be still practised by the Romish Church.

The Via Appia is a tolerably wide street,
with its ancient pavement in a far better condition than the modern at Rome. There are
still elevated *trottoirs* on the sides for foot
passengers, and the marks of wheels are even
now visible. There are the remains of shops
on both sides, the walls of all of them painted,
and the colours and designs perfectly fresh, as
if but just finished. The generality of them
are very small, and reminded us of those in the

Burlington Arcade, which they resemble as to
magnitude, and they are also very like the bazaars in Oriental cities.   In the public baking-
house, in which bread was found when it was
first discovered, is an oven, which, though some
thousand years old, might even yet be used;
and on a marble slab, in a coffee-house, are the
marks of cups, as if but recently set down!
Indeed, every thing looked so completely as if
the town had but just been deserted, that we
could almost have expected to have met with
some ancient Roman lingering in his native
city; but in these places, which some centuries
ago resounded with the cheerful hum of men,
solitude and desolation now reign, and the only
living objects besides ourselves and our guide,
were a wild bandit-looking shepherd, conducting
his sheep over pillars of marble, and through
stately edifices half buried in ashes.   The Amphitheatre is in such wonderful preservation,
that it might still serve for spectacles and
shows, and from the top there is a fine view
of Mount Vesuvius.   The Villa of Marcus
Arrius Diomedes is in an affectingly perfect
state; it really seemed so indelicate, penetrating into the haunts and apartments of a private family, that we half expected to have encountered some of them, coming to ask us the
motives for our intrusion, and to chide us for

our impertinent curiosity. The illusion at the moment was so strong that we forgot the many centuries that had elapsed since the poor master attempted to flee from destruction, with the keys of his house, and a purse of gold in his hand, and when the unfortunate females sought for refuge in the subterranean apartments, where seventeen skeletons were subsequently discovered.

We left Pompeii by the Herculaneum gate, beyond which are the tombs. Some of these are handsome, and some mutilated statues remain, as if in mockery of the efforts of frail mortality to rescue itself from oblivion.

The rain, which had hitherto good-naturedly kept off, now began to descend in such torrents, that we were obliged to abandon all idea of seeing Herculaneum. We however stopped at the Palace of Portici, which is built over it; in this particular resembling what is so frequently to be seen in the world, where the splendour and fortune of the favoured individual is founded on the depression and destruction of another, whose wrongs cannot be redressed, because justice to him would injure his rival's prosperity. Thus Herculaneum remains entombed, lest its excavation might injure Portici. The curiosities and treasures of the former are many of them deposited in the museum of the latter, and there are several very interesting pictures; also the skull of the unfortunate female who was found in the Villa of Diomedes, at Pompeii, and who, from being better dressed than her companions, was supposed to have been the mistress of the house. There is likewise the impression of her arm and figure upon the ashes which preserved this melancholy cast of her form, whilst they cut short the thread of her existence.

After Pompeii, the splendid apartments of Murat's palace had scarcely power to interest, though we could but be struck with the mutability of human events, in seeing the Bourbons now enjoying the elegancies and luxuries which were prepared for his own use by the unfortunate King Joachim.

We returned to Naples, much delighted with our morning's excursion, and greatly regretting that our limited time prevented our seeing more of its beauties, and those of the enchanting country around ; but we were compelled to proceed quickly, and consequently we were reluctantly obliged to abandon any farther excursions, which, under any other circumstances, would have been most gratifying to our curiosity.

LETTER X.

Embarkation in Steam-packet.—Isles of Lipari.—Stromboli.
—Straits of Messina.—Scylla and Charybdis.—Harbour
of Messina.—Beautiful situation.—Sirocco.—Earthquakes.
Shipwrecked Greeks.—La Virgine della Lettera.—Phænomenon of La Fata Morgana.—Duomo.—Marina.—Sicilian language, manners, and climate.

On the 29th of November we embarked, for
Sicily, on board the steam-packet El Real
Ferdinando, and we bade farewell to the continent of Europe. Before day-break on the
following morning, we were near the Lipari
Islands, and, as a volcano in an active state is
a sight not to be seen every day, we all rose
early to see Stromboli, the light-house which
Nature has placed in these seas as a beacon to
the wandering mariner, to guide him through
the pathless deep. It is an insulated rock,
with liquid fire constantly pouring down its
sides, and, boldly rising from the bosom of the
sea, it presents a most striking spectacle. At
sun-rise we found ourselves among the Lipari
Islands, and in the vicinity of King Æolus's
Palace, where in times of yore, he kept his
court, and where the artful " Jovisque et soror,
et conjux," promised him " formâ pulcherrimâ

Deiopeiam," to induce him to raise the tempest which scattered Æneas's fleet. Either the virago Goddess Juno had more compassion on a wandering female than on the Trojan hero, or the King of the Winds had had no interview with her this morning, for he sent us nothing but favourable gales and gentle zephyrs; and as the day more fully advanced, we found ourselves in front of the poetical Sicily, with the snowy mass of Mongibello, towering more than ten thousand feet aloft in the air, and soaring majestically above the range of subordinate hills. In the blue distance, on the left, appeared the mountains of the Calabrian coast, and in the foreground the Isles of Lipari dotted the surface of the briny deep. There were no signs of the Straits, and we seemed so completely land-locked, that really a more patient mortal than Hannibal might have imagined, as he did, that he was betrayed by his pilot, when in this situation. As we proceeded, however, the shores of Italy and the smiling hills of Sicily separated, and we were soon opposite the famous, or rather infamous rocks of Scylla; a low but rugged range of rocks, terminating in a steep and very precipitous promontory. If, however, never more tremendous than at this present moment, Homer must have had great talents for in-

vention, to have invested these regions with
such poetical terrors, for we could but smile at
the old saying—

" Incidit in Scyllam, cupieus evitare Charybdim."

Our pilot was skilful enough to guide us
safely through all these perils and dangers, and
after passing the Fanale, or Faro, we soon entered the celebrated harbour of Messina, which
is formed by a narrow slip of land, so exactly
in the shape of a sickle, that the ancients
feigned, Saturn flung his hither, down from
Heaven. It now, however, bears the name of
the Arm of St. Ranieri, and in its neighbourhood is the whirlpool of Charybdis, or Il
Garofolo, as it is termed by the Sicilians. This
is caused by the contraction of the water occasioned by the said arm, and changes with the
tide; but though we were often close to it, we
never saw any thing more remarkable in its
appearance than the ripple which the flinging
a large stone into the sea would produce.

We procured tolerable accommodations at
the Hotel Britannique, and as, thanks to the
Sirocco, and some dreadful storms, we were
detained here for more than three weeks, we
had time to become well acquainted with Messina. Its situation is most beautiful; superior,
perhaps, even to that of Naples, and the views

from the hills in the vicinity are enchanting.
Among these we frequently wandered, and
we were quite delighted with the romantic
variety of the scenery, which had a peculiarly pastoral air. Picturesque ravines and fiu-
mares, or dry beds of torrents, were tapestried
o'er with delicate shrubs, or clothed with rich
groves of orange and lemon trees, whose deep
green foliage was enlivened with their golden
fruits. Olive-trees lightly waved around, vines
hung in tangled festoons from tree to tree, the
cactus and the Indian fig grew in the wildest
luxuriance ; and the air, even at this late season of the year, was perfumed with the sweet
alysson, and other of our tender annuals. In
fact, there seemed no winter in this favoured
isle; none, at least, like our northern one, where

> ——" He comes to rule the varied year,
> Sullen and sad, with all his wintry train,
> Vapours, and clouds, and storms.

We literally found the climate too warm,
and we were compelled to take our meals in a
large sala at the top of the house, for coolness.
The Sicilians, however, have their siroccos and
their earthquakes ; the former, the " Plumbeus
Auster" of the ancients I presume, is so noto-
rious in its effects, that of any thing remarkably
dull, the *on-dit* is, that "era scritto nel sirocco :"

it quite unhinges the frame, and inspires nothing but lassitude and ennui. With regard to the earthquakes, poor Messina has not yet recovered from the dreadful one in 1783, when the Knights of Malta fitted out a squadron, and came to the assistance of the houseless, naked, sick, and starving inhabitants. "Use lessens marvels," it is said, and they talk now of a shock with as much *sang-froid* as we could do of a common tempest. They told us, however, that the sea-quakes were more formidable in their effects, two of which had been lately experienced. We felt, or fancied we felt, a slight earthquake one night, and of course I expected the house was to tumble down; however, nothing more serious occurred than a few bricks falling, which possibly might have been occasioned by the rats, which were very numerous and troublesome. It seemed as if some one were shaking the room violently; the light flashed from my eyes, and I could have imagined that I had been struck with an electric shock.

Messina, formerly termed Zancle, derives its present name from a colony of Messineans in the Morea, who fleeing from thence, took refuge here in ancient times. Whilst we were here, a vessel of Greeks, likewise abandoning their native land, was wrecked on the coast, but the poor creatures were all put into durance vile, and condemned to the Lazaretto; which considering the Messinese are themselves only a set of Greek refugees, was a reception any thing but courteous. There was something so classical, so Ulysses-like in Greeks shipwrecked in these regions, that we longed to become acqainted with them, but we however saw no one whom the utmost stretch of imagination could have converted into a hero —" the much-enduring man"— the heroic son of Laertes. The Virgin is the patroness of Messina, and she is reported to have sent the inhabitants a letter, which is said to be still among the records of the Senate-house, in which she exhorts them to keep constant to the true faith. She is from thence termed La Vergine della Lettera, but whether her epistle is dated from heaven or from earth, we did not hear. The phænomenon of La Fata Morgana takes place occasionally in the Straits, which is produced, it is said, by a very strong refraction in the atmosphere, which distinctly reflects terrestrial objects in the sky. We were not, however, fortunate enough to be treated with a sight of this singular spectacle, which is but of rare occurrence. It was across these Straits that San Francesco di Paolo passed over, seated upon his cloak, instead of a boat ; his servant,

who was placed behind him, for want of faith,
sunk to the bottom, whilst the Saint triumphantly
reached the wished-for harbour on the opposite
shore. The tower is still shown where Richard
Cœur de Lion lodged, when he stopped here
on his way to the Holy Land, and where Queen
Berengère met him, under the escort of Queen
Eleanor his mother; but with all our en-
deavours, we could see no one whom we could
imagine to be the descendants of the laughter-
loving Beatrice and " Benedict the married
man," the scene of whose adventures, in "Much
Ado about Nothing," is laid here. It was singular enough, that as we entered the harbour,
my head full of Claudio and the distresses of
the gentle Hero, the first ship that greeted
our eyes happened to be the Shakespeare.
Our courier one day brought us an offer from
the captain to convey letters for us to England, but the name had escaped his memory.
He most energetically assured us it was that of
" a great man in England," who, " like Voltaire,
wrote histories and tales ;" and we accordingly
went over a whole list of historians and novelists,
whilst he remained in utter astonishment at
our ignorance, till at length it turned out to be
our immortal dramatist.

Messina is most delightfully situated ; its
buildings extend along the sea, and up the

base of the mountains immediately behind, whilst its churches and houses are intermingled with groves of orange and lemon-trees, olives, and vineyards. From the Convent of San Gregorio, whose chapel almost rivals that of the Medicis in richness of decoration, there is a most magnificent view: you look over the whole extent of the Straits, which have the appearance of a noble river, and you see the rugged coast of Calabria to an immense distance. The Duomo is an antique building, adorned with the statues of the Apostles, as large as life, and the ceiling of the choir, representing the Deity in mosaic, reminded us of those at Pisa and St. Paul's at Rome. The pulpit of marble is ornamented with bassi relievi by Gaggini. But the great glory of Messina is its noble, and perhaps unrivalled, Marina; a magnificent drive, running close to the sea for some miles, where six carriages may drive abreast. There are some tolerable statues here, and the Sicilians set great store by that of Neptune, of the school of, or as some say, by Michael Angelo Buonarotti himself, in which the god is represented with his trident in his hand, and with Scylla and Charybdis enchained at his feet. The Corso is a tolerably good street, and divides the city into the marine and hilly divisions. The streets are clean, and were at this

time paving, under the superintendence of Mr.
Broadbelt, the American Consul. The numerous piazzas, or largos, are generally ornamented
with statues or fountains. The Italian spoken
here is very different from that of Florence
and Rome; but we were told that the Sicilian may almost claim to be a distinct language;
and Mr. Barker, the English Consul, observed,
it was full of expression, and worthy of more
attention than has hitherto been bestowed
upon it.

The costume of the upper classes here is
between the English and the French; something like our country towns, where every
one is behind the mode, but strives to make
amends for it by a little extra finery. The
lower classes still retain the graceful mantilla,
which is very superior to our formal bonnets
and pelisses. We were continually reminded
of the pictures in the old editions of Gil Blas
and Don Quixote, for there is a considerable
mixture of Spanish customs still intermingled
with the Sicilian manners. The rustics in
night-caps, mounted on donkeys, in Sancho
Panza style; the Monks in their robes; the
bare-headed Friar; the Lettiga between mules;
the goats brought down from the mountains;
the shepherd tending his flocks in the sequestered vales; all under a calm and serene sky,

tend to give something peculiar, something *Sicilian* to the scene; whilst the bagpipe resounding through the streets, seems as national here as in the Highlands of Scotland. We one day met with an old man at the door of a cottage, singing, or rather chanting his verses with great volubility in a sort of recitative, and accompanying himself on a two-stringed instrument, and we thought it was thus perhaps that the divine Homer first sung his immortal strains, and perhaps to as rude an audience.

The climate of Messina seems far milder and pleasanter than that of Naples; there we suffered considerably from the violent changes in the atmosphere—alternately broiling and freezing as we were exposed to the intense heat of the sun, or to the cold wintry blast. At Messina, on the contrary, though almost Christmas, we never experienced any inclemency of weather; and the Sirocco, which is equally prevalent at Naples, seems to be the only drawback to the agreeable and delightful temperature of Sicily. We much regretted we were not able to venture into the interior, but there are no roads, and at this time of the year the sudden swelling of mountain-torrents renders travelling unpleasant and even dangerous; we were consequently obliged to abandon the idea from motives of prudence.

LETTER XI.

Sicilian Brigantino.—Sirocco.—Augusta.—Brigands.—Light House.—English officers at Augusta.—Sicilian Maccaroni.—Syracuse.—Malta and Gozo.

On the 21st of December we embarked on board a small Sicilian brigantino, the Santa Maria del Porto Santo, and sailed out of the harbour of Messina with a tolerably fair wind. In the course of the night it suddenly veered round into an unfavourable quarter, and there was every appearance of the Sirocco returning. On the following day it began to blow, and the sea to swell, and we were for some hours most agreeably tossed off Mount Etna, but as I was not equal to remaining upon deck, I only *heard* of its magnificent scenery : green vales whose vivid freshness formed a fine contrast with the woody regions of the mountain ; romantic and picturesque rocks boldly presenting themselves to the sea, and precipices crowned with castles and toppling convents. On the 23rd the wind freshened into a gale, and the gale threatening to become a storm, the Captain resolved to put into Augusta, a small town upon an island on the coast of Sicily ; and about noon we anchored in its harbour.

In our cabin was an image of the Virgin,

before whose shrine was a lamp, which, in calm
and serene weather, was neglected, and was
frequently allowed to go out, to the great
offence of our olfactory nerves; but we were
somewhat amused with the devotion of the
crew, which rose and sunk with the wind. No
sooner did it begin to blow, than the lamp was
immediately re-lighted, and in proportion as
the strength of the storm increased, so did their
attention to the light, and when the tempest
howled the loudest, its flame was then most
carefully trimmed, and burned the brightest;
from which it would seem that the sailors
placed far more efficacy in feeding it with oil,
than in either propitiating the Deity with
prayer, or in using their own exertions to steer
the vessel.

For several days the Sirocco blew most violently and determinately, the greater part of
which period we spent upon shore, though
liable to be summoned to the vessel at the least
appearance of a favourable change in the weather.   On our first landing, we were somewhat
surprised at being all taken to the Quarantine
Office, and when it was ascertained that we
had not the plague, then we were handed over
to the Police and Passport offices, but, however, no sooner did they discover that we were
English, to whom the Sicilians are very partial,

than it was immediately " *va—bene, bene!*"
Our accommodations here were of the very
poorest description, and it was with difficulty
that we procured even these. There are no
hotels, or inns, for strangers; indeed, few would
visit Augusta but from necessity, there being
little to induce the traveller to wander thither;
but, however, it was better than our brigantino,
with her cargo of myrtle wood. It was a curious place to spend Christmas in; a small
island on the Sicilian coast, at the foot of
Mount Etna, which, in honour of the season,
put on several additional layers of snow; and
not more singular were the flowers we frequently collected in the meadows; jonquils, ra-
nunculuses, anemones, and candy-tuft, which
were growing in profusion, and the wildest
luxuriancy, in the open air. We thought of
Proserpine's fate, but I never was interrupted
by the grizzly old Pluto, who probably finds
one lady as much as he can manage in his
Tartarean domains.

On Christmas day, we were nearly attacked
by a party of brigands, who surrounded our
house with evidently hostile intentions, armed
with heavy bludgeons, watching our movements, and apparently intending to waylay us
when we left the town. We were enabled
to baffle their plans; but as the only fastening

to our door was a piece of wood thrust through
the staple, I fully expected, as the Irishman
says, " to wake some morning and find our
throats cut."

One evening, as we were rambling about the
island, the sound of music floating on the air,
induced us to go in search of the invisible
harmonist, when close to the sea-shore, and
thrown into strong relief by the light of the
pale moon, which was sailing in majesty through
a cloudless sky, we beheld a round chapel, and
before a small shrine to the Virgin, was a
silver-headed old man at his devotions, playing
a very sweet hymn ; by him knelt two young
men, one accompanying him, the other chanting, whilst prostrate on the ground, and wrapped
in their graceful mantillas, were thirty or forty
women and children, who filled the chorus in
a most harmonious manner, whilst the sound
of the waters was heard between each cadence
and dying fall. We never saw a prettier spectacle, or heard music that pleased us better,
than these Sicilian vespers.

Augusta is a poor little town, situated on a
small island, about two miles long and three
quarters broad, separated from the main land by
a back-water, which is navigable for small boats,
and over which a bridge is thrown, which is
commanded by the Citadel. The Light-house, a

pretty little fort, which appears like a ship at sea, is situated at the entrance of the harbour, which, though a noble one, is but little frequented. The Commandant of the fort, in order to conceal his having sold the powder contained in its magazines, partly destroyed it by blowing it up, which act of treachery he is expiating by imprisonment for life. King Ferdinand was so fond of this castle, that he is said to have shed tears when he heard of the injury it had sustained. From Augusta there is a noble view of Mount Etna, which, though forty miles distant from thence, looks as if it were in its immediate vicinity. The sea coast is seen from the head-lands near Catania to Syracuse Point, and the range of Hyblean Hills forms the back-ground. St. Dominick is the patron saint of the city, whose image we saw carried in grand procession through the town. The convent and church dedicated to him are the finest here; for the Duomo, though large, contains but little worth notice. In some of the churches, and particularly before the shrine of La Madonna dei Poveri, were some most singular votive offerings; every part of the human body, formed in wax, hung up by those who had been cured by her of diseases, in what seemed, to us, a most indecent display. To judge from the

wens and other horrible spectacles, the Virgin
must be endowed with very superior medical
and surgical abilities; but we were reminded
of the ancient custom of the Romans, who
were wont to hang up something in comme-
moration of any extraordinary deliverance.
The Town-hall is ornamented with the high-
sounding and sonorous inscription of "Senatus
Populusque Romani," which, considering what
a poor little place Augusta is, borders closely
upon the ludicrous. Yet even in this out-of-
the-way spot, strange to say, we met some
of our cosmopolite countrymen, who having
married Sicilian ladies, were settled here, and
one of them had contrived to muster round
him many little English comforts. They
soon found us out, and their kindness and
hospitality caused us to pass several very pleasant and agreeable hours in this retirement.
They talked to us of Sicily, and we told them
of England, and they absolutely seemed to
gasp for intelligence of what was going on in
the world, rumours of which seldom reached
them in this their banishment, for such, to
military men as they were, it must have seemed. A Sicilian Field Officer in the Neapolitan
service often accompanied them. He was a
polished, gentlemanly man, quite of the old
school; he had been Governor of Girgenti

for ten, and of Taormina for six years, and
was now retired to his native town, where,
as he observed, " Il s'ennuyoit beaucoup, for
there was no theatre, no conversazione." He
seemed particularly partial to the English; and
he told us, both his countrymen and himself
much regretted Sicily was not under our Government, rather than that of the Neapolitans,
whom the Sicilians appear to hold in utter
abhorrence. I shall not easily forget the utter
astonishment with which he viewed a sprig
of *myrtle* in my sash, for the Sicilians heat
their ovens with it; and when we informed
him that in England we ornamented our
green-houses and drawing-rooms with this
beautiful shrub, with a truly foreign shrug, he
exclaimed, " Mon Dieu ! est il possible !" In
spite of his subsequent bow of deference,
and his submissive, " I am bound to believe
you, Madam," I am convinced he thought
I was trying to impose upon his credulity.
We had an opportunity of seeing a good deal
of the Sicilian manners here, for at this season
of the year it appears to be the fashion to visit
in the evening, and a general salute always
went round when the parties separated. We
saw here the apparatus and process of making
maccaroni, which is so extremely simple, that
I wonder it is not constantly made in England,

in private families, instead of being imported. It is so infinitely better when eaten quite fresh, and before it has had time to become hard and dry, that most Sicilian families make it at home, just before it is wanted, and indeed it forms one of their principal articles of food. The paste, composed of simple flour and water, when of a proper consistency, is pressed by a screw through a plate full of holes, each of which has a peg in the centre, to make it hollow ; the whole is set in motion by a wheel turned by the hand, and the maccaroni is then laid in the sun to harden.

After frequent attempts to leave Augusta, and as many failures, we at length succeeded in rounding Syracuse Point, and we came in sight of the poor remains of that once celebrated city, which we viewed at a most tantalizing distance. The Island of Ortygia, on which they stand, appears by no means extensive. The last sun of 1825 set behind the Hyblean hills, as we took leave of the majestic, the beautiful, the sublime Mongibello, the fruitful source of so many poetical fables and extravagancies, with its cultivated base, its woody region, its snow-capped summit, and its crater, which all spring at once from the bosom of the sea.

" Off Cape Passaro !" were the first sounds

that greeted us on the 1st of January, 1826.
With a tolerable breeze we soon lost sight of
Sicily, and by the time the sun began to de-
scend in the horizon, appeared in the distance
Malta and Gozo.

> " Calypso's isles,
> The sister tenants of the middle deep,
> Where for the weary still a haven smiles."

As we neared the entrance of the magnificent
harbour of La Valette, at whose mouth several
pirates are suspended, the evening gun sounded.
" *Iddio !*" exclaimed the Captain, clasping his
hands with a theatrical look of despair ; but he
was mistaken, we were *not* too late ; and most
fortunate for us it was that we were not, for a
dreadful storm was impending, and right glad
were we to find ourselves transferred from the
Sicilian brigantino to Beverley's very excellent hotel. Those who have never travelled
can never know what comfort is, for it is by
comparison alone that we learn to appreciate
it. Ever since we left Naples, we had been
roughing it, and I cannot describe to you how
positively delightful to the poor weather-beaten
wanderers appeared the clean apartments, the
neatness and the tidiness of every thing around
in Malta, where we intended to spend a few
days, to refresh ourselves after our fatigues.

LETTER XII.

Malta.—Bay and Cave of St. Paul.—Order of the Knights of Malta. — Duomo.—Palace. —Maltese. — Hospitality.— Caleeshes.—Arrival of the Marquis of Hastings.—Malta, a Missionary Station.

THE Maltese term their island " the flower of the world." To the patriot, his first best country ever is at home ; but I have gazed at the Maltese landscapes till I have really thought them pretty. Sea views, perhaps, they should rather be termed, for the dark blue Mediterranean calmly sleeping in the deeply indented bays, or dashing furiously over the rocks, generally meets the eye wherever it is turned. This little barren rock in the midst of the Mediterranean, with no fresh water but that which falls from Heaven, no indigenous production but a few jujube trees, and no soil but what is brought from afar, has, by the hand of man, been covered with magnificent edifices, almost impregnable fortifications, and, by the prowess of its brave knights, its name has been enrolled high in the annals of glory. The names of L'Isle Adam and La Valette alone would be enough to consecrate this spot in the imaginations of all those to whom valour and mental courage are dear ; but it has higher claims to interest, for in Holy Writ, under the name of Melita, it is famed for the memorable shipwreck of St. Paul, and for his sojourn of three months on the island. The bay which was the scene of his escape, is still pointed out, and retains his name ; and at Civita Vecchia is shown the spot where " he shook off the viper, and felt no harm," since which time neither snake nor venomous animal has dared to enter Malta,—so runs the story. There is a statue of the Saint here, which has a fine effect as seen athwart the dark gloom of the cave where it stands, the stone of which is said to have the miraculous power of curing diseases, and of never diminishing in quantity. The Maltese also claim for their island the Grotto of Calypso, though this honour is disputed with them by Gozo.

The celebrated Order of the Knights of Malta derived its origin from the charity of some rich citizens of Amalfi in Italy, who, in 1050, by rich presents to the Caliph of Egypt, obtained his permission to erect a church and two hospitals at Jerusalem, which establish-ments were originally supported by the alms and contributions of the southern Italians and their Norman conqueror. Godfrey endowed them with an estate in Brabant, and many of his brethren devoted themselves to the per-

petual service of way-worn pilgrims. As the
association acquired importance, the Abbot
Gerard, feeling the weight of this charge, proposed to his brethren to renounce the world,
and to take a religious habit; and in the time of
the Grand Master Raymond du Puy, between
the years 1121 and 1160, the friars first became
soldiers, and were divided into three classes,
nobility, clergy, and serving brethren. When
not engaged in war, the various duties of the
hospital exclusively occupied their attention,
and the great men of Europe sent their sons
to Jerusalem to be trained up in religion, and
in knightly discipline and feats of arms. Every
country in Europe had Preceptories, thus called,
till 1260, when they were termed Comman-
deriés, from " Commendamus," the first word
at the commencement of their spiritual letters.
The Order was divided into the then principal
seven langues or languages of Christendom,
the English, German, Italian, Arragonese, Pro-
vencial, Auvergnese, and the common French.
After the Reformation, those of Castile and
Portugal were substituted for that of our
country, into which the Hospitallers first came
in the reign of Henry I. and their first priory
was erected by Jordan Briset, of Wellinghall,
Kent, at Clerkenwell, which was burnt by the
rebels in 1381. After the expulsion of the

Knights from Rhodes by the Turks, Charles V. presented Malta to the Grand-Master of the Order of St. John of Jerusalem, Villiers de L'Isle Adam, and they assumed the name of Knights of Malta, which their brave acts have rendered illustrious in the page of history. Vignes, Villiers, L'Isle Adam, and La Valette, are interred in a subterranean chapel in the Duomo, and the tomb of Cottonera is ornamented with a statue of that hero, with a Turkish and African slave enchained at his feet. The pavement of this cathedral is perhaps unique, and is by some considered the handsomest and most interesting in the world. It is entirely composed of the arms and mottos of the deceased knights, in magnificent mosaic, formed of the finest marbles. The ceiling, by Calabrese Prete, is well painted; but the frescos on the walls, chiefly representations of the heroic deeds of those who sleep below, are quickly yielding to time and damp. Unfortunately, this is also the case with those in the palace, a fine old building. It is a pity that some antiquary does not rescue them from the oblivion to which they will soon be consigned, for though certainly not quite equal to those in the Camere di Rafaelle, they are very interesting on account of the historic and heroic facts which they commemorate. The portraits of some of the grand-masters are still remaining, though it is to be feared they will be turned adrift at the behest of the first *tasty* Governor, for the hall of St. George has been converted into an elegant modern ball-room, and the old paintings quite expunged. At Malta, Maltese frescos were, perhaps, preferable. The armoury is highly interesting, and the suits of armour are so well arranged, that they would almost induce the spectator to believe that the mortal frames which once tenanted them, were still frowning from the vizarded and helmeted figures around. That of La Valette is still shown, richly inlaid with gold; besides which, there is an ample show of swords, spears, and other murderous weapons of offence and defence.

But for the poor knights, where are they? Alas for them! Well might Burke exclaim, " The days of chivalry are over." Of them whose deeds " once kept the world alive with lustre and with noise," nought remains but splendid tombs and stupendous fortifications to tell us such men were; and in the palaces and auberges, whose floors were once trod, per-chance, by L'Isle Adam or La Valette, now re-side the English merchant and the British fair. Occasionally may be seen wandering forth, like a ghost, an old-fashioned figure, clad in ha-bits formed a century ago, with an enormous

Maltese cross, the only token by which may be recognized a lingering relic of the illustrious Order of the Knights of Malta, looking, however, like a burlesque upon that glorious, that chivalrous race of men, whose prowess and whose exploits once filled all Europe with their renown.

In the Palace there is a room hung with some splendid tapestry, representing the animal and vegetable productions of warm and tropical climates. The great harbour, somewhat resembling a clumsy hand in shape, is separated from the smaller, where is the Lazaretto, by a tongue of land, upon which stands the chief city, La Valette. The brave Abercrombie sleeps at the entrance of the former, which is protected by the castle of St. Elmo, so famed for its vigorous defence against the Turks. The fortifications of Cottonera, Floriana, St. Angelo, and St. John, are really wonderful, and Napoleon might well have congratulated himself, which he is said to have done, on having a friend inside to admit him into the interior, as it would be almost impossible to enter by force. The streets of La Valette are clean and well-paved, but so irregular, that when walking in them, you are constantly ascending and descending hills and steps. The private houses are in a style of magnificence seldom to be met with; the rooms are large, spacious, and handsome, and the verandahs, flat roofs, terraces, courts, and fountains, evince the dubious situation of Malta, which required an act of Parliament to certify that it belonged to *Europe*. The faldetta and black mantilla, distended with silk, which form the national costume of the Maltese women, and the blue check, or white jacket and trowsers, sash, and long dangling cap of the Smiche, or caleesheer, give a peculiarity to the scene; and the olive complexions and brilliantly dark eyes of the inhabitants, their rude language, a *patois* composed of ancient Punic, modern Arabic, and barbarous Italian, forming a sort of Lingua Franca, remind you of the vicinity of Africa, whilst the English comforts and luxuries at the same time, make you feel *at Home*. The British inhabitants sit over fires of Newcastle coals, "just as we do in England," and stir them into a brilliant blaze, with that peculiarly national-looking implement, a poker, ever accompanied with Anglo tongs and shovel; whilst Tripoli and Tunis, the Morea and Crete, are talked of as familiarly as Bath or Cheltenham; and a trip to Corfu, or an excursion to Sicily, are proposed for change of air, as we should recommend one to Brighton or Ramsgate. We had every reason to be pleased with our sojourn at Malta; we came in idea but for a few days, and, like St. Paul, we tarried three months. On landing, we scarcely knew a single person ; but the Maltese,* though they have lost their barbarity, have *not* lost the hospitality for which they are famed in Holy Writ. They indeed " showed us no little kindness," and for courtesy to strangers, their island richly deserves to be termed, *par excellence,* " the flower of the world." We came in for all " the fun, frolic, and foolery" of the Carnival. There were masked and fancy balls, musical parties and dances innumerable. During the last two or three days, the natives paraded the streets in masks, and the English entered into it *con amore,* pelting each other with sugar-plums in a most determined manner. The caleeshes, which, from the nature of the country, are almost the only vehicles in use, even with the English, are singular-looking conveyances. First of all comes, full drive, a wildish-looking little horse in shafts, and by its side, at a long swinging trot, runs the bare-footed calesheer, his immense nightcap alternately sweeping one shoulder or the other, as the sun or rain requires the additional defence. Then, *not* upon springs, comes a sort of box or sedan chair, supposed to carry two, though that number is frequently doubled, nay,

* The English residents are here meant ; and their liberal, kind, and warm-hearted attention to strangers, makes the modern Malta of the nineteenth century, to compete with " the Island " when it " it was called Melita," in A.D. 62.

trebled. Last of all, like an after-thought, comes tearing away, a pair of wheels; and in this machine, off the traveller jolts, apparently to the eminent danger of dislocation either to his neck or limbs; but, though I frequently wished Cinderella's kind god-mother would have transmuted one of the enormous pump-kins sold in the market into a coach for my accommodation, I believe accidents are of very rare occurrence.

In consequence of the repeated piracies in the Mediterranean, we were strongly recom-mended not to venture to Alexandria in any but an English ship, which flag alone is re-spected. It was somewhat singular that the first vessels that sailed for Alexandria were the Ulysses and the Penelope; but the former, in spite of all his prudence and wisdom, did wan-der so egregiously out of his way, in sailing from Troy to Ithaca, and took so long a time to effect it, that we were apprehensive of en-trusting ourselves to so erratic a gentleman; and as it was unpleasant to choose between man and wife, we accordingly took a passage in the Eliza. In the interim, Sir Charles Col-ville arrived, whom we had intended to meet at Cosseir; but though he had enjoyed the journey, or rather voyage, extremely himself, it was rather appalling to me to hear him say it was, in his opinion, unadvisable for a lady to venture through Egypt, and all our friends recommended our returning to England, and proceeding by a China-ship. However, I was not to be daunted, and we continued our preparations for our Egyptian campaign. Two or three days before our departure, the venerable Marquis of Hastings arrived from England, with his amiable Marchioness and family, in the Herald frigate, and we were much gratified to see the enthusiastic affection with which he was received by the Maltese, by whom he was greatly beloved. C—— was presented to him on the 3rd of April, by Sir Frederick Hankey, when there was a great levee, and he had the honour of dining with him on the following day ; in the evening there were some splendid fireworks exhibited, the voluntary compliment of the Maltese to their noble and illustrious Governor, and one they had never paid to any of his predecessors.

In his absence, the island had been governed by the Lieutenant-Governor, General Woodford, and both he, and his elegant and accomplished lady, were, from the peculiar urbanity and affability of their manners, universally popular at Malta.

This little barren insulated rock, which, it is said, was colonized by the Phœnicians fifteen

hundred years before Christ, in many points
of view is particularly interesting to those who
are anxious for the spread of Christianity ; and
to them it is highly important, as the head
quarters of the Missionary labours in the Mediterranean.   The excellent and highly-respect-
ed Mr. Jowett, with whom we had the pleasure of being acquainted, was at this time at
the station, and was labouring most earnestly
in his vocation.   From him we procured some
Arabic spelling-books, which we afterwards
were enabled to distribute to some of the wild
Arabs we subsequently met with in our journey.
The schools at Malta seemed in a flourishing
and a prosperous state, but it was singular,
considering the island belonged to the English,
that they had no church here, and that the only
place where the Protestant form of worship was
performed, was at the Chapel in the Palace.

After a very delightful three months *séjour*
at hospitable Malta, in April we again began
to think of pursuing our route.   The island
had now assumed a very different aspect to
what it presented on our landing on the 1st of
January.   Winter had fled to the churlish regions of the north.   " Plumbeus Auster" no
longer reigned lord of the ascendency.   Storms
were hushed, and gentle zephyrs supplied their
place.   " Heaven's breath smelt most wooingly

and sweet ;" the little patches of soil were covered with verdure; the elegant pepper-tree,
with its pendant branches, formed an agreeable
shade ; " the flowers appeared upon the earth,
and the fig-tree put forth her green leaves ;"
the air was perfumed with sweet alysson, which
communicates so peculiar a taste to the Maltese
honey ; the barren fortifications were tapestried
with minute flowerets, and the daisy, the star
of home, which, wherever the British wanderer
turns his steps, recalls dear " merry England"
to the memory, decked the sterile rock of
Malta.

LETTER XIII.

Departure from Malta.—German Missionaries.—Service on
board.—Alarm of Pirates.—Arrival at Alexandria.—Landing.—Consul's House.—Pompey's, or Diocletian's Pillar.

As the evening gun fired on the 5th of April,
we sailed out of the great harbour at Malta,
bade farewell to Europe, and with a fair but
not strong breeze, we proceeded towards Alexandria. Our fellow passengers were some German clergymen, sent out by the Church Missionary Society. Mr. Kugler, destined for
Abyssinia ; Mr. Krusè, with his wife, bound to
Grand Cairo. We felt deeply interested in

their welfare; they were quite young, but
evidently wrapped up in the good cause they
were engaged in.   They had forsaken their
country, their friends, and all that makes life
dear, to preach the Gospel in the dark corners
of the earth, and we could but look upon them
in the light of self-devoted martyrs.   Our cabin
was separated from theirs by a very slight partition, and it was amusing, and by no means
unedifying, to hear the warm theological dis-
cussions carried on between them and the officers of the ship ; the manly, but artless simplicity and singleness of heart of the former,
engaged with the shrewd and worldly good
sense of the latter ; but the Germans had ever
the advantage, as much as the sacred cause and
object to which they were devoting their ener-
gies, was superior to the cotton cargo the others
were in pursuit of.   On Sunday we had divine
service on board, and with the blue sky for our
canopy, upon the pathless deep, which knows
no other master than the Almighty, it was far
more impressive than in the full-choired cathedral,

> " Where through the long-drawn aisle and fretted vault,
> The pealing anthem swells the voice of praise."

For several days we saw nothing but the heavens and the sea.   The evenings were lovely,
and after the glorious sun had set in a flood of

gold, when the silver crescent of the moon appeared in the west, and the stars emitted a brilliant light, it were impossible to conceive a more enchanting scene. A ship in full sail, with a steady wind and calm sea, is a magnificent sight, and that sea was the classical Mediterranean! When in the neighbourhood of Crete, the birth-place of Dardanian Jove, "a sail a-head" was the cry! The Captain's round, ruddy face fell — a little—and *but* a little. We were in the neighbourhood of the pirates. The wind suddenly veered round into an unfavourable quarter; the telescopes were handed round with the utmost anxiety, and dreadful stories of the atrocities of the corsairs were immediately in circulation. Excepting C——'s pistols, there was not a single weapon of offence or defence on board, and consequently resistance was out of the question. The Eliza belonged to a Quaker, who would not allow any arms to be taken; but as self-defence is the first law of nature, it surely was scarcely right to risk the lives and liberties of his passengers for a scruple. Whilst we were anticipating boarding, captivity, and slavery, several ships bore down upon us—hailed us—and—passed on!

On the 13th the coast was descried, and it was the land of Africa! Low sandy cliffs presented themselves, and a swarm of flies proclaimed our vicinity to that country, where they were once sent as a plague to its hard-hearted monarch. Cape Deras we saw in the morning, and Arab's tower in the evening. On the following day, Pompey's Pillar was distinctly visible with a glass, tall and slender as a needle; and on the 15th, Alexandria was the cry; we had reached our wished-for haven! Soon down came Giovanni, (a Maltese servant whom we had engaged in the place of our Swiss courier,) breathless with rage, and unintelligible from passion. " Tak'em! tak'em! the Turk," was all he could utter for some time, pointing expressively at his master's feet. C——'s slippers, which had been accidentally left on deck, were not forthcoming, and Giovanni, immediately attributing their disappearance to the Turks on board, came down to communicate his wrathful suspicions to us.

When I went upon deck, I had ocular demonstration that we were arrived in another quarter of the world. There sat, or rather squatted cross-legged, a turbaned Turk, and around him stood several others, very ill-looking and very ill-dressed. They surveyed Mrs. Krusè and myself with looks of intense curiosity, as if perfectly astonished to see females emancipated from the seclusion of the Harem. Then came on board one in authority, to de-

mand our names, &c. It was an excellent
scene. Our honest, square-built, John Bull of
a captain, blushing, and looking half-daunted,
half ashamed, before the proud, lord-like looking
Turk, "for he understood not one word of their
lingo, not he;"—Giovanni Maltese was loudly
called for: poor Giovanni, who had hitherto
been the laughing-stock of the crew for his
foreign ways and habits, was now exalted into an interpreter. " The captain of the port
sent saluti (or compliments) to our captain."
" Much obliged," was the laconic reply. Soon
after, off came another boat to us, and Mr.
Salt's Janissary, Selim, a remarkably handsome,
well-looking, and well-dressed person, seem-
ingly of some importance, leaped upon board.
He immediately recognised and shook hands
with Giovanni, saluted me with " Good morning, Madam," salaamed C——, and finally carried our letters of introduction to the Consul
on shore. In due time he returned, with a
very polite invitation from Mr. Salt to his
house; and with him came two Indian servants, who had accompanied Sir Charles Col-
ville hither, and whom he had kindly desired to await our arrival. Sheik Chaund, a
Mussulman, was clad in the light cotton angrica and turban of the East, and Matiste, a
Portuguese, a native of Goa, had a face as

black, and hair as curly as a negro's. To my great surprise, who had never seen the Oriental form of salutation from an inferior to a superior, the former bowed almost to the ground at my feet, touching his forehead with his hand. The *mélange* of nations in the little boat in which we went on shore, was curious. Before our English selves, squatted, cross-legged, the Janissary Selim, in his Turkish dress; Sheik Chaund, in his Indian costume, held an umbrella over my head, to shelter me from the noontide sun, the Goa Portuguese sat behind, and we were rowed by native Egyptian sailors; Europe, Asia, and Africa! When we landed, poor indeed were the wretched objects that crowded around us, dark, dingy, dirty and ill-dressed. Donkeys were in waiting for us, for carriages are almost unknown here, and as I had left my side-saddle in the ship, you may conceive my consternation at seeing none but men's saddles brought for my use. However, as I could not resolve to mount *en cavalier*, as the Oriental Frank ladies do, I seated myself as well as I could sideways, every minute expecting to be jolted off, but the Janissary held me on, on one side, and Sheik Chaund obsequiously held the umbrella over me, on the other, and the donkey trotted on—and I—could have laughed at my own situation.

The road, if road it could be called, was rough, and passed over innumerable hillocks of sand and rubbish. We met several Arab parties. The women hid their faces, and they were riding on camels! "An Arab wife!" exclaimed Selim, who was acting the part of cicerone, and anxiously showing off his English, for my edification. In a narrow, a very narrow place, we came suddenly upon a string of loaded camels, which it was necessary for us to pass, and they stretched out their ugly necks one way, and they stretched them out the other, and they looked half determined to eat me up, as they stalked, stalked, stalked on close to me, so close that I could have touched them. C—— called out, "Do not be afraid;" and the Janissary told me not to mind; however, I could but think them very monstrous-looking creatures, and I sincerely wished myself safely in England. At last we reached Mr. Salt's country house, which was built very much in the Italian style, with one long sala in the middle, upon which all the other apartments opened, and with a flat-terraced roof. We were received by the Consul with the utmost civility, but I thought of the Arabian Nights, when, on his clapping his hands, a black slave made his appearance, fortunately, however, not with a scimitar to cut off our heads, with

which Zobeide treated the Caliph Haroun Alraschid and the three Calendars, but bearing
refreshments. Coffee, in beautiful little china
cups, which would have delighted many an
old dowager in England, in delicate stands, or
saucers of filigree gold, was brought upon a
silver waiter by the Mussulman Abdallah.

From the window we looked over a garden
of date-trees and saw Pompey's Pillar; over a
dusty, brown and undulating plain we beheld
Cleopatra's Needle. A Turkish mosque rose
in front—camels with their Arab drivers slowly
stalked by, and donkeys with Turkish riders
sitting cross-legged on their back.

"'Twas strange, 'twas passing strange,"
to see these objects; what we had so often read,
and heard, and talked of; we could scarcely
believe our own identity!

In the evening Mr. Salt's Cancelliere, or
Secretary, a young Venetian, offered to escort
us to the far-famed Pompey's, or, as it is now
discovered to be, Diocletian's Pillar. It is a
noble column ; one tall, superb, unbroken mass
of granite; standing like a monument of olden
time, it seems to tell of by-gone days, and yet
this survivor of its own times seems quickly
approaching to destruction, for the shaft has
left the base considerably, and a gap of considerable dimensions now intervenes. As we

stood contemplating this fine Pillar, which stands on a considerable elevation, the glorious sun was setting in the west, the silvery crescent of the moon was shining on high, and daylight gradually disappearing in all the softened brilliancy of an Egyptian evening. The Lake Mareotis, with the Canal, lay before us, with numerous Cangias gliding on its bosom. Alexandria, with its mosques and minarets, was at a little distance: a noise of rude merriment floated on the air. " It is the Ramazan," observed the Venetian. As we returned through the arched gateway of old Alexandria, the Turks were prostrating themselves at their evening devotions. This was indeed a day of days in my life ; one does not often meet with so much to excite in this " worky-day world !"

LETTER XIV.

Franks at Alexandria.—Cleopatra's Needle. — Costume of Egyptian Women.—Flies.—Native Music.—Camseen.— Plague.—Public Baths. — Visit from the Aga of Alexandria.—Curiosities from Thebes.—Mr. Salt.

ON the morning of the 14th of April, for the first time, I saw the sun rise over a garden of date-trees, in which Mr. Salt's house

was situated, and as their light feathery tops
waved and danced in the morning beams, I believed myself to be actually in Africa, for hitherto I could have fancied I had been in a dream.
It being Sunday, Mr. Thunberg, the Swedish
Consul, Mr. Madden, (the traveller,) and many
of the European Residents called, and this seems
to be the principal manner in which the Christian
Franks celebrate the day in Egypt.   The upper
part of the principal Sala was furnished in the
Oriental fashion, with deep sofas and very thick
cushions, at once serving for the accommodation of Europeans and Turks, and as this was
our morning sitting-room, as well as where the
Consul received his guests, we had an opportunity of seeing a curious *mélange* of nations
and customs.   The visitors generally walked
in unannounced ; sometimes appeared a stately,
dignified, well-dressed Turk, with his graceful
salaam, in which I was always carefully and
most respectfully included.   He, perhaps, was
followed by an Italian resident, or a Greek ad-
venturer ; an English captain upon business, or
an Arab Fellah with a complaint.   We were
somewhat amused with one who came up in a
most intense rage ; and after a long story of his
grievances, he most significantly and energetically concluded by giving *himself* a violent box
on the ear, with " Giovanni Maltese."   Mr. Salt's

head servant, a Maltese, and he had been quarrelling, and the Consul was obliged to go out
and make peace ; a circumstance, he observed,
of no unusual occurrence.

C—— accompanied Mr. Salt on a visit of
ceremony to one of the Consuls, where he saw
several Greek ladies, in the costume of their
country, sitting cross-legged on the sofa, and a
few Italian and French, but no English. Indeed, I believe it to be almost universally re-
marked, that however migratory our countrywomen may be in disposition, they seldom *settle*
abroad, for all the Consuls' wives are foreigners. They seemed enjoying the " dolce far
niente" of Oriental climates, which to use an
Irish expression, is perhaps the only thing that
Europeans can do in these sultry countries.

In the evening, as Mr. Salt seemed to think
there was no danger, C—— and I took a *tête-
à-tête* walk to Cleopatra's Needle. We passed
some fine shafts of granite, and over numerous
heaps of rubbish and excavated mounds of
earth, apparently the former foundations of the
houses of ancient Alexandria. No traces of
cultivation were to be seen, but desolation
reigned around ; and in an out of the way,
neglected spot, close to the sea-shore, where
once the great ones of the earth held their
fantastic revels, stood the obelisk which bears

I 2

the name of that cunning gipsy, who queened
it so bravely over the lords of the world, and
for the sake of whose *beaux yeux* an empire
was lost by the love-stricken Antony.

A few yards distant, prone on the ground,
and deeply embedded in the sand, lies the
fellow obelisk ; two sides of which are very
perfect, but the others are much injured, and
covered with lichen and moss. We walked over
this fallen monument of greatness, which, it is
said, was at one time to have been taken to Eng-
gland ; but the ancient Romans surpassed us in
this respect, for whilst we cannot contrive to
carry away an obelisk which is on the sea-shore,
they were wont to convey them from Thebes to
the city of Rome. Some Turks in the vicinity
stared to see two Frank strangers wandering
unprotected among their ruins : the dogs,
half canine, half jackal in their nature, each
from his strong hold on his own hillock of
sand, barked and yelped at us most furiously.
A stone was flung, whether meant for them or
us, in offence or defence, we knew not, therefore as it was growing dusk we prudently
wended our way homewards, passing many an
Arab party in our way. At the doors of their
low and miserable huts, sat the Fellahs, with
their wives by their sides, dandling and fond-
ling their babes with paternal exultation :

happiness illuminated their dingy countenances, and affection dwelt in the smile with which they proudly exhibited them to us, as we walked by.

The costume of the Egyptian women consists of a coarse blue shift, descending to their feet, with fashionably large sleeves; a piece of cloth tied over their faces, leaving the eyes visible, and another, in the style of the mantilla, over their heads; and this, when they meet any one, they draw over their faces. I imitated them in this particular, by always holding my shawl up to my face, and keeping my veil down; but though my English attire excited the utmost attention, and in particular my black jean half boots, a white face and black feet, being what they could not comprehend, yet I was constantly treated wherever I went with the utmost deference and respect, and though they furtively watched me, whenever the men saw it was observed, they immediately turned away. A good lesson for Bond-street and Regent-street loungers, who think it gentlemanly to stare a woman out of countenance.

It is not easy to describe what a terrible torment the flies were, particularly at meals; and though I was at first surprised, and indeed almost annoyed, to find our servant constantly taking his station behind me, and waving a chowree, or Indian fan, over my head, I soon found it was by no means a useless ceremony, or one of mere show. This being the fast of Ramazan, during which period the faithful Mussulmans never eat whilst the sun is above the horizon, they feast and amuse themselves for hours after it is set, and in consequence we every night heard native music; there was something wild and by no means unmelodious in the sound, wafted from, and softened by the distance.

On the 17th, the morning was lovely, but soon afterwards a dense and heavy fog came on, which lasted for an hour or two, and then the Camseen, or Hamseen, began to blow : the terrible wind which prevails more or less for fifty days in Egypt during the spring, and whose effects are so dreadful, that were it to continue for more than two or three days consecutively, all animated nature would be destroyed. It has the enervating and dispiriting effects of the Sirocco, and sweeping across the deserts of Africa, it brings with it dense and moving clouds of sand. Though every window and door was closed, all parts of the house were filled with it, and it penetrated into our hair, our food, and our dress. Fancy to yourself the most dense and gloomy November

London fog you ever saw, with a dark and lurid atmosphere, impregnated with dust, and accompanied by a hollow mournful sound, and you will have a faint idea of the Camseen; but the blast heats instead of cooling; the skin is parched, and a violent thirst ensues, which it is almost impossible to assuage. It blew incessantly for three days, with but one short interval, when a shower of rain fell for twenty minutes, and Mr. Salt observed he had never seen it more violent. This wind is most unhealthy, and is generally the precursor of that dreadful scourge the plague. Several *accidents* had already occurred in Alexandria, which is the delicate way of announcing its commencement, and we were consequently anxious to set off before it had more generally spread. During the plague season, almost as much a thing of course in Egypt, as the return of the spring, the Europeans entirely confine themselves to their houses, holding no communication but what is absolutely necessary with the exterior world; their houses are barricadoed with as many precautions as if the city were besieged.

> " The sullen door,
> Yet uninfected, on its cautious hinge
> Fearing to turn, abhors society ;"

and the months of seclusion, when " the pestilence walketh in darkness, and the sickness destroyeth in the noonday," appear to be of the most awful and appalling nature. We could not be sufficiently thankful to Divine Providence, for guarding and protecting us from this terrible danger.

C—— paid a visit to the public baths, and was rubbed, pinched, steamified, shampooed, and purified in the most approved Turkish fashion. He described the sensation as most delightful; but though they thrice in the week are appropriated to the use of females, and the Consul told me, I could go, if so disposed, I could not resolve to venture all alone, and I was consequently obliged to rest satisfied with Lady Mary Wortley Montague's account. In his walks, C—— met with a German, a former fellow-voyager of ours from Messina to Malta, whom we had denominated Pharaoh's baker, as he was going to Egypt to serve Mahomet Ali in that capacity. His fine hopes had been disappointed, as is frequently the case with Europeans who go to Egypt in hopes of employment, and, though at liberty, he was wandering about in a very disconsolate state, and was most happy to accept C——'s offer of recommending him to his countrymen, the German Missionaries, who gladly engaged him as a servant.

One evening, as the Consul and we were sitting at tea, quite in the English fashion, and talking over our friends in the green Isles of the West, a considerable bustle was heard on the stairs, and to our great surprise, in walked— the Aga of Alexandria and his Tahlanjee !* The former was a good-looking, middle-aged man, with very polished, and even dignified manners, clad in a handsome, but sober suit of brown, and with a white turban on his head ; the latter, a Neapolitan Renegado, was gaily dressed in a scarlet vest, covered with gold. He possessed his country's energy and vivacity, and addressed me at once with all the airs of a *petit maitre*, questioning me about my travels, and talking to me in Italian of " Lady Mahree, and her nice children, Miss Bathurst, balls," &c. The Aga only spoke Turkish,—and his conversation turned upon Tripolizza,—the Greeks, the Pasha, &c. ;—both he and the Tahlanjee taking the opportunity of abusing the French vehemently, as a sort of compliment, which they considered as acceptable and pleasing to the English. They took tea *à la mode Anglaise ;* and at retiring, they salaamed me in the most graceful and respectful manner, and shook hands with C—— with the greatest cordiality. As the Consul offered to attend them down stairs, the Aga stopped him with the utmost energy, and it

* Aide-de-camp.

was quite amusing, to see the Turk and the Englishman striving who should be the most polite. This call was a most unusual and unprecedented one, for Mr. Salt had not returned the last, and he therefore attributed it to curiosity on the part of the Aga to see his English guests. I was in my usual costume, and you can have no conception how perfectly uncomfortable I felt without my veil, for the women so invariably cover their faces in Egypt, that I was quite ashamed of showing mine at Alexandria.

We were fortunate enough to be present, when Mr. Salt opened a packet of curiosities from Thebes, which was sent to him by his agent, who was established there for the purpose of making the collection. Some of them he pronounced to be very rare and valuable, particularly the image of a Persian King in silver, which, to his great annoyance, and to its great detriment, they had been endeavouring to clean, and had removed the venerable dust of ages in a very rough manner. It was covered with the Persepolitan arrow-headed character, which has, I believe, never been deciphered. There were also several mummy necklaces, with small, and by no means unpretty ornaments hanging to them, resembling delicate seals; also several scarabei, and other trinkets, of some of which the Consul kindly made me a present.

What a pity it was that the members of our Government should have been seized with such an unlucky fit of economy, when Mr. Salt offered his collection of curiosities to them for sale, and which, in consequence of their refusing to purchase them, have now passed into the hands of the French, who gave ten thousand pounds for the whole, for, from his knowledge, and power of procuring what was most valuable, they would doubtless have been a noble addition to any museum. Mr. Salt was rather a fine-looking man, with a considerable degree of lassitude in his manners, which gave C—— an impression he was at that time suffering under a liver complaint. When engaged in conversation, however, this vanished, and from having been much with the literary and politically Great, possessing a well-informed mind, and considerable taste for literature and the beaux arts, he had great powers of entertainment, and was a very amusing companion. He showed us his paintings, his poetry—he appeared delighted to meet with some one who could enter into his pursuits and feelings—and it seemed a refreshment to him, to turn from the price of cotton, or from some trifling dispute of English Captains

or Arab Fellahs, to the works of Madame de
Stael and Walter Scott. I confess, I never expected to have discussed the merits of Corinne
and Rob Roy at Alexandria! On the 19th, in
spite of the Camseen, and his kind wishes for us
to prolong our stay, we took leave of our kind
host, trusting to meet in England at some future period. Alas! we little thought his end
was so near, when we bade him farewell.

LETTER XV.

Embarkation on the Canal of Mahmoudieh.—Maash.—
Cock-roaches.—Journey from the Canal to El Aft.—Na-
tives.—Scenery on the Nile.—Flirting scene.—Giovanni,
Cameriere to Napoleon.—Boulac.

In the afternoon of the 19th, attended by
the Janissary Selim, we mounted our donkeys
and rode to the Canal of Mahmoudieh, where
our Maash was waiting for us. The Camseen
had sunk, the moon shone brightly, the evening was delightful, we talked of Cleopatra,
and we agreed that every thing was very novel,
pleasant, and agreeable. We met several boats
laden with cotton ; it required some dexterity
to keep clear of each other, and, in passing
rapidly, the rigging not unfrequently caught,

to the mutual detriment of both vessels. On a slight dispute arising, Selim caught up his silver stick, his badge of authority, and silence on its appearance immediately ensued. A heavy dew beginning to fall, C—— recommended my retiring to the cabin, which was about six feet square, and four feet high, so that for the first time in my life I positively found myself *too tall!* On the lamp being lighted, to my great consternation, we discovered thousands and ten thousands of cock-roaches running merrily about in every direction, and absolutely over our couches; and we had also the pleasure of finding our boat was infested by rats, which paid us repeated visits during the night.

The morning beamed fresh and lovely, and, about noon, we reached the point where we were to disembark, and to proceed to the Nile overland, as the water in the Canal was not deep enough for us to continue upon it; several boats were moored there, chiefly laden with cotton. A rude tent was pitched, beneath which reclined Turks, and Arabs, and Egyptian Fellahs, in their various costumes, the green turban betokening the wearer to be a descendant of Mahomet. Arab women were on the banks, in their blue robes, and half naked infants were crawling and running about in every direction. Whilst they were moving our luggage, we had a couple of chairs placed beneath some dwarf willows, which gave just enough shade to make us sigh for more, it being intensely hot.   Numerous water-mills emitted a droning sound ; several kites hovered over our heads, flapping heavily their wings. The children crowded round us, sat down, eyeing us with looks of curiosity, and held out their hands for " bucksheesh ;" whilst some respectable men, approaching us, would fain have entered into conversation with us, had we understood their language.

The Janissary hired, or, perhaps, rather seized ten camels for us, in the name of the Government, upon which all the drivers simultaneously ran away, expecting that they were to have, in consequence, no remuneration. This caused considerable delay, and more than an hour elapsed ere our little caravan was ready, and I now found my side-saddle of the greatest use.   C—— and I rode at the head, my donkey attended by Selim, and the ten camels, tied together, led by Sheik Chaund, followed with our luggage, whilst the rest of our attendants brought up the rear. The first adventure was my donkey endeavouring to run under the camels, and it was with some difficulty Selim rescued me from the impending danger. Then crash came down one of the camel's loads. It proved to be the property of Mr. Salt's gardener, who had asked permission to accompany us to Cairo, but, though a faithful Mussulman, the fall betrayed the cargo to be wine! We then entered a desert tract, where not a shrub or blade of grass were to be seen, and the soil resembled the fissured surface of a horse-pond when dried up by intense heat. All around us appeared the mirage, a most beautiful delusion; lakes in the distance were apparently to be seen, and a fine river, on whose calm bosom trees and buildings were distinctly reflected; so complete was the deception, that it was some time before we could be convinced it was not the Nile we beheld.

In about three hours' time we reached El Aft, but as we had outstripped the camels, and a date-tree was our only shelter from the ardent rays of the afternoon sun. C —— asked for a house. " What for, want house?" asked Selim, with much *naïveté*, who seemed to think a house was only to *sleep* in. In one we attempted to enter, the owner was shaving, and sherbet was preparing; I was, therefore, put into the cabin of a Cangia, which was neither high enough for me to stand in, nor was there any description of seat to sit upon, so that I was forced, *bon grè mal grè*, to lie down upon the floor upon my cloak; but whilst waiting

for our baggage to come up, I became so faint
from want of refreshment, some hours having
elapsed since breakfast, that C—— was obliged
to go in search of some, saying " Haram" to
the Reis as he left me. " Haram," we were
told, means secret, and is always held sacred.
Though there were none but rude sailors on
board, none of them attempted to intrude upon
me, or to molest me, whilst I was alone ; and
the Reis roughly reproved a man, who, not
knowing the cabin was occupied, was about to
enter.

The only boat large enough to be safe,
was a Cangia, in miserable repair, which,
to add to its delights, had but lately had a
cargo of sugar, so that the ceiling was positively encrusted with flies, and the floor was
swarming with fleas ; however, as we hoped to
reach Cairo on the following day, and having
no other alternative than to return to Alexandria, we resolved to engage it. About 6 P. M.
we got under weigh, and our escort Selim returned to Alexandria, leaving us with our two
Indian attendants, and our Maltese servants.
As C—— spoke Hindoostanee, and I myself
Italian, and Sheik Chaund and Giovanni, Arabic, they served as interpreters between us and
the crew. We passed Foua and Salwyah at
sun-set, and on the following morning we

found ourselves under the lee of a sand-bank, opposite Khafir Daour. The wind being too strong to proceed without danger of foundering, our Cangia, with two or three others that accompanied us, was aground, and their respective crews upon shore, fast asleep. We were forced to adopt *" patienza"* for our motto, and we amused ourselves with taking a walk on the banks of the river, though it was with difficulty we avoided treading on the men who were lying scattered about in every direction, wrapped in immense cloaks. As soon as our Reis perceived our intention, he insisted on accompanying us, as he made signs it was unsafe for us to venture alone ; and, after attempting for some time to converse with us, kissing C——'s hand, he ran and collected some flowers, which he presented to him. A Frenchman would have offered them to me ; however, every nation has its customs, and I am convinced the Reis intended them for me, whose property they immediately became. In our walks, the women in the villages, and on the banks, eyed us with the most intense curiosity. Some of them were much ornamented with gold, and their veils were tied up between the eyes with a string of small silver bells. Their chief occupation appeared to be the drawing and carrying of water ; the children, generally in a com-

plete state of nature, were frequently much
frightened at our appearance, and one of them,
on meeting us, ran quickly away, crying out
" Mamma, Mamma," in as broad a tone as any
little Scotch boy could have done. The men
laughed good-naturedly, but not disrespectfully
at our foreign appearance, and turned away
their eyes, exclaiming, " Haram !"   One morning, I felt myself suddenly caught hold of, and
turning, in some degree of alarm, I beheld a
woman in the blue dress of the country, completely veiled, offering her hand, and exclaiming, at the utmost pitch of her voice, " Salamat !
Salamat !" I returned the salutation, and gave
her my hand in return, upon which she made
signs for me to follow her to her house, in a
village at a little distance, but I was afraid of
accompanying her, as the invitation did not
extend to C——. She, however, offered her
hand to him in a very friendly manner, and
seemed very well pleased at his putting some
piastres into it.

We saw nothing of the so much boasted
fertility of the Delta, and the country was by no
means as luxuriant as is customary in the immediate vicinity of rivers in general. The land
appeared all arable, and a very light soil ; there
was no pasture ; but there were wheat, barley,
flax, and quantities of melon beds, with which

many of the numerous islets were entirely
covered. The Nile was very low, and the sailors
were constantly obliged to jump into the water, to
push the boat off a sandbank, or to tow it along
the banks. We passed numerous buffaloes wal-
lowing in the water, their noses upturned to
Heaven, quaffing the ambient air ; and there
were beautiful white batta birds, standing and
admiring themselves in the river. The scenery,
on the whole, was very monotonous, but the
climate was delightful, the heat being pleasantly attempered by fresh breezes. A fine
cloudless sky—a wide dusky-brown river, which
frequently assumed the appearance of a lake —
low shelving banks—small mud villages, with a
few date and other fruit-trees—a lone mosque—
Fellahs tilling the ground, and planting melons
—half naked countrymen fishing—women in
their blue dress carrying water—the ox turning
water-mills—the cooing of doves—the caw-
ing of rooks—the cry of the pee-wit—and the
sweet notes of the bulbul—were the chief
sounds and sights that greeted us between
Alexandria and Cairo. The banks were occasionally perforated most regularly and curiously in perfectly straight lines, by the sand
swallow, to the number, perhaps, of a thousand
holes, and the male birds kept watch in front
of each domicile. At Sallaggar the ground was

covered with the Convolvulus arvensis; I
thought of Rousseau, and "voila la pervanche,"
as home and all its charms rose to my mind,
and I involuntarily exclaimed, " This grows at
Windmill Hill !"

At Nadir we saw one of the telegraphic
towers, which are to be built every twelve
miles, for the purpose of giving information
what boats ascend and descend the river.
Near Kal el Gazi, we stopped for fire-wood,
and *pomegranate* was brought, rich in all its
scarlet honours. Whilst waiting, I accidentally turned my eyes to the shore, where was
the Reis, who at first I actually thought was
possessed. There stood the old man, sometimes lifting up his hands, as if in an attitude
of astonishment, sometimes wiping his beard,
then prostrating himself on the ground, and
touching it with his forehead. Anon, jumping
up, he began again, and went through the
whole of the mummery anew. I at last found
out he was at his *devotions*, not, perhaps, the
less fervently performed from perceiving he
was observed. Whilst this holy farce was acting, a very different scene was carrying on at
a little distance. A party of native women approached with their merchandise, chiefly consisting of some flat wheaten cakes. The dusky
belles at first cautiously kept their dirty sarrees,

or mantillas, over their faces *with their teeth*, but in the eagerness of chaffering, the envious veils that obscured their dingy charms from the garish eye of day, by degrees deserted their posts, and disclosed their features to view. Their eyes were small, and sunk in their heads; their noses flat ; their mouths good, and with very fine teeth, which were much set off by the darkness of their complexions. There was a vivacity and archness in the expression of their countenances, which saved them from being absolutely plain. One or two of them wore gold bangles, necklaces, and ear-rings ; the rest were attired in the common blue dress of the country, the lower part of the face being dyed with indigo, and their nails stained with henna. Whilst they were bargaining, a coarse-looking sailor, one of our crew, flung himself on the grass, and kept on humming a song, evidently sarcastic and pointed,· which made some look ashamed, and forced others to laugh. After the marketing was over, the women all sat down, huddled together, on the ground, and the sailor approached them, and seated himself among them. His sullen countenance suddenly brightened up, and he cocked his chin in the air, as importantly as any dandy in town showing off to an admiring circle of demoiselles. With an air of familiar gallantry, he patted one on the shoulder, which was coquettishly repulsed. He then put his hand into his vest, and produced a dirty rag, and a coloured cord, which were as eagerly contended for, as the famed apple of the Goddess Atè by the three rival goddesses. With a very self-satisfied and triumphant manner, but with a contemptuous and sarcastic look, he bestowed them on the favoured fair, who, evidently gratified with this distinguishing mark of attention, tore them in pieces, and distributed them to her companions, who all crowded round their hero, as if he were a little god. It was an excellent scene, and as good a satire upon flirting as I ever saw. Flirting in Egypt!

The dandy was suddenly summoned to the boat. What a transformation! No more smiles, no more graces; he once more became a coarse-looking, ill-conditioned sailor, doffed his clothes, and fell to towing.

At midnight we were roused by a noise of fighting and quarrelling. The knight of the rag, the hero, had got soundly bastinadoed, because he had *accidentally* laid his hand upon some fruit in another vessel. It seemed to be the husbands of the ladies who had been flirting with him, who took this opportunity of avenging themselves. Our servants tried to stop the clamour, by telling them there were a Cowasjee and a Mhurra (a gentleman and a lady) in the cabin, but they would not be pacified, till the Cowasjee made his appearance *in propriá personá* among them.

On the morning of the 23d we came in sight of the Mokattam Mountains, in the vicinity of Grand Cairo. The Nile was here covered with small islets, and we passed the wrecks of some boats, which justified the Reis's precaution in so frequently coming to anchor. By his own account, he seemed troubled with every disorder under the sun, and would need have C—— prescribe for him. In vain did C—— assure him he was not a medical man; a Frank and a physician are synonymous in the imagination of an Oriental, and he asserted " the Cowasjee knew every thing."

This being St. George's day, we gave Giovanni a glass of brandy in honour of the King. " *La festa del Rè d' Inghilterra,*" exclaimed he, with the utmost glee, promising to drink it " *al suo salute.*" On the principle of the earth that dwelt with the rose till it imbibed its fragrance, poor Giovanni should have been a great man, for he had lived with several distinguished characters. He had been Cameriere to Napoleon when in Egypt, had personally attended him, and constantly slept in his room; he told us, it was his custom to walk up

and down half the night *thinking*, till, overcome with sleep, Giovanni, who remained in
attendance to take off his boots, would venture
to rouse him from his reverie. He described
him, as "*fastidioso, come una Signora, per la
pulizia*," and spoke of him as a very kind and
considerate master; and once, when he was
wounded, he informed us, that he (Napoleon)
used to insist on his taking his medicines, and
"gave him water in his own silver goblet."

Giovanni had also lived with Lewis Buonaparte, with Menou, and likewise with several
distinguished Englishmen. In describing one
of his numerous masters, he said, " He always
dressed like a lady," and maintained his asser-
tion, saying, " at least he always wore a faldetta."
On farther inquiry, it turned out to be the High-
land costume, which he imagined to be a lady's
dress! What would the martial Highlanders
say to this? However, I think Mrs. Graham
mentions that the South American heroine assumed this attire when fighting, as the most
feminine she could adopt. He had also lived
with Sir Frederick Henniker, and was with
him when he was attacked in Syria; likewise with Dr. Bromhead and Mr. Cooke; he
attended the latter when he expired on his
camel and was interred at Elim; and with the
garrulity of old age, he was very fond of tak-

ing every opportunity of reciting his adventures.

At 3 P. M. we came in sight of Cairo, or Misr, as it is termed by the Arabs; and after passing Soubra, the Pasha's Garden house, in the evening we anchored off Boulac, having been five days and nights in our crazy Cangia, instead of the twenty-four hours we had anticipated when we embarked.

LETTER XVI.

Grand Cairo.— British Consulate.—Style of living there.— Overland Passage to India.—Affray.—Visit to Mahomet Ali.—Native Music.—Camseen.—Soubra.

THE Scotchman, William Thompson, so well known to Egyptian travellers as Osman Effendi, who was made a prisoner and a Mussulman in 1806, and set at liberty by Burkhardt, who found him at Djidda, now the third Interpreter, or Dragoman to Mr. Salt, came on board early in the morning to receive us, and to escort us to the British Consulate. A horse was brought for C——, and a donkey for my accommodation, and we proceeded through the streets of Boulac, and along a wide but very dusty road to Grand Cairo, the first appearance of which was any thing but striking ; minarets seemed to be the only ornamental buildings, and I could but think how wofully the young man in the Arabian Nights must have been disappointed, when he beheld the city of which he overheard his father giving his uncles such glowing accounts. We crossed the famous Esbequier Birket, sometimes a lake, now a large square, and we then defiled through the sinuosities of some such very narrow streets, that I fully expected in reality to have met with some of those adventures which the fair Amine feigned to deceive her husband, who, by the by, must have been of a most suspicious temperament to have doubted the veracity of her statement, for the wonder, in an Oriental city, would be, how one escaped, rather than how one met with accidents. Immense windows and projecting balconies overhanging the road, form-ed an agreeable shelter from the sultry sun. At length we ultimately reached the British Consulate, situated in the most strange, out of the way place imaginable, where from Mr. Maltass, the Vice-Consul, we experienced a very hospitable and courteous reception. His residence was an old Mameluke house, so singular and rambling in its construction, that it would have been admirably calculated for the scene of a romance. An immense

gateway opened upon a court, partly surrounded by a sort of cloister, beyond which
was the dining-room, the roof of which was
curiously painted, and at the bottom played a
fountain, accompanied by musical glasses. This
looked upon a garden of oleanders, date, and
pomegranate trees, which opened upon the
public promenade. A very narrow staircase
led to the upper stories, which seemed to defy
all plan, but most of the rooms were apparently constructed upon the principle of security
and privacy. Many of them had curiously
carved window frames, with painted glass and
window seats. There was one apartment so
secret, that it would have been impossible to
have discovered it, had it not been pointed out
to us, the access being through a sliding pannel.
Upon the flat terraced roof was a sort of framework to catch the wind, and in the upper part
of the Gran Sala, or reception room, was the
Divan, which is an immense window-seat, fitted
up with cushions like a sofa. This was invariably offered to the principal visitor, but
though it was certainly a most luxurious
lounge, we preferred the European chair. Here
we saw even a greater variety of nations, if
possible, than at Alexandria;—Turks, Greeks,
Armenians, Indians, Levantines, Africans, Italians, French, and English, were coming in

and out all day long; and as we resided at the Consulate for nearly a fortnight, their different manners were very amusing. Our style of living was as follows:—At break of day, coffee was brought to the door of our respective apartments, and at noon we all assembled to a *dejeuné à la fourchette* in the dining-room. This is the usual hour of dinner for the Egyptian Franks, but in compliment to the English visitors, that meal was deferred till four p. m.; the interim was passed in reading, writing, sleeping, or in making and receiving calls. Frequently the English travellers and foreign Consuls at Cairo dined with us; and after I retired from the dining-room, coffee and tea were brought to me, *à l'Anglais*, in the Gran Sala, by a domestic in Turkish costume. In the cool of the evening we rode out, or took walks in the public garden, which is the chief promenade of the Franks, but where, however, we frequently met Turks, who, *en passant*, always salaamed us most courteously. There was a grand-piano in the late Mrs. Salt's apartments, which was in very tolerable tune, and not much deteriorated by the climate. I confess, I never expected to play quadrilles and Irish melodies at Grand Cairo! Our countrymen, that we met here, were imprudent enough to assume the Turkish costume, a practice most strongly deprecated by Mr. Salt, as being a species of disguise which rendered it impossible for him to be responsible for their safety. At his suggestion, we never altered our English dress; and though it certainly rendered us conspicuous, it ensured us respect wherever we went. The Turkish attire, is, however, so very becoming and handsome, that it requires some philosophy to resist so tempting an opportunity for wearing it. It alters the appearance so completely, that it is almost impossible to recognize any one, and I had been some time in the room with a gentleman whom I imagined to be a young Turk, ere I discovered he was an Englishman, and an acquaintance. We frequently met here Mr. Galloway, a civil engineer, a clever young man, in high favour with the Pasha, who was employing him in lighting the Palace at Soubra with gas, and in many other ingenious works. He was much interested in, and exceedingly sanguine about, the over-land passage to India, which he demonstrated to be perfectly feasible. The plans laid down, were, to have steam-packets from Alexandria to Cairo, which were to communicate with those at Suez, by means of the ancient canal, which might be easily re-opened, or the seventy intervening miles be passed in a few hours by camels, relays of which might be stationed in the desert;

and to prevent all danger of infection in case of plague, an albergo, or caravansera, was to be built outside the city walls, which was to have no communication with the interior.

One night, after the gentlemen had left the British Consulate, they fell in with a considerable skirmish in the streets. They would not have been Englishmen had they not joined in the affray, which originated in a Sardinian, who had been sued for debt by order of the Sardinian Consul, attempting to evade his creditors by proclaiming himself a Mussulman. The Turks upon this rescued him, when the Franks, indignant at the apostacy, again endeavoured to seize the Renegado, and a dreadful uproar took place, in which the former ultimately prevailed, but a French colonel, who to his shame be it spoken, joined with their party, was stabbed in the back, it was said dangerously, by one of the infuriated mob. On the following day the Sardinian was taken before the Pasha, and an honorary dress was given him, to the poor Consul's great vexation, who appeared terribly annoyed at this termination to the affair, as indeed were all the Franks at Cairo. *Mais, à quoi bon?* "Might overcomes right," as the old proverb observes, all the world over.

One evening, C—— paid a visit of ceremony to the Pasha. He was introduced by Mr.

Maltass, and was very graciously received. Mahomet Ali appeared about fifty-five years of age, though Mr. Salt told us he was very fond of being thought much younger ; short in stature, thick-set, with a high forehead and aquiline nose, he had a penetrating look, and an expression which evinced him to be no common man. His dress was plain, and his only ornament, a dagger studded with diamonds, with which his coffee-cup was also enriched. He was surrounded by attendants, who obsequiously watched his every movement. Immediately after C—— took his departure, he called for the chess-board, which was a sign something had gone wrong in his affairs, as it is his never-failing resource when any thing occurs to vex him. Report said, he had that day received intelligence that the star of the Greeks had gained a decided ascendency over his. After their return to the Consulate, some native musicians arrived, whom Mr. Maltass had kindly sent for to amuse us. There were four of them, clad in blue vests and turbans. They sat down on the ground at the bottom of the apartment, and the lamp cast a lurid flame upon their swarthy and wildly expressive countenances. Their voices were clear and strong, and they sung loudly, most loudly, some not unpleasing airs, accompanying themselves on a two-stringed instrument, something between a mandoline and a guitar, from which far more harmony was produced than could have been anticipated ; another played on the guitar, and all joined in chorus. I could almost have fancied myself one of the heroines in the Arabian Nights Entertainment.

During our stay at Cairo, the Camseen frequently blew, filling the house with all the dust of all the Deserts of Africa, and inspiring every one with lassitude and ennui. The weather was oppressively hot, the thermometer, even at sun-rise, being often as high as 82°, and we could do little more than lounge about, and drink sherbet and tamarind water.

In addition to all this, the Consulate swarmed with every species of insect, crawling, creeping, jumping, flying, buzzing, and humming about one, to such a tormenting degree, that I really believe it must at one period have served as an Indian Pinjrapole ; and had we been disposed to have studied entomology, this would have been a glorious opportunity. It was almost ludicrous to hear the various complaints, of the different annoyances, and to see the woful countenances exhibited. Occasionally some of the party had their eyes nearly closed with bites and stings, and of course this was attributed to an incipient ophthalmia. Osman

Effendi's advice and prescriptions, however, prevented that dreadful disorder, which the dews, the dust, and the flies of Egypt, are really enough to produce, without coming in contact with the disease in others.

In the intervals of the Camseen, however, the weather was far from unpleasant; and one afternoon, escorted by Osman Effendi, we rode to Soubra, the Pasha's Garden-house, on the banks of the Nile, where are the water-works, in the superintendence of which, poor Belzoni, on his first arrival in Egypt, was originally employed. The exterior of the palace presented a somewhat mean appearance, but the interior was handsomely fitted up, and we saw it in high style, as the Pasha and his ladies were shortly expected, for the approaching feast of Bairam, and every thing was ready for their reception. The ceiling of the hall on the ground-floor was painted so as to resemble a chintz curtain, and in one of the state apartments, round which sofas were ranged, were a fountain and basin in the centre, and an Arabic sentence, from the Koran, was suspended, framed and glazed, against the wall, signifying that " One hour spent in the service of God is worth a hundred thousand years." A handsome staircase, something similar to that at Ashburnham Place, opened upon a room, or sala, somewhat

in the shape of a Greek cross; each deep recess was fitted up like a Divan, with Turkey
carpets and sofas, and at each corner was a door
opening into an elegant apartment. That appropriated to the use of the chief Sultana was
most superbly and magnificently ornamented
with a profusion of gold, and furnished with
handsome carpets, low sofas, ottomans, and pillows; and there, perhaps, never was a place
more fitted for luxurious ease, or better adapted
for the inhabitants of the Castle of Indolence.
There was a handsome, but old-fashioned pier-
glass at the bottom of the room, where, in some
little niches and recesses, were several elegant
little toys, and we were amused to see an English
sixpenny paper fan carefully installed among the
curiosities of the Cairo belles. Two other apartments were elegantly, but more simply fitted
up, for the accommodation of the other ladies,
and a beautiful little bath, and pretty little
dressing-room, filled up the fourth angle; so
that if the Turk confines his lady fair, it
must be acknowledged he tries to render her
seclusion as delightful as possible, by giving
her every possible comfort and luxury. The
Pasha's own bed-room was small and plain.
His couch seemed to consist of nothing but
several tiers of pillows; in an adjoining room
he holds audiences. The gardens were prettily,

but somewhat formally laid out, and the pavilion there recalled those of the Caliph Haroun Alraschid to our recollection. In the centre played a fountain, and several alligators spouted water into a marble basin; round which ran a colonnade or verandah, supported by light fantastic pillars of white marble. At each corner were apartments and baths elegantly fitted up in the Turkish style, and here it is the great delight of the Pasha and his ladies to repair, and, as Osman described it, " to romp and play together," amusing themselves with trying to push each other into the water, and such pretty little infantine and innocent sports. The road from thence to Cairo, about three miles distant, was bordered with mulberry-trees. As we returned, we thought of the old song

" My heart's in the Highlands, my heart is not here;"

when poor Osman, after a few minutes abstraction, said with great *naïveté*, by way of apology for his silence, " I was thinking how green the fields are looking in Perthshire." I could not resist saying, " I hoped he would, ere long, return thither;" I longed to add, " and to his fathers' God." I think he perceived what I meant, but he seemed by no means offended with my observation. In our way home, we passed the Copt quarter, where the old wood-

en houses appeared like receptacles for vermin,
plague, and disease, and through the Esbequier
Berkit, where were the palace of the Pasha's
son-in-law, and the house of the Sheik of the
Serpent Eaters.

LETTER XVII.

Arrival of Sir Hudson Lowe.—Citadel.—Joseph's Hall and Well.—Palaces.—Slave-Market.

WHILST we were at the Consulate, Major-
General Sir Hudson Lowe, with his Aide-de-
camp, arrived. They had left England nearly
at the same time with ourselves, and had travelled by Vienna and Constantinople. It was
at Smyrna, in his way from thence to Cairo,
that the base and unmanly attack was made
upon the General, which was mentioned in
the newspapers. A Frenchman made his way
to the door of his apartment, avowedly with
the intention of assassinating him, but was
prevented from accomplishing his dastardly
purpose by the master of the Hotel. Sir Hudson Lowe knew nothing of this till the following morning, when Lord St. Asaph and
several Englishmen called upon him to make
enquiries concerning his health, and he then
heard of the attempt upon his life on the pre-

ceding night, and, by their advice, he never again, whilst there, slept on shore. As it was rumoured that the French had made a vow he should not pass through Egypt in safety, the Consul and Vice-Consul were under very considerable apprehensions for him; he, however, never exhibited the slightest appearance of alarm, but rode and walked about Cairo with all the coolness and intrepidity of an English officer, and seemed to have no more idea of danger than any of the rest of the party.

One afternoon we made the grand tour of the Lions of Cairo, which the Camseen had hitherto prevented our visiting. Our procession was most curious. First of all rode two Janissaries heavily armed; then followed in file, it being scarcely possible for two to ride abreast, the General and his Aide-de-camp, C——, Mr. Maltass, Osman Effendi, and myself—all upon donkeys, which went scuffling through the streets at a prodigious rate. Each of the party was attended by a dirty, half-naked, Arab driver, besides other attendants. The Turks laid down their pipes as we passed, and I distinctly heard the cry of " Frankistan " as we trotted by.

We rode through streets so narrow, that a person in the centre might easily have touched the opposite houses at the same moment, and we passed long files of loaded camels tied toge-

ther, guided by one man. We saw Turks on
donkeys, and Mamelukes on horseback, " pride
in their port, defiance in their eye," riding down
every one before them, purposely and offensively sticking out their tremendous shovel-
shaped stirrups ; one Chieftain, in particular,
seemed to wish to evince in what utter contempt
he held the Franks ; but when he saw a *female*
among the party, it is impossible to describe the
change that instantaneously took place in his
whole demeanour ; the proud and contemptuous
air with which he surveyed the gentlemen, was
to me altered to one of the most perfect courtesy
and civility ; and the most polished Frenchman could not have reined in his steed with
more grace, or have expressed more gentlemanly regret at my being annoyed and alarmed, by my donkey accidentally running against
his horse. Though it was evident he held the
Christians in abhorrence, he saw that I was a
woman, and he treated me with deference and
respect. Indeed, I must say for the Turks, in
general, whatever their other faults may be, that
their manners towards our sex as far exceed
those of our countrymen in courtesy, as their
graceful costume surpasses that of the Franks
in magnificence and grandeur. Then we saw
women mounted on camels, riding on immense saddles, towering aloft in the air, and
shrouded in their black cloaks, looking really

very tremendous and awful. In a narrow,
a *very* narrow street, a vicious camel, at the
head of a long file, had chosen to lie down,
and completely filled up the narrow way, roaring and bellowing most tremendously. In vain
did the driver beat it, and the Janissaries goad
it with their silver sticks; it only redoubled
its cries, and stretched out his long neck, and
opened its ugly mouth, and seemed to threaten
death and destruction all around. The gentlemen being mostly military men were brave *by
profession,* and were consequently not to be
daunted by an angry camel; but alas for
me, who was a woman and a coward! I do
not think I ever felt more thoroughly frightened in my life than whilst in the vicinity
of this frightful creature, which, however, I
eventually passed in safety. We saw the exterior of the principal mosque, into which it is
death for a Christian to enter; and ascending
the citadel, Osman pointed out the spot where
the Mamelukes were massacred in cold blood
by the orders of Mahomet Ali. From the top
is an extensive view over the city, and from
thence Cairo really appeared to deserve the
epithet of Grand ; for the Nile, the tombs of
the Caliphs, and the Pyramids, are all seen at
once. We saw Joseph's Hall, and from thence
proceeded to Joseph's Well ;—not, however, he
who flourished more than seventeen hundred

years before, but he who lived twelve centuries
after Christ.

It is, however, a pity that we may not believe
these structures to have been the work of the
Patriarch, rather than of the Prime Minister of
Saladin. Joseph's Well is very curious, and
the citadel is entirely supplied with water
from thence. We descended by a dark and
very steep gallery, till we came to the first
landing-place, and then hearing there was nothing but an ox turning the wheel to be seen,
if we went to the bottom, we agreed it would
be as well to be satisfied with the *on-dit*, without going in person to ascertain whether this
were a fact, or whether the old saying be correct, that " Truth lies in a well."

On emerging from our cool and gloomy retreat, we were beset in so furious a manner
by a crowd of mendicants, that Osman was positively obliged to draw his sword upon them
before he could rescue me from them, as they
seemed determined to lay violent hands upon
me. We then proceeded to the two palaces,
which the Pasha, like a kind husband, was
erecting for his wives. They were built on
nearly the same plan with that of Soubra, and
by-the-by, I wonder that among the freaks and
fancies of the present day, no architect has
adopted it for an English house, as it would be

admirably adapted for parties : the grand sala
to be devoted to dancing, the deep recesses to
conversation, and the corner rooms to music,
reading, cards, and refreshments. In one of
these halls was a fountain, and an aqueduct of
marble, down which little marble fish seemed
to glide. They were fitted up with even more
splendour than those at Soubra, and one of the
baths was quite a *bijou*, so exquisitely elegant
was it in its construction. It was supported
by light and airy columns of marble; and the
beautiful and simple ornament of the crescent,
the badge of the Ottoman power, accompanied
by a single star, was everywhere to be seen.
The gentlemen all took off their shoes before
entering these *sanctum sanctorums* of the Oriental beauties, which is the eastern mark of
respect; whilst I ran here and there and every
where, claiming the privilege of my sex, which
here was of use, though the workmen stared
to see a woman at such liberty. I, however,
am inclined to think that all that we are told
of the imprisonment of the Seraglio is a great
mistake. I suspect the Turkish ladies are under
no greater restraint than princesses and ladies
of rank in our country, and the homage that is
paid them seems infinitely greater. The seclusion of the Haram appears to be no more
than the natural wish of an adoring husband,

to guard his beloved from even the knowledge
of the ills and woes that mortal man betide.
Whilst he himself dares danger in every form,
he wishes to protect " his Lady-bird"—" the
light of his Haram," from all trouble and anxiety. He would fain make her life " a fairy
tale ;"—he would not even let " the winds of
Heaven visit her face too roughly ;" and as
we carefully enshrine a valuable gem, or protect a sacred relic from the profane gaze of
the multitude, so does he, on the same principle, hide from vulgar ken, his best, his choicest
treasure, " his ain kind dearie." The Turks,
in their gallantry, consider the person of a
woman sacred, and the place of her retreat, her
Haram, is always respected. Nay, there have
been even instances where persons have fled for
protection to their enemy's Seraglio, and been
thereby saved ; so that I found that in Egypt
I was likely to be the guardian of the party,
and that in my utter helplessness I might possibly be a panoply from danger to my pro-
tectors themselves. In fact, Mr. Salt seriously
recommended that I should always carry all
our most valuable papers and money about me
for safety.

We returned through the principal bazaars,
where the shops were all open, and the master sat
on an elevated stone platform in the midst of his

goods; but there was no show or magnificence, none of the jewels and cloth of gold, and splendour that we picture to ourselves in an Oriental bazaar. In the Slave-market, a sort of piazza, or square, were several negroes seated on a mat, who seemed very much gratified with some money C—— threw to them. Some Nubian girls then came out, their hair greased and frizzed in the latest and most approved Nubian fashion, but whilst I was considering whether it were right and delicate to annoy their feelings by gazing at them, the tables were turned completely upon me, for they fell to laughing, and grinning, and quizzing, and pointing at *me;* my English riding-habit seeming far more *outré* to them, than their curiously-plaited hair did to us. I thought of the French ladies, and of the Duchess of Angoulême's little bonnet.

LETTER XVIII.

Pic-nic at the Pyramids.—Ride thither.—Sphynx.—Ascent and Interior of the Pyramid of Cheops.—Hippopotamus.

THE 2nd of May was the day appointed for our pic-nic to the Pyramids. We started long before day-break, and traversed the streets of Cairo by the lurid light of flambeaux. Soon

after we passed the gates of the city, the stars
" 'gan to pale their ineffectual light," and
" young-eyed day," appeared in the East,
whilst a flood of liquid amber proclaimed the
approach of the sun, and every minaret, cupola,
and airy grove of date-trees was tinged with a
roseate hue, or burnished with living gold. The
air was fresh even to coolness, as we were fer-
ried over the Nile, and right glad were we to
hail the glorious luminary as he appeared above
the horizon. We passed the Island of Rhoda,
on which, tradition states, the infant Moses was
exposed, and where the chosen servant of God
was saved from impending destruction by the
compassion of Thermusis, the daughter of Pharaoh.   Here also is the famous Nilometer, and
during the overflow of the Nile, the citizens of
Cairo are wont to repair hither, and, smoking
their long pipes, enjoy beneath the broad
spreading sycamore, that quietude and luxurious indolence to which the climate so much
disposes them.   The village of Ghiza, on
the opposite shore of the Nile, is considered
by some to be situated on the site of the ancient Memphis.   After passing this place,
we crossed a very fertile plain, covered with
corn, where we could have imagined the Pyramids close to us; but their immensity
deceived us, for they were still several miles

distant. We then came to a barren tract,
where were goats browsing, buffaloes rumi-
nating, camels grazing, and several Bedouin
encampments. The men were " sitting in the
tent door in the heat of the day ;" the women were within, working at the mill, and
making bread. The Sheiks came forward and
saluted us most respectfully, and when they
saw me, they called out " Haram."

As we wound along the plain, you cannot
conceive how picturesque our party appeared.
The heavily-armed Janissaries—Osman in his
Mameluke dress—some of our English friends
in their splendid Turkish costumes, rich in
scarlet and crimson, green, blue, and gold—
our Turkish, Arab, and Indian attendants,
whose dark complexions, wild countenances,
and fantastic dresses, harmonized well with
the scene, and I could have fancied we were
a caravan bound to Mecca, or a party flying
to the Desert for safety. I, in my English attire, was the only humdrum among the whole,
and perhaps the only one who could have
walked in London without being mobbed.

By the time

" The sultry sun had gain'd the middle sky,"

we came into the neighbourhood of the
Sphynx; *the* Sphynx, of which every one has

heard so much, and here the soil presented such immense fissures, and such heavy beds of sand, that whilst wrapped no doubt in some very sublime speculation, down fell my donkey, and over its head went I,—I was picked up by a Bedouin Arab, who was offering me some cucumbers and melons at the moment— but, though more frightened than hurt, this *contretemps* was enough to quell my courage for the day. However, that you may not attribute my fall to my bad riding, I beg to observe that several others of the party made a similar obeisance with myself to the Sphynx, by involuntarily prostrating themselves in the dust before her. The Sphynx presented an African countenance, and her hair was dressed much in the same style with my Nubian friends in the Slave-market. The sand, which at times has been cleared away, has again collected, and it was at this time nearly embedded in it.

We at length reached the Pyramids, which were founded by Cheops, Cephrenes, and Mycerinus, between 815 and 1032 years before Christ, and which stand in the Desert, as if intended for the time-pieces of creation, by which the flight of centuries may be counted, as by the gnomons of our dials we reckon that of hours. There is nothing in their

immediate vicinity with which to compare
them, and their very immensity deceives the
spectator.   They rather look like excavated
mountains, than edifices reared by man, and it
is only by our own insignificance that we can
comprehend their enormous magnitude. We
all immediately commenced the labour of ascending; but I can truly say those ladies who
have accomplished the arduous task *without*
feeling alarm, and *without* encountering difficulty, must have had very differently constituted nerves to mine, and their faculties, both
physical and mental, must have been far
stronger. We scrambled up the door-way, and
continued along a ledge on the North side, till
we came to the North-East angle, and here the
tug of war began. I was fairly pulled up by
the friendly aid of the party, most of the
rugged stones by which we clambered being
two or three feet high. My heavy cloth habit
was but ill suited for the attempt, and I soon
found neither my courage nor my strength
were adequate to the undertaking. I however did not relinquish it till I had been repeatedly entreated to desist, and I was at
length glad to veil my cowardice under the pre-
tence of conjugal obedience, as C—— was really
seriously alarmed for my safety. I therefore
accepted Osman's proffered services, and re-

mained with him, *téte-à-téte*, for about half an hour, suspended, like Mahomet's coffin, between heaven and earth, upon the north-east angle of the Pyramid of Cheops. It was a curious situation, looking over the valley of the Nile on the one side, and the immense deserts of Africa on the other, surrounded by pyramids and tombs, in company with a Scotch Turk! Osman made an excellent cicerone, and soon convinced me that we were in the old burial-place of ancient Memphis, and I saw, or *fancied* I saw, (which was almost as good,) evident marks of the old bed of the Nile, which ages ago is said to have flowed close to these edifices, but whose course was altered by Menes, the first acknowledged mortal King of Egypt, and the founder of that city, which was destroyed by Nebuchadnezzar, 574 years before Christ. Shortly afterwards down came Sheik Chaund, supported by two Arabs, saying " his head turned round before he could reach the top ;" and I then congratulated myself on my prudence in not having attempted to proceed farther, the more so, as the gentlemen, on their return, all told me I had lost nothing but the honour of carving my initials on the top *myself,* which, however, was done for me by deputy. The descent was truly frightful ; I was compelled to jump from stone

to stone, and one false step would have precipitated me to the bottom, and dashed me to
pieces ; but however, after all our exertions,
perils, and dangers were over, I do not think
we ever had a more amusing repast, than that
we partook of, spread on the ground, something in the Arab style, in a sort of recess, *over*
the door of the great Pyramid of Cheops, and
under the shelter of some huge projecting
stones. At its conclusion, a *saddle* being
brought for my pillow, I partook of the general *siesta*, sleeping undisturbed by the ghost of
Cheops, till it was time to visit the interior
of the Pyramid ; and this, having the fair
Pekuah's fate fresh in my mind, I was determined nothing should prevent my exploring.
Osman pioneered, holding my hand, and conducting me up and down, through passages,
dark, steep, narrow, and more gloomy than
imagination can fancy, till we reached the
King's chamber, a large and lofty room, with
a flat roof, formed of immense blocks of granite, and with a sarcophagus hewn out of one
tremendous piece, placed considerably out of
the centre, which resisted our every endeavour
to break off a piece by way of trophy.

The flickering light of the flambeaux glared
strangely and terribly upon the dark walls,
throwing each individual into bold relief ; and,

as our voices resounded in the sepulchral chamber, methought they had a hollow and unearthly sound. The approach to this room was very unpleasant ; the gentlemen strode from side to side over a dark abyss, small holes being cut for their feet ; but I ascended by a steep, very narrow, slippery, and highly-polished ledge, or abutment, of granite. The return was even worse than descending the Pyramid, and I could but think of the terrific bridge of a hair's breadth over which faithful Mussulmans pass to Paradise. I once nearly lost my footing, when I was fortunately caught by the nervous grasp of one of the Arab attendants ; but my sensations were more dreadful at the instant than I can describe, and on emerging from the dark passages, after visiting the Queen's chamber, which is smaller than the King's, and has a vaulted roof and a recess, glad indeed was I again to greet the cheerful light of day, and to breathe once more a purer atmosphere. Some of the party descended into the Well, and found dust and dirt, bats and darkness, for their trouble ; and they also paid a visit to the Pyramid of Cephrenes. In the cool of the evening we returned home, stopping to see a young hippopotamus in a tank, where it plunged and floundered about, and opened its wide and ugly mouth, and displayed its fish-like neck with great self-complacency. It however seemed good-natured, allowed C—— to pat it like a dog, and appeared to be of a far better disposition than the unfeeling brute its keeper, who displayed much unnecessary ferocity and wanton cruelty towards the unoffending Fellahs that crowded round us. The surprise they testified at the indignation I openly expressed at this tyrannical treatment, shows, I fear, that such barbarity is not unusual at Cairo. It was late at night ere we reached the Consulate, all agreeing, however, that we had had a very pleasant day, and that our *pic nic* at the Pyramids had gone off much better than such parties generally do. Having ridden between twenty and thirty miles in the course of a tremendously hot day, you may conceive how glad I was to lie down after all this exertion, and to dream of Cheops, Cephrenes, and Mycerinus, on my couch, after having paid a visit to their cemeteries.

LETTER XIX.

Cangia.—Benisouf.—Gebel Sheik Hassan.—Miniet.—Caves of Beni Hassan.

On the evening of the 6th of May, preceded by the two Janissaries, and accompanied by

Osman Effendi, we rode down to Boulac, and again embarked upon the Nile. Our Cangia had been well cleaned and purified by our own servants, and we found every thing so arranged as to present a tolerably comfortable appearance. The principal cabin was about six or seven feet square, and four high, with three windows on each side ; and these, and the two doors, were so disposed as to allow a free and a thorough circulation of air. In this were our couches, a table, and two chairs; behind, was a smaller cabin, about four feet square, and in front, was an awning, beneath which were sofas placed, where, in the cool of the day, we not unfrequently took our meals. Our luggage was stowed below, and my Takhtrouan, or native litter, being placed in the centre of the boat, formed an excellent partition between us and the crew, which consisted of a Reis and ten men. The Cangia was forty feet long, and ten broad, with one tremendously large latteen sail, and another of smaller dimensions. We lay that night moored under the lee of a sandbank, close to the strangely-painted Customhouse, where we were grievously tormented by flies and musquitoes.

As there was a report that the Nile was infested by river-pirates, it had been arranged, for the safety of the whole party, that we should all sail together; but as Sir Hudson Lowe was detained, by the horses, which he had purchased at Cairo, not being embarked at the time appointed, we separated, and, by his accidentally passing us in the night, we did not again meet till we reached Djidda.

On the following morning, May 7th, we set sail at 8 A. M., and passed several islands, with buildings and gardens upon them ; Ibrim Pasha's Palace, a large ruined building, romantically covered with ivy, and the Military College. We saw in this neighbourhood immense rafts of pottery, formed by huge earthen pots lashed together, with men guiding them, floating down the river. It was intensely hot, the thermometer being at 97° in the cabin, although the wind was so fresh that we scudded for some time under bare poles, and at last such a hurricane blew up, that we were compelled to anchor for the night in the neighbourhood of the Pyramids of Dashour. We were roused the next day (May 8th) by a discharge of musketry, which proclaimed the termination of the fast of the Ramazan. We saw here numerous Pyramids of different shapes and sizes, some very irregular and of a singular construction, totally differing in appearance from those of Ghiza. One of these is called the False Pyramid. The wind continued favourable the whole of this day, but the river was so agitated, that it was as roughly unpleasant as the sea.   At sun-set we reached Benisouf, a tolerably large place, where there was a good deal of shipping, and an armed yacht.   It was a lovely evening, and we enjoyed a delightful walk on the shore, along a canal, as far as the tomb of a Mahometan peer, or saint.   In the West was visible the delicate crescent of the new moon, which was a most joyful sight to the Mahometan devotees, as its appearance had put an end to the fast of Ramazan.   " A single star was by her side."—'Twas Vesper hung his silver lamp on high, and as he shone in all his beauty, and cast a flood of radiance upon the waters, we could no longer wonder at the inclination of the Orientals to worship the starry Host of Heaven.   The Egyptians feigned that the soul of Isis delighted to reside in this planet ; and so lovely is its appearance, that it really appears like a beneficent deity, in these Eastern climes, when " the springs and dying gales," the cool atmosphere and calm serenity of evening, succeed to the heat and turmoil of the day.   On the 9th the river presented a very different appearance from the turbulent aspect it had assumed on the preceding day.   We were regularly becalmed, and the surface of the water assumed a glassy smoothness, in which every minaret and tree was faithfully reflected. We were towed along by the sailors, who chanted wild and by no means unpleasing airs; and after their labours were over, they enjoyed their hardly-earned repose, stretched on the ground beneath the shade of some friendly rock.

A Persian gentleman, whose Cangia kept company with ours, very frequently came on board for society, being apparently very much *ennuyè* with his own. Unfortunately, C—— and he could only converse through the medium of an interpreter, though he seemed anxious to become better acquainted. At Gebel Sheik Hassan, is the residence of a famous Mahometan Saint, and as the usual hurricane blew up about sun-set, we anchored for the night at Fieslem. At Sherone, which we reached the following day at noon, the hills, which had hitherto approached very near the Nile, receded to a considerable distance, and an extensive plain presented itself, covered with date-trees. We then came upon some steep cliffs and bold headlands, where there was a remarkable echo; but as C—— was trying its powers, the Reis very earnestly entreated him to desist from "making the mountain speak," as it was that, in his opinion, which caused the wind to rise, the customary evening gale happening at the moment to spring up. The scenery here

was very fine; the precipices rose abruptly
from the glassy waves, which faithfully reflected their image on the deep stream, whilst
the sighing of the wind, the flapping of the
immense sail, and the ripple of the water, were
the only sounds that broke the calm serenity of
the evening.

Sandy hills and low uninteresting banks
then presented themselves, till at noon on the
following day, (May 11th,) we reached Miniet,
the largest and neatest town we had yet seen,
where there was the appearance of some commerce, indicated by extensive lime-kilns, some
large buildings, and a cloth manufactory, which
was under the superintendence of a Maltese.
Our crew here chose to go on shore, ostensibly
for provisions, but they detained us for more
than three hours, with a thermometer above ninety degrees, and our boat moored close to a hot
sand-bank, whilst they were under the barber's
hands, and amusing themselves with smoking
with their friends. Fortunately for us, there
was a very pretty reach of the Nile here, with
which and " *pazienza*" we were forced to be
content, it being too sultry to venture upon a
promenade. It was with considerable difficulty
we got them on board at last. At sunset we
reached Beni Hassan, where are the ruins of
four villages, which the Pasha will not allow

to be inhabited, on account of their being no-
torious for the resort of robbers. The famous
caves here are cut out of a mountain, which is
most curiously perforated and honey-combed;
and up the steep side of which we scrambled,
over ruins and mounds of sand, which gave
way under our feet, till we reached a range of
ancient Egyptian temples, which are literally
excavated out of the solid rock. Of these we
counted twenty-six, some of which are of very
considerable dimensions, and some are filled
with sand, and communicate with each other
in a strangely romantic and mysterious manner. The chief room of the principal temple
is supported by pillars; behind this is a smaller
one, with a recess and a deep well. The walls
are generally covered with paintings and hieroglyphics, the colours of which were very vivid,
when the dust with which they were encrusted
was rubbed off, and the designs were still quite
perceptible. The prospect, as viewed from the
interior of the temple, through the massy and
ponderous pillars of the portico in front, was
singular and magnificent. The setting sun
cast a flood of golden radiance and liquid
amber on the fertile plain beneath, and its
boundary hills. Far as the eye could reach,
the windings and meanderings of the Nile
were distinctly visible, and the solitary white

sail of a Cangia alone appeared gliding upon
its peaceful bosom.   The wild air of our Arab
attendants seen athwart the gloom, stealing
cautiously among the ruins—now lost in the
darkness of the caverns—then emerging into
light—their fierce cries, their loud halloos, the
occasional flash of fire-arms, the hollow echoes
that reverberated through the subterranean
communications, together with the noble chambers, the deep caverns, the fallen pillars, all
combined to make the scene highly impressive.   In imagination we flew back some thousand years, when these temples were first excavated in honour of false deities; " the likeness
of things in heaven, of things in earth, and of
things under the earth."   We then thought of
the saintly fathers of the Desert, who among
these fallen fanes, forsaken shrines, and altars
overthrown, in the early ages of Christianity,
retired hither from the temptations and persecutions of a heathen world, to serve the only
true God in solitude and peace.   Now, these
caverns, which once offered a refuge to the holy
eremite, are the lurking-place of banditti and
the lair of wild beasts ; and the Reis pointed one
of the latter out, which was distinctly visible,
stealing stealthily through the gloomy recesses
of the perforated mountain.   Whilst lost in
these musings, and whilst we kept a watchful

eye upon the ground to mark the traces of the hyæna, in whose neighbourhood we were conscious we were, and of the robber Arab, in whose vicinity we feared we might be, how were we startled to see—a footstep! not such as alarmed poor Robinson Crusoe in his desert island—naked—toe and heel impressed upon the ground—but the true London right and left dandy sole, as if some Bond-street lounger or dashing dragoon had just left the ground. Oh what a bathos! Egyptian priests, holy anchorets, robber Arabs, and centuries of antiquity fled from our sight, as we involuntarily flew back to St. James's-street.

As we descended, we passed extensive ruins, deep pits, numerous excavations, when the Reis, suddenly stopping, pointed out — the bones of a man! Perchance the victim of the robber of the Desert!

The evening was lovely, as indeed they almost ever are in Egypt, when after a sultry and oppressive day, the cool and refreshing breeze springs up, and the air, rarified by the heat, assumes a peculiar purity and elasticity, which is unknown to our northern climes.

" In the still hour to musing dear,"

when the daylight gradually faded into a softened twilight, there was something very delightful in gliding on the surface of the vast river, abandoning the mind to all the soft and wildly-pleasing reveries of fancy : the past, the present, and the future, all melting into one bright chaos: Oriental scenery and European imaginations combining to form a fairy scene of enchantment, quite beyond the verge of probability, yet just within the verge of possibility.

LETTER XX.

Life on the Nile, and Scenery.—Sheik Ababdè, the Ancient Antinoe.— Monfalout.— Siout.—Djebbel Heredy.—Alarm of Robber Pirates.—Intense heat.

To those who, for the sake of the beauties of nature and the wonders of art, could abandon, for a short period, their English comforts and luxuries, the life upon the Nile, though monotonous, would, from its strange novelty, be by no means undelightful. An ardent sun—a majestic river — dusky forms are seen. The eye no longer falls upon European elegance— the ear is no more greeted by European sounds. The heat, too intense for exertion either of body or mind, admits only of a luxurious, do-nothing sort of existence — and it is pleasant to lie upon the couch and allow the thoughts

to assume a romantic, tropical colouring, unlike—oh! how unlike our European coldness
and frigidity, where the useful and the expedient are always preferred to the grand and
the noble! Could we transcribe the fleeting
fancy of the moment, in all the vividness of
the original conception—could we catch the
passing and fugitive idea, it would be truly
poetical — but, alas! the very sun, the very
clime that inspire and excite, at the same time
enervate the brain, and unnerve the hand, that
would fain perpetuate thoughts so strange, and
yet so wildly pleasing.

In the morning, it is delightful to rise with
the sun, and, ere he has attained any height in
the heavens, to walk by the banks of the majestic Nile, so famed in history, both sacred
and profane, in poetry, and in romance. An
agreeable breeze springing up, generally at-
tempers the atmosphere, braces the frame, and
enlivens the spirits. Then, when the sultry
sun drives most living objects to seek the
friendly shade, it is pleasant, at noon, to glide
along in the Cangia, and lazily reclining on the
couch, to watch the objects that apparently
move before the eyes:—There is now a low and
level sand-bank, and a herd of cattle have come
down to quench their ardent thirst—then, a
bold promontory, or steep head-land, clothed

with the purple haziness of heat and distance, closes the scene, and we are apparently sailing on the smooth bosom of a peaceful and glassy lake. Farther on, a fine reach of the river opens upon us, and a fresh breeze taking the crew by surprise, runs the vessel aground, and "Hamesha ma — Halle — la — yah" — in drowsy chorus is chanted as it is pushed off again. Then will the waves often ruffle and fume, verily, as if old Father Nile were indulging in a little fit of anger; but his ire is short-lived, and we again glide on, as if this choleric gentleman were the most benign and placid of river deities; such as we have seen him at the Vatican, where in marble majesty he lies, mighty, grand, and composed, despite the myriad of little sprites that play about him and around him. Whilst this calm and dignified serenity continues, his waves assume a glassy smoothness in which every object is distinctly reflected, and where the river goddesses might arrange their toilet by the aid of this superb natural mirror. Now we come upon the clumsy buffalo, lolling and awkwardly disporting in the water, as if more at home there than on land, with head uplifted, and expanded nostril, quaffing the ambient air—that element, purer than even the aquatic one he de-

lights in. On a sandy islet, half-a-dozen storks
may be seen in a composed attitude, standing
upon one leg, contemplating themselves in the
river,—then stalk — stalk — stalking on, till,
alarmed by the nearer approach of the Cangia,
they heavily rise in the air and vanish to a
place of greater security. A sullen plash, pro-
claims that a creeping crocodile, winding his
unwieldy, lizard-like form along, has also deserted the sunny bank where he was basking,
and plunging into the stream, he hides himself
from the curious ken of the voyager. Then
upon the surface of the water, in the distance,
appears a black spot—what is it? What can it
be?—It approaches—it elongates;—'tis a man!
A hardy native, who unmindful of crocodiles
and river serpents, himself scarcely less amphibious, is fearlessly swimming across the Nile.
A solemn stillness reigns around during the
sultry noon-tide heat, and the sounds that
alone disturb the sleepy monotony, are, the
drowsy creak of water-mills, the ceaseless cry
of the pee-wit, the wild shriek of the water-
fowl, and the lazy flapping of the sail, when
the breeze has entirely died away. But when
least expected, a sudden gust, a violent eddy
of wind comes down from the mountain, flings
the vessel on its side—threatens to overturn

it—the sleepy crew are aroused,—all are on the
qui vive—consternation reigns on board—every
thing is upset,—the interior economy of the
cabin is totally deranged. The gale, however,
proves as transient as unlooked for; the Cangia is
righted, and all again resign themselves to sleep,
or to the reveries and musings of the Nile.

On the morning of the 12th a strong north
wind carried us to Sheik Ababdè, the ancient
Antinoe, which was built by Adrian in memory of his favourite, who devoted himself to
destruction, and threw himself into the Nile, on
a soothsayer's declaring that the Emperor would
prove unfortunate during his lifetime. A heap
of dust is all that now remains of the Imperial
city. Desolation reigns around with extensive ruins and heaps of rubbish, wearying alike
the foot and the eye. These had been lately
ransacked by Mahomet Ali, in search of treasure. Prostrate on the ground were fine granite columns, and beautiful friezes were imbedded in the sand. We saw marble pillars on
dunghills, and handsome carving over a stable !
In character with the scene was a funeral afar
off in the Desert, which we had seen crossing
the river. Man was gone to his long home, and
loud were the wailings that floated on the air.

One morning, when I awoke, I discovered an
immense tarantula under my pillow, and close

to my cheek, like the toad at Eve's ear! You may conceive my horror and consternation at the sight. In the afternoon of the same day we saw crocodiles, for the first time, dis-sporting in the cool waves, floating like logs upon the water, or sunning themselves, each on " a bright little isle of its own." The appearance is that of an immense lizard. " It is shaped, like itself, and it is as broad as it has breadth : it is just as high as it is, and it moves with its own organs : it lives by that which it eats, and the elements once out of it, it transmigrates : it is of its own colour too;" and as Lepidus observed to Mark Antony, one may safely acknowledge that it is indeed " a strange serpent."

Off Monfalout, as we were sailing before a fresh breeze, we came crash up against another vessel ; and the noise of the encounter, the loud vociferations, the vehement reproaches, and the mutual accusations, but ill accorded with the calm serenity of the evening. To prevent a repetition of the accident, it was thought advisable to come to anchor for the night. On the following morning, (the 13th,) we took a long walk on the banks of the Nile, and met with a boat moored in a little creek, which they told us belonged to an English Cowasjee, whose party we saw riding on donkeys at a

little distance. There was here an extensive
plain extending on the left, and we beheld a
large serpent swim across the river. We were
becalmed near Siout in the evening, and the
banks were here very prettily fringed with
palms, mimosas, tamarisks, and other shrubs.
This city, the capital of Upper Egypt, and the
principal residence of one of the Pasha's sons,
is in latitude 27° 10'. It is supposed to occupy
the site of the ancient Lycopolis, which was
so termed from the jackal having been particularly venerated here. Tradition says that
our Saviour and the Virgin took refuge here
in the time of Herod's persecution; and, in
consequence, many Copts retire hither to spend
their last days. The mountains in the neighbourhood, Djebbel el Kofferi, are much perforated, and were formerly the burial-places of
the ancient Egyptians, and these catacombs are
termed Sababinath. In front of these are numerous small white buildings with cupolas, the
tombs of the modern inhabitants.

At a distance, Siout, with its mosques and
minarets, looks somewhat important; but on a
nearer approach, the narrow streets and houses,
built of unburnt brick, present a very mean
appearance. The city stands on a fertile plain,
about a mile or two from the river, by which
it is inundated at the period of its overflow.

We rode thither from our Cangia on donkeys along a causeway, somewhat elevated above its surface; but though our white faces and foreign costumes attracted general attention, and though we were also using green umbrellas, which sacred colour, it is said, none but Hadjes may use with impunity in Mahometan countries, we met with no other molestation than the old observation of "Haram." Having a letter for Signor Rossi, a Venetian, residing here, we rode up to his house, and down he came in Turkish costume, but we really could scarcely keep our countenances to see the excessive surprise depicted on his countenance at perceiving an English gentleman and lady at his door. As he spoke no English, and C—— but little Italian, the awkward task of introducing ourselves, and of explaining who and what we were, necessarily fell upon me. He gave us a most courteous reception, though the interior of his mansion, one of the best there, as he told us, presented any thing but a comfortable appearance to European ideas. This was a Copt-house;—perhaps, the Mahometan may be superior, or they must be poor indeed. Signor Rossi had been six years in the country, having been employed in Mr. Brine's sugar manufactory; but he seemed thoroughly disgusted with Egypt; and from his account, it must, indeed, at this present moment, be a wretched place for a European to *reside* in. To our surprise, we found the General and his Staff had out-sailed us, and had reached and left Siout on the preceding day, having passed us in the night. This somewhat nettled our Reis; and having laid in a fresh stock of provisions, we again set off, he being determined to overtake them. In consequence of this resolution, we continued sailing all night, and passed Tahta and Gow in the dark.

On the following morning, (May 15th,) our boat was hailed by a person in Turkish costume, riding on a camel. He proved to be an Englishman, Mr. Wilkinson, who was amusing himself with making a survey of the Nile. He came on board and took some refreshment. At noon we met a boat full of tropical beauties; their faces positively blacker than coal, and their hair plaited and braided in the Nubian fashion, which much resembled the head-dress of the Sphynx. They showed their white teeth, and grinned, and nodded most graciously to me, and I smiled, and bowed in return. The wind was too fair to allow us to stop to explore the grottos and excavations of the mountain Djebel Heredy, in which the Reis told us treasure had been discovered, and where are the crystal surface and pillars which Sir Frederick Henniker compares to Sindbad's valley of diamonds. The name is derived from a Mahometan Santon, who tradition states migrated into the body of a serpent, under which form he is still supposed to reside here, and is venerated as an oracle.

We passed Girgè at about 10 p. m. It is so termed from our patron Saint, St. George, and there is a monastery here dedicated to him. By the light of the moon, it appeared a considerable place, and looked rather important, springing apparently from the very bosom of the water. The two following days we were regularly becalmed. The river assumed a glassy smoothness, like a silvery lake, and we were obliged to track for the greater part of the time. The scenery was very fine. The mountains, totally barren, and devoid of all verdure and vegetation, were of a considerable height, and bold and precipitous. They here approached close to the river. The heat was intense, and I felt so overcome, that I thought I was going to be seriously ill, till a glance at the thermometer, which was above 100°, very satisfactorily explained the cause of my languor and depression. It is impossible to describe how strange it was to find every thing we touched much hotter than blood heat. The furniture even in the cabin was unpleasantly

warm, and it was almost startling to feel what
we were accustomed to find cool, thoroughly
heated. We saw several wild geese here, and
such numbers of crocodiles, that the Reis requested C—— not to bathe. On the 18th the
thermometer rose to 110°. The atmosphere
was clouded with a heated fog, and the distant
headlands were obscured by a purple vapour.
The heat was too intense to think of seeing
Dendera at this time, so we passed that place
and Kennè; but scarcely had we come to anchor for the night, in the neighbourhood of
Keft, or Coptos, when our slumbers were disturbed by the report of robbers. C—— immediately arose, and, calling all the sailors
on board, they pushed the Cangia off into
the middle of the river, when we had the
pleasure of seeing forty or fifty men's heads
stealthily peeping over the banks, evidently
watching our movements, with apparently a
hostile intention; and probably, had we not
been on the alert, the boat would have been
plundered by these river-pirates. We fortu-
rately escaped; but I passed a very anxious
night, and right glad was I to hail the dawn
of day, which alone put an end to my apprehensions.

LETTER XXI.

Arrival at Thebes.—Visit from the Cacheff of Luxor.—
Superb Temple.—Cacheff's House.—Magnificent Temple
of Carnac.—Sesostris.—Egyptian Dynasties.

At day-break we met the General's boats returning from Thebes, which place, having completely got the start of us, he had visited on
the preceding day. About noon, the Reis began to look out for a large sycamore, the land-
mark by which he was to recognise Thebes.
A Cangia was moored in its neighbourhood,
and a tent was picturesquely pitched beneath
its friendly shade, in the neighbourhood of a
water-mill. These were the property of Mr.
Hay, who, with Mr. Bonomi, had been residing here some time, amusing himself with
making excavations and discoveries. Scarcely
had we come to anchor, ere we were beset by
wild-looking natives, offering necklaces, scara-
bæi, and other curiosities for sale, with the same
eagerness with which the Waterloo people bring
relics to travellers. Our gravity was quite put
to flight by the sudden entrance of a cat—
through the window. Had she been alive she
would have been invaluable, on account of the
rats which infested the Cangia; but this was a

staid old mouser, of the time of Pharaoh perchance, looking as demure and as wise, however, as any of the tabbies of the present day,
though probably three thousand years had rolled
over her head in her mummy form. We took
possession of her, and of some of the other curiosities, which were here offered in such profusion, that they seemed to lose their value by
their numbers.

In the afternoon we crossed over to Luxor,
and the Cacheff sent us a present of some cucumbers, and an invitation to dinner! C——
then went to pay him a visit, and to make my
excuses, saying it was not the custom for English ladies to dine where there were none of
their own sex to meet them. In about an hour,
whilst, exhausted with heat, I was reposing in
the cabin, Giovanni came running to the door,
saying, " his master was coming, *con tutt' i Sig-
nori.*" Starting up, and looking out of the window, I saw C—— returning, accompanied and
surrounded by an immense crowd of Arabs and
wild-looking natives. After holding a short
audience under the awning in front of the
cabin, C—— brought the Cacheff and one or
two of his principal attendants inside, and introduced them to me. They seemed, and expressed themselves much pleased with their reception, exclaiming, " C—— was good, and I

was good, and every thing was good." They
likewise appeared highly delighted with the refreshments offered, particularly with the brandy
and water, which they quaffed with the greatest glee, the rest of the suite all the time peeping in at the doors and windows, and eyeing
me with as much curiosity as we should view a
rhinoceros or hippopotamus.

We then proposed going to see the Temple,
when the whole party volunteered accompanying us, and a strange and motley group we
were. This majestic building is nearly choked
with modern huts, heaps of sand, and mounds
of rubbish, broken pottery, dirt, and filth. In
many of the walls, sticks are inserted for the
accommodation of pigeons, which bird is particularly venerated by Mahometans, as the life
of their Prophet was once saved by a dove;
and these, together with the circular pots, resembling men's heads, peeping over the battle-
mented walls, had a most singular effect. At
the principal entrance of the Temple stand two
noble obelisks, in perfect preservation, with colossal figures, in a sitting position, half imbedded in the sand. After passing through a majestic Propylon, we saw some fine sculpture and
paintings, representing battle-scenes. From
thence, a double row of immense pillars, seven
in number, with the lotus flower and bud for

the capital, led to a court surrounded with pillars, beyond which was another portico and several interior apartments; but such confusion reigned around, that it was difficult to form a correct idea of the original building, which, when perfect, must have been most grand, and even in ruins, is still superb. C—— ascended the top of one of the Propyla, whilst I remained in the court below, upon which my friend, the courteous Cacheff, most politely brushing the dust off from a low wall with the skirt of his own robe, waved to me, and made signs for me to come and sit down by him whilst waiting for C——'s return. He then invited us into his house, built of, and amongst the ruins; and very like an owlet's retreat it proved. Ascending a rude staircase, we entered an apartment of tolerable size, the walls and floor of which were composed of beaten mud, but at the superior and elevated part of the room were carpets and sofas, upon which the Cacheff placed us, myself on his right, and C—— on his left hand, whilst our respective attendants seated themselves on the ground. He then asked us several questions in a very polite manner; coffee in the usual beautiful little China cups was brought, and pipes; but I had some difficulty to keep my countenance, when, after smoking one of the latter for a short time, he most courteously offered it to *me*. Repressing a strong inclination to laugh, I declined it, observing that "the English ladies did not smoke ;" upon which he presented it to C——, and then to our head servant, Sheik Chaund, who however very properly refused it, "as being too great an honour for him." An ewer and basin of water were then brought in, and we took our leave, highly amused with our *soirée* at the house of the Cacheff of Luxor.

Returning to our boat, we passed several female figures of granite, sitting gazing pensively on the Nile, the ceaseless flow of whose waters they had been watching for probably more centuries than I had lived years. The Cacheff very generously offered any, or all these statues to C——, but fortunately for the future traveller and antiquary, they were too cumbrous and ponderous to be pleasant travelling companions across the Desert, although I certainly should have liked to have had a female friend with me occasionally. Could we have animated these said statues, what an agreeable gossip we might have had with them concerning King Sesostris, and other heroes of the olden time, when Thebes, like London, was populous, and animated, and great, and powerful ; but we were forced to leave

these granite ladies to their meditations upon
the Nile, where they still remain, as if fixed
there by the wizard wand of some potent en-
chanter. They reminded me of Zobeide's
palace, where she found all the inhabitants
turned into stone. The Arabs, by the by, do
consider statues as nothing more than the
actual bodies of men and women which have
been petrified.

At sun-rise, on the 20th, we mounted our
donkeys, and set out to visit Carnac, the majestic ruins of which appeared in the distance,
towering in their magnificence most sublimely
above a grove of trees. After traversing a low
tract of land, which is annually flooded by the
Nile, we came upon the Temple, and here I
doubt whether even Sir Walter Scott, with all
his powers of description, would be able to convey even a faint idea of the overwhelming grandeur that awaits the spectator. An avenue of
Sphynxes, which, though partly ruined, are
still distinctly visible, reaches from Carnac to
Luxor, two or three miles distant. In every
direction sweep fine colonnades; and innumerable courts and halls puzzle and bewilder the
imagination. The walls are covered with a
profusion of sculpture and painting; and Mr.
Hay, who had kindly undertaken the office of
Cicerone, pointed out to us in particular some

very spirited battle-scenes, as also the discoveries
he had lately been making, by excavations, and
by clearing away the accumulated sand, so
that I had the pleasure of being the first of
my countrywomen to behold what had been
hidden for ages from the light of man, and was
now brought to sight by his indefatigable exertions. We saw two noble obelisks standing,
with a third prostrate on the ground, and a
column of majestic proportions in insulated
grandeur, all its comrades having fallen. There
were also the fragments of a colossal granite
statue, the limbs of which were still very perfect, and another of equal dimensions, but more
mutilated and broken. A fox stealing among
the ruins was quite in character with the scene.
The roof of one of the sanctuaries, which is
in excellent preservation, is painted blue, and
covered with golden stars, which had a very
fine effect ; but what struck us most, and literally overwhelmed us with astonishment, was
a truly majestic forest of gigantic columns,
the greater part quite perfect, though one or
two in a falling state were yet suspended in
the air, as if the angel of destruction in passing
over, had stayed his destroying hand, touched
with the magnificence of the scene ; or

" As if the spoiler had turn'd back with fear,
    And, turning, left them to the elements."

From the top of one of the propyla, which
we ascended, we had a sort of panoramic view
of the scene. In every direction, diverging
like the radii of a circle from a common centre,
we beheld vast avenues of immense pillars,
gigantic ruins, majestic fragments, and an infi-
nity of propyla and gateways, which from
their numbers might have well entitled ancient
Thebes to have been denominated, *par excellence,* " Hecatompylos, the city of a hundred
gates." Upon one of the colonnades had lately
been discovered the name of Seconthis, and of
his successor Osorchon, written " The beloved·
of Amon, Scheschonk." According to Blair,
Seconthis flourished 874 before Christ. He is
by some thought to have been the Shishak of
the Scriptures, who sacked Jerusalem 970
before Christ; though Sir Isaac Newton considers Shishak to have been the same with
Sesostris : but whoever may have founded or
inhabited Thebes, enough remains at the end
of two or three thousand years to show that at
one period, it was, perhaps, the grandest city in
the world, and to prove that the inhabitants of
Africa, however we may now maltreat them,
were at one time very superior to ourselves
in some respects, for what modern building
would survive the flight of so many centuries ?
Amongst all the majestic buildings at Thebes,

probably Carnac reigns preeminent, and such is
its wonderful majesty and strength, that it seems
as if nothing but Almighty power could have
destroyed it, when for the sins of the nation
"the Lord God destroyed the idols and caused
their images to cease;" when "He poured his
fury upon Sin, the strength of Egypt, and cut
off the multitude of No;" when "He set fire in
Egypt, and No was rent in sunder." Oh, the
greatness and the littleness of man, which,
whilst he debased himself to worship "the likeness of things in Heaven above, and in the
earth beneath, and in the water under the
earth," could at the same time have raised such
grand, such magnificent structures to the honour of false gods!

The walls of Carnac and the other buildings
are covered with the names of our countrymen,
who have sought a little transient fame by in-
scribing them where those of heroes are passed
into oblivion and forgotten. In some of the
smaller apartments, some late travellers, turning
out the owls and bats, had taken up their abode,
disputing with them the possession of these
fallen edifices. Had we not been pressed for
time, I cannot but say I would most willingly
have followed their example, by spending more
weeks than we could spare hours at Carnac;
but delighted with what we had seen, we re-

turned to our boat, a burning sun having tried our enthusiasm and antiquarian zeal to the utmost.

The name of Thebes * is supposed to be derived from an Egyptian-word, Thbaki, which signified " The City." It was partly destroyed in the days of Moses, by Salatis, the Prince of the Agaazi, or Ethiopian Shepherds, and the founder of the dynasty of Shepherd Kings, who behaved very cruelly to, and wrested the lands from their original owners, and destroyed the dynasty of Cushite, or Egyptian Kings, which was begun by Menes in what is called the second age of the world. This Shepherd dynasty was, in its turn, overturned by Sesostris, who called Thebes by his father's name, Ammon No, made the decorations in the sepulchres of the West, and founded Diospolis, on the opposite side of the river, to which latter place all that the Scripture mentions of Ammon No relates; for, though the Nile divided Diospolis and Ammon No, they were considered as one city, as appears both from profane history and the prophecies of the Prophet Nahum, who describes Thebes very exactly, if the

* Theba was also the Hebrew word for the Ark which Noah was ordered to build. " Thou shalt make thee an ark (Theba) of Gopher wood."

word *river* were substituted for that of *sea,* as
some say it ought to be. This city was a
second time nearly destroyed by Cambyses,
525 years before Christ, and was again plundered by the soldiers of Ptolemy Lathyrus,
since which period it has never recovered its
importance.

Medinet Abou, some say, signifies " the Town
of our Father," and was so called by Sesostris in honour of his father. In the ancient
language its name was Ammon No. The tomb
discovered by Belzoni is now ascertained to be
that of Sesostris, or Amun Mai Rameses, and
that of Bruce is said to be that of Rhamses
III. Most of the great structures of Thebes
are supposed to have been constructed about
the latter end of the 18th and the beginning
of the 19th Diospolitan dynasties; and Dr.
Richardson arranges them thus in point of
time. First, the Temple of Isis, behind the
Memnonium ; *next,* the *body* of the Memnonium ; then the body of the smaller Temple at
Medinet Abou ; next the Temple at Luxor ;
then the large Temple of Carnac, and last of all,
the large Temple at Medinet Abou. M. Cham-
pollion differs from Blair in many of his dates ;
he conceives Sesostris, who some think flourished at the time of the Trojan war, to have

been Rhameses Sethon, who reigned 1300 years
before Christ.   He succeeded Amenophis, in
whose reign the Israelites left Egypt, who was
the successor of Rampses, or Rhamesis, who
succeeded Sethro Egyptos, the founder of the
19th Diospolitan dynasty.   Although national
vanity made the ancient Egyptians represent
the various dynasties as successive, it is thought
many of them were collateral, as Egypt was
said to have been divided into seven districts
where monarchs reigned:—Diospolis or Thebes,
Memphis, Tanis, Bubastis, Sais, Sethron, and
Elephantine.   This would account for much
of the confusion and uncertainty which reigns
in the early accounts of the history of Egypt,
and it would appear that the Diospolitan monarchs, by whom most of the noble structures
of Thebes were built, at the time, or soon
after the Israelites sojourned in Egypt, were
a distinct race from the Pharaohs of Scripture;
but as the hieroglyphics are deciphered, fresh
discoveries may be anticipated.

LETTER XXII.

Biban Ool Moolk.—Tomb of Sesostris, or Amun Mai Rameses.—Arab attendants.—Tomb of Rhamses III.

MR. HAY and Mr. Bonomi breakfasted and
dined with us on board our Cangia ; and in the
evening of the same day, we again mounted
our donkeys and proceeded to Biban Ool Moolk,
the Valley of the Tombs of the Kings. As
we advanced, the road gradually became more
wild and desolate, till we entered the valley,
worthy to be termed the Valley of Death.
The scenery was fit for the pencil of Salvator
Rosa, and the only living creature we saw
was a gazelle which peeped over the rock,
when in an instant all the Arabs and dogs
were in full pursuit with wild halloo and shout,
which re-echoing and reverberating among the
hills, strangely sounded among the surrounding stillness. The defile became narrower and
narrower, the mountains assumed a more savage
appearance than we had ever before seen, even
among the deepest recesses of the Alps. Not
a blade of grass,—no verdure, nor vegetation
were visible—all nature seemed to be dead,
and even the scorpion we picked up was cold and
stiff. At the head of this valley were the Tombs,

o 2

and we entered that of King Sesostris, or Amun
Mai Rameses, lately discovered by Belzoni,
by a steep descent or staircase, at the bottom
of which was a door, which Mr. Salt has had
placed there to keep out the external air. I
thought of Aladdin and his cave, as from a
painted corridor we passed into a room filled
with spirited sketches, and then by another
staircase we found ourselves in a large subterranean hall, and a handsome arched room,
where stood the alabaster sarcophagus. One
of the lateral apartments has a projection all
round, and was termed from thence by Belzoni
the side-board room : it was, when first discovered, full of small figures of perfumed wood, from
six to ten inches long, covered with hieroglyphics, many of which are still remaining. The
walls of all are covered with the most spirited
paintings, the colours as fresh and as vivid as if
finished but yesterday, and it was with difficulty we could believe they were some thousand
years old. One room is in an unfinished state,
and, from this circumstance, is, perhaps, more
startling and affecting than those which are completed, for it has the appearance of having been
just left by the workmen, who were intending
shortly to return to complete their performances.
There was something wonderfully striking, and
even awful, in thus traversing these majestic

suites of subterranean apartments, excavated
in the bowels of the earth ; and I really could
have fancied myself visiting some of the palaces
in the Arabian Nights, constructed by magi-
cians or genii. Our Arab attendants were
highly delighted with all they saw, and one
of them, who had particularly devoted himself
to me, and insisted upon being my squire
wherever I went, amused us considerably by
his way of doing the honours. He was particularly pleased with a huge ox in a procession, to which he turned my attention, making
a chucking noise, as if to bid it go on ; as
Michael Angelo exclaimed " cammina" to the
equestrian statue of Marcus Antoninus ; and
when, after examining the figures with mature
deliberation, he and his companions had discovered their eyes, noses, mouths, &c. with the
greatest joy and glee they pointed them out to
us, expressively touching their own features at
the same time, as if doubting our capacity to
comprehend them ; and upon some of the party
writing their names upon the wall, they immediately fell to imitating them, by scribbling
something also, as if they thought it were some
magical ceremony.

From thence we proceeded to the Tomb of
Rhamses III. which is known to travellers by
the name of Bruce, who discovered it ; and the

approach to which an immense number of bats
seemed willing to dispute with us. However,
we effected an *entrée*, and descended into a
long corridor, on both sides of which were
several small rooms, full of the most curious and interesting paintings, in which were
delineated various domestic scenes, weapons of
offence and defence, implements of agriculture,
boats, household utensils, chairs, baskets, and in
the famous Harpers'-room, were the two figures
so particularly described by Bruce, playing
upon harps.

After our exertions, we sat down upon
some rocks at the mouth of the caves to rest
ourselves. The scene was savage and wild
beyond description. Rocks and mountains
confusedly hurled around, met the eye in
every direction, whilst the full moon, rising
in majestic splendour at the head of the valley, darkened the gloom of the excavations,
deepened the shadows of the caverns, and
threw the rocks into bold relief. The bats,
fit denizens of such gloomy places, flitted
around us from tomb to tomb, as if convey-
ing messages from one ghost to another, or
imparting intelligence of one mummy to its
mummy brother. On the ground, in deep repose, were stretched our donkeys, our dogs,
and our half-barbarous attendants.

A solemn stillness reigned around, which was only interrupted by the heavy whirring of the leather-winged bats. A more awfully impressive scene I never beheld, and to complete the picture, it only wanted a band of robbers stealing down the mountains: fortunately, however, that addition to the scenery, of which we were really in some degree apprehensive, was spared me, and is reserved to grace the journal of some future heroine, whose wandering star may lead her to visit the tombs of the ancient Kings of Egypt; but as it was growing very late, we at length deemed it would be expedient to return, and we had a pleasant moonlight ride home, after leaving the wild, the dreary, the desolate valley of Biban Ool Moolk, undisturbed by either the ghosts of King Sesostris, or of Rhamses III. and unimpeded by the more formidable appearance of robbers of the Desert.

It is scarcely possible to believe that these noble suites of subterranean chambers were excavated wholly for the purpose of serving as the burial-place for one person, however distinguished he might have been. Ezekiel, 594 years before Christ, in his vision of Jealousy, and in his description of the chambers of imagery, and of the abominations therein practised, in the 8th chapter of his Prophecies, 7th to

12th verse, has exactly delineated the tombs of the Kings of Thebes, and possibly has explained the idolatrous uses to which they might have been appropriated.

The Israelites were ever prone to imitate the Egyptians in their idolatrous practices, and it seems pretty well ascertained now, that some of the noble structures of Thebes were erected during their sojourn in the country, or soon after their departure. Abraham went down to Egypt B.C. 1921, about 430 years after the Deluge. Joseph was sold into Egypt B.C. 1729; he was advanced to power by Pharaoh B.C. 1715; his family came into Egypt B.C. 1705; and the Exodus of the Israelites took place B.C. 1490, which is about the end of the 18th, and beginning of the 19th dynasties of the Diospolitan Kings; when and by whom it is supposed that the tombs were excavated, and many of the chief buildings at Thebes erected, so that the Israelites might have acquired a knowledge of the rites, which some think were practised in the tombs, before they left Egypt; but they kept up afterwards so constant an intercourse, as may be seen by the denunciations of the Prophets for their reliance upon Egypt, that any similarity of manners cannot be a subject of surprise. It is true there is no appearance of smoke upon the walls of the tombs which we visited, and the colours of the paintings are perfectly fresh and vivid, which militates against the idea of these having been used for secret mysteries; this circumstance induces some to believe they were only used as sepulchral chambers. Dr. Pococke, however, I think, mentions, he saw several others discoloured by smoke.

LETTER XXIII.

Memnonium.—Medinet Abou.—Colossal Statues.—Shammy and Tammy.—Mummies.—Curiosities discovered in the Tombs of the Kings.

ON the morning of the 21st, our party assembled early, and we proceeded to the Memnonium, by some supposed to be the Tomb of Osymandyas, the hero of the 16th dynasty of Diospolitan Kings, who flourished B.C. 2272, and deserving of fame, as being the first person who collected a library! Here, prone on the ground, lay the magnificent remains of the colossal statue, which is by some called the greater Memnon. The countenance is fine and placid, and the features good. Upon the fragments of the lesser Memnon, whose head, by the indefatigable exertions of the adventurous, but ill-starred Belzoni, has been installed in the British Museum, is the name of that unfortunate traveller,

engraved by himself. We were much struck
with the imposing appearance of some colossal
statues, standing in front of the temple, supporting a sort of portico, with their arms crossed
on their breasts, and looking as if they only
waited for the word of command to start forward.
From this noble and majestic ruin, we crossed
the plain to the Temple of Medinet Abou, the
effect of which is, at a distance, somewhat disfigured by the modern mud huts which have
been erected against and upon the walls, and
which really have the appearance of wasps'
nests. We entered by a comparatively modern propylon, and passed into a temple, with
several small lateral apartments, in some of
which our Cicerones had very recently been residing. We there saw the ruins of a palace,
which would have made the buildings of Rome,
the Palatine and the Coliseum, " hide their
diminished heads," on so tremendously grand a
scale was every thing here. It was constructed
of enormous masses of stone, fourteen and
twenty feet large, and these were covered with
spirited sculpture. On one of them have
lately been discovered the figures of a king
playing at a game resembling chess, with a
lady in a standing position. After I thought
we had seen all, I was struck with astonishment at the superlative magnificence of a court,

into which we subsequently passed. It was surrounded by a majestic gallery, or colonnade, the ceilings and walls of which were ornamented with superb sculpture and paintings, as indeed was every pillar, and also the exterior of the temple ; spirited battle and hunting-scenes were represented, and dreadful scenes of devastation and cruelty pourtrayed. The principal hero of the piece, both here and elsewhere, is generally represented as of colossal height, in comparison to his antagonists, whom he is depicted as mutilating, butchering, and sacrificing in the most cruel and barbarous manner. Many of these seem to be deprecating his vengeance, and praying for that mercy which the victor denies. The *tout-ensemble* of this court is certainly somewhat heavy ; but there is such a ponderous majesty about it, that it seems as if it might defy even the ravages of time itself. In the centre may still be seen the remains of a Christian church, and most poor and mean they are. In the dust we distinctly saw the fresh marks of a wolf's foot! The cool observation of " Probably he slept here last night, and is now in the neighbourhood," was not particularly pleasing to my womanish feelings ; and I cannot but say I looked with some degree of nervous apprehension into the different apartments, fearful lest the ravenous animal, having taken up his abode in one of them, might spring upon me from thence.   In this neighbourhood we saw a profusion of cornelians and agates imbedded in the sand.

We then proceeded along an avenue of broken and mutilated Sphynxes, to where the famous statues, Shammy and Tammy, as they are termed by the Arabs, are sitting in colossal and solitary grandeur : generations have passed away, centuries have rolled over their heads, yet still, like the twin Genii of the plain, do they remain in mournful majesty, gazing on the ruined scenes around.   Awfully sublime and imposing is their appearance : they recall Nebuchadnezzar's golden image to the mind, whose height was threescore cubits ; and with a very slight stretch of imagination, one could fancy that the spirits of the haughty founders of the magnificent temples around, raised to the honour of false gods, are doomed, for a punishment, to remain spell-bound upon these plains, to witness these proud fanes crumble into the dust, and to hea,

> " Aghast, the voice of time, disparting structures,
>   Tumbling all precipitate, down dashed,
>   Rattling around, loud thundering to the moon,
>   While murmurs soothe each awful interval
>   Of ever flowing water."

They are facing the East, and tradition states, that the figure termed Memnon, Tammy, or Salamat, was wont to pay his homage to the God of Day by a strain of melancholy music issuing from him on the first appearance of the sun. The pedestal is covered with the names of persons who testify that they heard this miraculous harmony. This statue was thrown down by Cambyses, but was subsequently built up, and by an inscription lately deciphered, it is ascertained to be that of Amenophis, or Phamenoth II. who flourished 1700 years before Christ, and was cotemporary with Joseph. We were neither early enough nor fortunate enough to hear the melody, but there is something so strikingly impressive in the insulated grandeur of the twin statues, their situation on the plain is so grand, and the scenes around so fine, that I can fancy a highly-wrought enthusiast might easily give himself up to the delusion, and that imagination must be cold indeed, that could be unmoved at the feet of Memnon. In the immediate neighbourhood lies a colossal statue, biting the dust; —in the background are the Temples of Medinet Abou, and the Memnonium;—afar off are the excavated and perforated Mountains, containing the Tombs of the Kings;—in the front rolls the Nile, beyond which are Luxor and

Carnac, with the range of hills behind:—surrounded with such prodigies, which have lasted so many centuries, what ephemera did man appear; and yet they were the work of our fellow-mortals!

We had now been up for several hours, and the sun was become intensely hot; we had been wandering among these interesting scenes so long, that at length I became quite exhausted with heat, fatigue, exertion, and excitement; and the party kindly proposed adjourning to the house of a Greek, a *ci-devant* agent of Mr. Salt's, where we might have both shade and shelter from the sun, and where we might obtain some repose and refreshment. Here we were treated with some *modern* coffee and cakes to eat and drink, and with some *ancient* bread to look at, which had just been discovered in the Kings' Tombs, and which was supposed to be not less than three thousand years old! We also saw some bows and arrows, wrapped in cloth of a saffron hue, and of very even texture; shoes and sandals of leather, made right and left, and some curious models of boats, such as were formerly used to convey the dead across the river. The figures were well done, about six inches high, and the mummy-corpse laid out exactly as is represented in the paintings in the tombs. There was also a granary, where was a ladder, with a man above in the loft, and a woman grinding corn beneath. Had we seen these in Regent-street, we should have imagined them to have been the workmanship of Dutch toymen, just imported, from their very fresh and perfect appearance; but these were the performances of Egyptian artists some thousand years ago! We likewise saw a curious and low old-fashioned European-looking chair, such as may be still frequently seen in nurseries in England. Such, perchance, were used in the court of King Sesostris; and perhaps this identical one might have had the honour of supporting the weight of an Egyptian Monarch. Grinning ghastlily and horribly around, "revisiting the glimpses of the moon" in their fleshly forms, were ranged several mummies, their countenances uncovered, and their features disclosed to view. They were erect, and standing against the wall. I passed close to them, and ere I had perceived in what neighbourhood I was, I had almost touched them. A sickening and a loathing sensation came over me, at being thus surrounded with the dead. Yet,

> " These have walk'd about, how strange a story !
> In Thebes's streets, some thousand years ago,
> When the Memnonium was in all its glory.

How did we long to prevail upon one of them

to unfold the secrets of their prison-house,
and how much information might we have
derived from the least, the meanest of these
poor creatures, whom we cannot allow to remain quietly in his grave, had he vouchsafed
to speak; yet how terrified should we have
been, had one of these lack-lustre eyes but
rolled in its orb, or opened its leathern jaws!
It is said, the Egyptians had a tradition that
they were to rise again at the end of three
thousand years, but it may be presumed
they anticipated a more glorious resurrection
from the grave than the being thus ignomi-
niously torn from their tombs, and exposed
and examined in a manner so revolting to
humanity, to satisfy the curiosity of the traveller. For my part, I see little difference
between the resurrection-men in London, who
steal the bodies of the dead for the purposes of
science, and the mummy-seekers in Egypt,
who exhume them for curiosity. Why are
not the corporeal frames of the ancient Egyptians to be considered as sacred as those of
Europeans? And why should not those who
disinter the Egyptians expect to be haunted
by the ghosts of Amenophis or Rameses of
Thebes, as soon as by those of Mr. Smith and
Mr. Johnson of London? Most of these
mummies were wrapt in cloth of a saffron hue,

and a quantity of it, their former habiliments, was scattered about, but we were so pressed for time that we could spare but little for the investigation of objects so curious and so interesting: and, oh! how did we wish for some of those hours of frivolity and ennui, which, from the conventional forms of society, are necessarily often spent in civilized company, to devote to the wonders that surrounded us; but we saw so much in so short a period, that neither my physical nor my mental powers were competent to appreciate properly all I beheld. In comparison with what we had just viewed, Pompeii appeared modern, and bread out of the Tomb of King Sesostris made that in the Italian ovens of no curiosity.

We breakfasted with Mr. Hay and Mr. Bonomi in their tent, and were favoured by them with a sight of some very spirited and correct sketches of the paintings and sculpture on the different temples, particularly those lately discovered by themselves, and which I imagine and believe will one day be given to the public. After which, the thermometer being at 105°, you may conceive I was not sorry to lie down upon my couch, being half dead with fatigue, for it was then near noon, and we had been in constant exertion of body and mind ever since daybreak.

LETTER XXIV.

Kennè.—Preparations for the Desert.—Temple of Dendera.—
Specimen of Egyptian Deceit.

HAVING struck the main-sail of our Cangia in the afternoon of the 22nd of May, we began to descend the river, and falling down the stream, we reached Kennè in the evening. This place appears to be of some degree of consequence, from the circumstance of its situation. All the caravans bound for Mecca, from this part of Africa, necessarily pass by it, and there is a considerable manufacture of earthenware. Indeed, such immense quantities of the fragments are everywhere to be seen, that there are numerous hillocks, resembling the Monte Testaceo at Rome, formed in consequence. The banks were at this time covered with the encampments of the caravans of Moggrebyn Hadjes, and a noise of rude merriment and native music floating on the air, induced C—— to turn his steps in that direction, but he returned quite disgusted with the exhibition of Almahs, or dancing girls, which he had been witness to, which, however, he said seemed to create great amusement and delight among the spectators.

On the following morning (May 23rd,) C—— paid a visit to the Cacheff of Kennè, Ibrim by name, and a Greek by birth. He found him in a more than usually respectable Divan, engaged in looking out of the window at his horses, which were training for the parade. Sheik Hoseyn and his son, native merchants, then came down to our Cangia, and breakfasted with us in the European style, apparently much delighted with all they saw, and declaring every thing was " tayeb, tayeb," good, good. They brought me a present of some preserved dates from the ladies of their Haram, which *galanterie* I returned by sending them by Giovanni some silk handkerchiefs. Sheik Hoseyn undertook to transact every thing for us in the marketing way, to procure provisions for our campaign in the Desert, and the day was devoted to laying in water and other stores. The water of the Nile is probably superior to that of any other river in the world, after having been purified,—(which is necessary before it is taken,) by filtration through a paste of almonds, in a porous jar, and standing for some hours. Before this, it is dark, and full of sediment, but it then becomes beautifully clear and transparent. These precautions were not taken, and we suffered severely in consequence, as the stock of water laid in, in mussuks or skins, to last till we reached Djidda, proved to be so bad that we could scarcely use it. This was the fault of our attendants, as the Nile water generally keeps good for an immense length of time : probably ours would have been better had it been bottled, after having been properly filtrated, which unfortunately was not done.

In the evening we fell down the river, and crossed over to the opposite side to see the Temple of Dendera, the ancient Tentyra. The village is prettily situated, about a mile from the river : here we procured a guide, and proceeded to the Temple, which is considerably disfigured by the *modern* ruins about it. We passed through a Propylon, covered with sculpture, of which one enormous stone had fallen from the top, as if to show the traveller a specimen of the ponderous dimensions of those with which the edifice is constructed. We then entered the Dromos, or area, and in front of the Temple we saw six fine columns, or pilasters, and a magnificent Pronaos, or portico, supported by eighteen majestic pillars, entirely covered with superb sculpture and paintings. This is in the highest state of preservation, as are the Temple and inner apartments, though these last are almost choaked up with dust and rubbish.

The walls are also literally covered with magnificent sculpture and paintings, and upon the ceiling are the figures which the French erroneously supposed to have represented the Zodiac, which idea was more fanciful than correct. The bats flew about us in numbers, raising a most disagreeable dust, so offensive to our olfactory nerves, that after passing through a low aperture, and up a dark and narrow staircase, the walls of which were covered with sculpture of a somewhat inferior description, we were glad to emerge into fresh air, and to find ourselves upon the roof of the Temple, where, to our great surprise, we discovered the ruins of a modern town, in a far more dilapidated state than the antique edifice upon which it was founded. Here we in vain searched for the famous circular Zodiac, which, by the descriptions of the Temple we had read, we were aware must be in this neighbourhood; but after a great number of pantomimic signs had passed between us, the Arab guide made us understand it had been taken away, and this we subsequently found was positively the case, a Frenchman having carried it off to Cairo! What a Goth! to dismantle this majestic building for the purpose, in a man-

ner more rude than even the Turks themselves! We, however, saw the spot where—
alas! that I should say—it *had* been. The exterior of this noble Temple has been somewhat
injured by exposure to the air and dust, but
the sculpture with which the walls are covered
is still very visible. We likewise saw large lions'
heads projecting, like conduit pipes, to carry off
the water. Behind is a smaller temple, completely covered with figures, with a narrow dark
gallery round two sides, where the bats were
reigning sole occupiers. On the right hand of
the Propylon by which we entered, and in the
interior of the court, is a small temple, termed
by Strabo the Tymphonium, wonderfully perfect, with a portico, interior Sanctum Sancto-
rum, and the remains of something like an
altar, or idol. A gallery, imbedded in the sand,
part of which had lately been excavated, appeared to run round the whole; this is supported by superb pillars, two of which only are
visible, and of these but little more than their
magnificent lotus capitals. C—— observed that
the figures in the Temple closely resembled
those he had seen in India, and in fact it was
here that the Sepoys, when brought into Egypt,
prostrated themselves in adoration, thinking
they saw their own deities before them: a
curious circumstance, which proves there is

strong affinity between the worship of the ancient Egyptians, and that of the modern Hindoos. On this Propylon are evident marks of attempts having been made forcibly to extract a stone, which however, fortunately, have proved unsuccessful : the adjacent parts have been sadly defaced, which evinces that these noble edifices suffer more from the modern Goths and Vandals who affect to admire them, than from the devastations of time. At a little distance from the Temple are another Propylon, and half a dozen detached columns, apparently of later construction. The view from hence is striking and singular, from the contrast and the variety it presents; on one side is a desolate and barren desert, extending to the foot of the mountains ; on the other, a rich and fertile plain, reaching down to the banks of the river, beyond which appears a chain of hills, which at this time were tinged with the roseate hues of the setting sun. This Temple is said to be more modern than those of Thebes, and there is a peculiar massiveness in its appearance, which though it takes off from the elegance, adds to the grandeur of the whole. It seems calculated to defy the attacks of time ; and when we subsequently saw the excavated Caves of Elephanta, we were strongly reminded of the style of architecture in the Temple of Dendera.

As we returned to our Cangia, a venerable old man, with a white beard sweeping his breast, accosted us, and offered us some coins, and a curious old lamp for sale, which latter he valued at a piastre and a half; but we had here a specimen of Egyptian deceitfulness and cunning, for no sooner had we agreed to take it at this price, than he immediately raised it to two piastres, and when we had consented to this, he said he must have still more; upon which, disgusted with his extortion, we left him without our lamp. Upon reaching Kennè we found there were great rejoicings there, and firing in honour of the taking of Missolonghi.

LETTER XXV.

Camseen.—Walk by the Nile.—Caravans of Moggrebyn Hadjes.—Preparations for departure.—Inopportune visit of the Cacheff of Kennè.

On the following day, C—— repeated his visit to the Cacheff, to request he would expedite our departure, and as he went *en militaire,* he experienced a most gracious reception.

To our great dismay, instead of the clear horizon of yesterday, clouds of sand, of a lurid hue, now hung over the Desert—that desert upon which we were about to venture! The sultry and oppressive Camseen began to rise; the atmosphere became of a purplish colour; sudden gusts of wind fitfully blew, and instantaneously raised dense, but moving columns of dust, whirled them round and round in a most appalling manner, then gradually subsiding, a hillock, newly formed upon the level surface of the plain, marked where this, in India emphatically termed Devil, had been exerting his odious power. My heart sickened within me, at the idea of meeting the Simoon, or Samiel, in the Desert; and I thought of Volney's observation, "Woe to the traveller whom this wind surprises remote from shelter! he must suffer all the dreadful consequences, which sometimes are mortal." Such, I feared, might be our fate, were we there to encounter this poisonous blast, upon which the demon of destruction loves to ride, appalling all nature with his fiery breath,—this pestilential wind, that not unfrequently overwhelms immense caravans, and by whose power whole armies have been destroyed, for many attribute the loss of those of Cambyses and Sennacherib to the sultry Samiel or Camseen.

Our camels, of which we had hired between twenty and thirty, began to arrive in detached parties, and lay sprawling about in the sun and in the dust, apparently delighting in both. Dusky were the forms, and sooty the faces of their attendants, who were seen glancing about in every direction, clad in the loose blue Arab dress, or with a simple piece of cloth carelessly wrapped round them. In the evening, the force of the wind having abated, we emerged from our cabin to take our farewell ramble upon the banks of old Father Nile that noble river, which disdaining to be viewed but in full majesty, shrouds his infant stream in obscurity, and bursts upon the sight in full strength and vigour, fertilizing those plains which without his beneficial waters would be an arid tract of desert land. Like the stately edifices that adorn his banks, his origin and source, if not totally unknown, are at best but dubious; and from the mystery in which they are involved, perhaps an additional degree of sublimity is imparted; for the imagination left unshackled by time and place, is free to range in distant ages and unknown regions. How many interesting reminiscences are connected with " the Nile !" By its waters have wandered the steps

of the Patriarchs Abraham, Joseph, and Moses,
and it has been the witness and the subject of
the numerous miracles which were wrought
when "the Lord hardened Pharaoh's heart."
Upon its banks, "the serpent of old Nile," the
witching gipsey Cleopatra, kept her luxuriant
and fantastic revelries, holding the Kings and
conquerors of the earth aye subject to her
beck and nod. Still onwards flows the majestic
stream, undisturbed by the flight of time, the
ruin of dynasties, and the fall of empires, though
Persian, Grecian, Roman, Saracenic, and Turkish potentates have, in turn, held sway over
the devoted land, on which the awful voice of
prophecy has uttered such dreadful denunciations of woe and vengeance. From Dendera,
whose massive Temple lies choked in sand, even
unto Thebes, the city of a hundred gates, did
we view the meanderings of the Nile. Afar
off appeared, like a mighty fortress, the mountain within whose bowels lay many a crowned
head, who, when alive,

> " Kept the world awake
> With lustre and with noise."

In another direction, an arid and sandy tract
marked our vicinity to that desert of which
Bruce has given so interesting an account;
where dwells want, and rapine, and violence;

where range the wandering Bedouin, and the rapacious Arab. Beneath the bank were moored numerous Cangias and Maashes, and on the plain were dispersed caravans of Moggrebyn Hadjes, and detached parties of Arabs. Their tom-toms beat a wild and discordant sound, and gleaming fires and glimmering lights disclosed and threw into bold relief wild and dusky forms preparing and devouring their evening repast. Occasionally might be seen athwart the gloom, emerging from the obscurity of the distant desert, a solitary pilgrim, whose way-worn appearance and tattered robe spoke of a long and weary journey. He was a Hadje, a holy man, who had visited the sacred shrine at Mecca, and his sins were forgiven! With an air of confidence he entered the first tent, from his sanctified character, and from the well-known hospitality of the Bedouin, secure of a welcome, and of a friendly reception. Of an ample bernouse, which had seen better days, was his attire generally composed, whilst on his head he wore, not the green turban, but a venerable, high-crowned, conical hat of straw, exactly resembling those with which our witches are usually depicted; admirably adapted to keep the sun from the head, whilst its broad brim was well calculated to shelter the face from its ardent rays. By degrees the fires were extinguished, the tom-toms no longer were heard, the roaring of camels had ceased, the wild cries of the drivers were hushed, " Nature in silence bade the world repose," and we, too, retired to our Cangia, where, from being moored under the lee of a sand-bank, we were all night sadly tormented by musquitos and sand-flies.

On the following morning, May 26th, we rose at break of day, hoping we should be able to commence our journey ere the heat of day had set in. The fiery blast of the Camseen, however, still blew, though with abated force ; but though our cabin was stripped of all its comforts, and our things were placed ready to be packed upon the banks, there they remained till noon, for though we were ready, the camels and drivers were not. During the oppressive meridian heat, bitterly did I feel the want of my couch, but I consoled myself with the Janissary Selim's sage observation upon a similar occasion, that " the pains of the body are soon forgotten." Our Reis took up his station opposite the cabin-door, showing his white teeth and smiling most fantastically, quite in the Malvolio style, intending to look quite captivating ; and whenever he caught my eye, out came " bucksheesh," for he appeared to have great faith in the powers of female persuasion, and generally when he wished to carry a point with C——, he endeavoured to avail himself of my supposed influence. Seyd Hoseyn and his son, attentive to their own interest, also put in their claims for " bucksheesh;" our umbrellas, our knives and forks, our spoons, nothing was too high or too low for their desires. The sailors also screamed out " bucksheesh," and so often was the cry repeated, that it might well have been termed " the day of bucksheesh."

It would be difficult to give you an idea of the confusion that reigned around, both in our Cangia and on shore. Arabs were running in every direction, shouting, screaming, and scolding most vociferously;—The camels bellowed and roared—Sometimes a peculiarly pious one, just after he was loaded, tired of this worldly din and uproar, would set off upon the Hadje by himself;—whilst his driver was scampering after him—lo, and behold,—another of a more idle disposition seeking to evade the journey altogether, trotted off in another direction. No order or method appeared, but with the most complete Mahometan indifference and predestinarianism, every thing was left to take care of itself;—it seemed impossible that we could ever be ready;—I was in despair, our servants looked dismayed, whilst C—— used his utmost powers of persuasion and argument, to induce them to expedite matters.

In the midst of all this disorder, a more than usual bustle announced that something extraordinary was about to occur, and the appearance of a splendid train announced the approach of the Cacheff of Kennè, who had taken this most inopportune time to pay us a visit: I was so completely knocked up, that I did not feel equal to receiving him, and I therefore vanished into the interior cabin, though from the many inquisitive glances he cast upon the door, I suspect his visit was intended as much for the lady as to the gentleman. The Arab boats, as well as houses, are admirably adapted to peeping and listening, as the readers of the Arabian Nights will probably remember; and as I was not likely ever to see the Cacheff of Kennè again, I was positively vulgar enough to follow the example of the Caliph Haroun Alrasched, who was so extremely fond of peering about, and through a huge fissure I very leisurely contemplated a grave, good-looking young man, with a dignified and imposing appearance, handsomely clad in the Turkish costume, with the graceful Arab bernouse thrown over all as a surtout. Coffee was offered, but he took brandy-and-water in preference, which he seemed to like so well that he at last drank the spirit in a pure and unadulterated state, and made such large potations, that C—— prudently abstained from pressing it upon him, for fear of consequences. Whilst I was gazing at the Cacheff, to my great surprise, I found I was the object of equal curiosity to his attendants. I was without my veil, and the cabin-windows being all open, I was distinctly visible to them on the banks where they were standing, and they were all staring at me with the utmost earnestness, though without the slightest appearance of impertinence; however, as I could not brook the eyes of such a multitude, I immediately closed the casement.

At length the Cacheff took his departure; at the suggestion of his suite, he too immediately repaired to the spot where they were seated, as if he wished to have a sight of the wonderful white-faced female,—but I had taken care to be invisible. An Arab then took him up in his arms and conveyed him over a small stream, and he repaired to his Cangia, which, with several others, was waiting for him, the whole of which were most handsomely equipped and appointed; his, in particular, being covered with crimson cloth, and his rowers clad in the most splendid and magnificent dresses; the gorgeous pageantry of the whole far exceeding in magnificence any thing I ever saw at the Opera. His attendants tarried behind a few minutes to ask for "bucksheesh:" six piastres had we to pay for this visit! The great man then carried off every body in his wake; they all went to see the show. At last a gun fired—he was fairly off—the Cangia set sail, Seyd Hoseyn and the Arabs returned, and we had hopes that our business would be ultimately attended to.

LETTER XXVI.

Takhtrouan, or Native Litter.—Village of Sheraffa.—Ababdè Dandy.—Tombs.—Camels at their supper.—Garden.—Tomb of the Sultan's Son.

It was full 3 p.m. before there was any prospect of our setting off, and my courage was not a little daunted by being told that "the camels did not like the Takhtrouan." This was a native litter we had purchased at Cairo, for forty-five dollars, as the best and safest conveyance for me to cross the Desert, resembling, I do imagine, the cage in which Tamerlane carried Bajazet about with him. The body of it was about six feet long, and three broad, composed of a curiously heavy-painted open wood-work, something like the

Mameluke windows; and in this I lay as in a palanquin, which it a little resembled.   This was placed upon shafts, and carried by camels, one going in front, the other behind, as in a sedan-chair; the latter having its head tied down, in order that it might see where it stepped; and when they were in harness, it was raised nearly six feet from the ground.   Strange-looking creatures are camels to an English eye, and a fearful noise do they make to an English ear; they stretch out their long necks one way, and they poke them out another, and there is no knowing where one is safe from them; and I was to mount a litter conveyed by these singular productions of Nature, probably the first and only Englishwoman that ever ventured in a native Egyptian Takhtrouan!   My heart failed me terribly at this instant. I cannot but confess, and I was nervously alarmed at the sight of my unwieldy vehicle.   However,

> " ' Come it slow, or come it fast,
>   It is but death that comes at last,' "

thought I, as I sallied forth to ascend my Takhtrouan.   There were no steps, and we had neglected to take the precaution of bringing a ladder.   What was to be done?   Whilst I was hesitating, an Arab crouched down at my feet, and offered his back for my footstool.

Was it not the Emperor Valerian by whom the cruel Sapor was wont to ascend his horse in a similar manner? I thought of him, as in this conquering style I entered my Takhtrouan. The motion was very unpleasant at first, and what with my fear and fatigue, I had a sensation of sickness, almost to fainting, come over me; however, I supported it as well as I could, and you cannot conceive how very strange were my sensations when I found myself enclosed in a wooden cage, surrounded by wild Arabs, about to enter the Desert! C—— rode by my side upon a camel: at first he thought its movements were rough, but he ultimately preferred them to those of a horse. The getting on and off is somewhat dangerous to those unaccustomed to it, for the animal first rising with a spring behind, throws itself forward, then backwards, and then again forwards, so that it requires some degree of skill to preserve the equilibrium. At his own particular request, my Arab friend, who had hitherto so gallantly devoted himself to my service, was installed as my especial attendant, the Knight of the Takhtrouan; and he undertook to guard me across the Desert, thus securing to himself the opportunity of performing the meritorious Hadje; but in the Desert of the Thebaid did I experience, that—

" Men are deceivers ever,
    One foot on land, and one on sea,
    To one thing constant never."

My Arab Prince, as C—— termed him, proved a very recreant, " false to his god and to his lady fair." Scarcely had he performed half a mile of his pilgrimage, ere his devotion melted, his gallantry evaporated, and he complained that he felt the sand hot to his feet. He changed his mind, deserted me, took his bucksheesh, and returned to his amphibious life in the Cangia.

In about an hour and a half's time we came to a sudden halt. Our Arab attendants had become refractory, and refused to go on unless their full pay were advanced to them. C—— resisted this demand, till at length, as a compromise, he agreed to pay half; but in consequence of this debate, it was deemed advisable not to proceed farther, till we had come to a better understanding, and Seyd Hoseyn was sent for accordingly; for being completely at the mercy of our camel-drivers, it was not agreeable to commence our journey with a dispute.

Whilst our tents were pitching, my Takhtrouan was set down on the ground, close to the walls of a building, which I subsequently found was a tomb, and I amused myself with

gazing on the motley scene around. We were
in the vicinity of the village of Sheraffa, upon
the borders of the Desert. Beneath a neighbouring tree a caravan of Moggrebyn Hadjes
had taken their station. An old man, with a
mussuk of water upon his back, and a tin-pot
in his hand, went from tent to tent, and from
caravan to caravan, selling water to the thirsty
pilgrims. An itinerant musician, performing
on an instrument resembling a guitar with two
strings, drew forth far more melody than could
have been anticipated. This he accompanied
with his voice, chanting, or rather vociferating,
a sort of recitative to us, till the present of a
piastre sent him to display his powers of harmony elsewhere. I thought of Lalla Rookh,
but no stretch of fancy could enable me to convert him into a Feramorz. As the Takhtrouan
is the conveyance used only by persons of the
highest distinction on their pilgrimage to Mecca, mine, consequently, attracted very considerable attention; and I am convinced I was
taken for a sultaness or princess at least, by the
curiosity evinced by the inhabitants of the village to see its contents. The women crowded
round my litter with the utmost *empressement*,
and accosted me with an air of the greatest
kindness and cordiality. They were attired in
the usual blue cotton vest of the country, and

were ornamented with beads ; but though they seemed deeply interested in me, and well-disposed to be on the most friendly terms, our intercourse and conversation were necessarily limited to their shaking and kissing my hand, and to our mutually exclaiming " Salamat, salamat — Tybe, tybe." Their manners were most pleasing and courteous, and I could but think of Ledyard's observations in praise of our sex.

A funeral passed by, accompanied with the customary train of attendants, and with the usual lugubrious cries, and loud and outrageous wailings. The mourners stopped their lamentations to gaze at my Takhtrouan, and then —began again. Convenient grief !

A blind beggar, conducted by a little boy, came to the door of our tent, to solicit relief. He was precisely the figure-painters assign to the unfortunate Belisarius, and I thought of the ill-starred General, as, with a piastre and a sigh given to his distress, he thankfully retired. If true the tales narrated of Turkish oppression, tyranny, and ingratitude, peradventure this poor man might once have been " in fortune's lap high fed," though now doomed to " solicit the cold hand of charity," and though now no ray of light could ever re-

illumine his visual orbs, which, vainly turned
to heaven, were for ever quenched in endless
darkness.

A singular, but a strikingly handsome figure,
with a commanding and martial air, attracted
my attention; the more particularly as he
seemed to take myself and my Takhtrouan under his immediate protection. The only covering to his manly and well-turned dusky form,
was a coarse white cloth, thrown carelessly but
gracefully and picturesquely round him. His
features were remarkably fine and regular, and
his intelligent countenance was lighted up by
bright and wildly-expressive eyes. His coal-
black hair was frizzled at the top, and from
thence, parted with the utmost care, hung several hundred curls, so arranged as to fall in
clusters behind the ear, each individual ringlet
being terminated in a sort of tassel; through
the whole was passed a wooden bodkin, which
some authors are vulgar enough to imagine is
there placed to scratch the head; we more charitably supposed it was to dress the hair, in
case it should be discomposed. The *tout ensemble* had so good an effect, and was so extremely becoming, that could Truefitt or Wood-
man dress heads in this fashion, I have no
doubt this style would be quite the rage among

our Exquisites. Over the shoulder of my incognito hung a pouch, two swords were by his
side, and in either hand he carried a lance or
javelin, of strange and antique form. At first,
I imagined his devotion to me was accidental;
but when with an inconceivably chivalrous and
patronising air I perceived him take up his station for the night at the door of my tent, like
Malek Adhel at that of Mathilde, I thought
it time to enquire who my self-installed knight
was, who had thus succeeded to my recreant
hero of the Nile, and I found he was a Bedouin of the Ababdè tribe of Arabs, who had
offered to guide and escort us through the
Desert to Cosseir; and as these wandering gentry, if not allowed to defend, are very apt to
offend you, C—— had accepted his services;
thus paying a sort of tribute, or black mail, for
safety in their domains. We had no cause to
repent our bargain, for our Ababdè proved a
true and trusty guide, and was of a most
obliging and courteous disposition.

When the evening was closed in, we made
our escape from the din and clamour of the
caravans, to stroll among the neighbouring
tombs, which were on the borders of, if not
absolutely in the Desert itself — an immense
tract of land, covered with small and by no
means inelegant edifices and cupolas, which

latter were not unfrequently overshadowed by
a spreading tree. In Eastern countries, the
cities of the dead often exceed in pomp and
grandeur the abodes of the living; and between a Turkish and an English burial-ground,
there is as much difference, as between the lovely and serene evenings of Oriental climes, and
our dark and dreary November nights. Every
thing that can alarm or disgust is kept out of
sight, and there is a sort of decent woe, of
luxurious grief, very different from either the
gloomy vaults and charnel-houses of England,
or the *petit-maitre* French foppery of *Père la
Chaise*.

There is " ample space and room enough "
for the tenants of the grave, and the arrival of a
new comer is never the signal for the ancient
holder of the tenement to turn out, as in the
crowded churchyards of London, where every
spot of ground is of value; this may be one
reason why you seldom hear of Turkish ghosts;
besides, if they wish to walk, they can do so in
the desert, without annoyance to or from their
neighbours, which disembodied spirits, " revisiting the glimpses of the moon," are apt to
cause in England, where a ghost cannot take
his round without the whole parish being up
in arms.

Looking towards the Nile, we perceived a

dense fog hanging over its waters, of which, when on it, we had never been conscious; but perhaps this evaporation, together with the dusty winds and the glare, may be among the causes that render ophthalmia so general a complaint in Egypt. C——, from being more exposed than myself, suffered considerable inconvenience with his eyes, but I never experienced the slightest, as I never went out without a veil, which probably saved them considerably. Returning to our tents, we stopped to see our camels take their evening repast. They were kneeling in a formal circle, and eating their supper with the most profound gravity and decorum, imitating their masters both in manner and style of deportment. The provisions were placed in the centre, in the Turkish fashion, to which they helped themselves with the utmost civility and politeness.

There is something very sociable in the Oriental repast, and after the labours of the day were over, it was pleasant to see our attendants sitting down on the ground to enjoy themselves, round one common dish, into which every one plunging his hand, helped himself, *sans cérémonie*, and, I used to think, there was more heart in this unsophisticated meal, than in the chairs, table, knives and forks, and other etceteras of European civilized life.

At the door of our tent, we found suspended a small lamp, sent by the Sheik of the village as a present. These little marks of attention, these *gages d'amitié*, are very pleasing, and they incline one to feel well disposed to the donor.

Surrounded by Turks and Arabs, Moggrebyn Hadjes, camels, and camel-drivers, I passed my first night in a tent upon the borders of the Desert, but

> " Far from my heart was trembling fear,
> For thou, my gracious God, wast near;"

and I slept as well, and as soundly, as if we had been beneath the gilded roof of a stately palace.

On the following morning, Seyd Hoseyn and his son arrived early. They sat in the door of our tent, administered justice, and soon brought our refractory camel-drivers to an amicable accommodation of differences. On taking their leave, the venerable old man approached me with a most insinuating air, of course I thought to make his parting compliment. " Bucksheesh," whispered he; I positively blushed for him, for I had hitherto considered him as something of a gentleman; but this spoilt all!

Whilst breakfast was preparing, we strolled about in the vicinity of our tent, and an old man observing we were looking at a garden in the neighbourhood with some curiosity, courteously made signs for us to follow him, and opening the door, he introduced us into literally a wilderness of sweets, which had originally been laid out with much taste, but now seemed neglected and allowed to run to waste. There grew the date with its wavy and elegant fern-like leaf; the doom with its fan-shaped branches; the sycamore bearing figs; the pomegranate with its scarlet honours, contrasting so gaily with the vivid green of its foliage; the cotton with its yellow corolla and cistus-marked petals; the citron and the lime with their sweetly-scented and exquisitely white blossoms, embosomed in their darkly rich and deep-hued leaves. All these in bright profusion appeared doubly beautiful, from the contrast of the surrounding sterility, and we made our way through tangled thickets and intermingling boughs, till we suddenly came upon a small glade, or opening, where a young man of distinction, richly dressed, was sitting on the ground, performing his devotions, whilst his attendants stood round in the most respectful manner. The gay hues of the Turkish-costume had a good effect, seen among the thick foliage and arched branches, and the whole re-

minded me of a scene in the Arabian Nights.
Salutations and "Alicum salaam" were mutually exchanged in the most courteous manner,
and we continued our route.

The Camseen, though dying away, and blowing with abated force, was not yet over, and
the breeze, instead of cooling, consequently
heated, and filled our tent with sand and dust:
the thermometer, at noon, rose to 105°, and
this, under canvas, we found most oppressive.
We therefore took up our station under the
friendly shade of a noble tamarind which overhung the neighbouring tomb, and having our
chairs and table placed beneath, we sat there
for some time, and I began a letter to my
friends in England, dated "from the tomb."
In the Scriptures and in Eastern stories we
often read of persons dwelling in the tombs,
and taking up their abode there, which formerly
seemed strange ; but I now comprehended that
they might be a very agreeable retreat.   This
was, we were told, " the sepulchre of the Sultan's son."

By a small door we entered into an open
court, which was surrounded by high white
walls, and where were the graves of several of
the family, magnificent sycamore and tamarind-
trees overhanging the whole, round the stems

of which, equal to those of English oaks, were placed jars of water, for the benefit of the weary and the thirsty traveller : a charity which can only be appreciated by those who have been in dry and sultry climates. An apartment of about fourteen feet square, with a vaulted roof, perforated so as to admit the air and a subdued and chastened light, whilst the glare and heat were excluded, contained the principal tomb, which was handsomely hung over with crimson cloth, and richly embroidered with Arabic sentences and ornaments ; at the head of it a lamp was burning — the Sultan's son slept beneath. Who and what was he ?—a tyrant or a benefactor to mankind ? He was—the Sultan's son !

As I knelt on the threshold, not knowing whether a woman and a Christian might enter the interior, and as I gazed on the coolness and calmness within, contrasted with the hubbub, toil, and trouble without, I felt indeed the tomb to be a refuge from the din and turmoil of this "dim spot which men call earth," and I was half disposed to envy those who had made their escape from thence. Greatly to our surprise, I was told I might enter ; but how much more were we astonished, when a deputation from the Sheik of the village informed us " we might *dine* within if we pleas-

ed." At first, a sort of natural loathing came
over me, but however,

" The dog-star was raging, a shade was a boon,"

my repugnance melted before 105 degrees
of the thermometer, and we dined with—the
Sultan's son! Unlike Don Giovanni's com-
mander, he did not however pay us a visit
during our meal. No! such freaks are only
played by our light-hearted, light-heeled European ghosts. A Turkish one would be too
sedate ; and, undisturbed by the Sultan's son,
we made our repast in his tomb.

LETTER XXVII.

Desert of the Thebaid.—Caravan —Alarm of predatory
Arabs.—Caravansera.—Village of Bir Ambar.—Legayta.
—Arrival of Caravans.

WE felt how doubly delightful was the retreat of the tomb when the time approached
for us to bid it adieu ; it was so cool, so calm,
so peaceful, and presented such a contrast to
the confusion and hubbub that reigned without. There were caravans going and coming;
our own camel-drivers running about in every
direction, hallooing, screaming, and shouting,

till at length Giovanni came in quite dismayed, to request C—— would come and "gridare"— scold them all well. He accordingly went, but soon returned, for he said, he could not answer for himself, they were so provoking.

The sun was sinking in the west ere we again commenced our journey. Amidst a crowd of wondering spectators and wild-looking natives did I once more attempt to enter my Takhtrouan, but just as I was on the point of ascending, I was suddenly arrested with the information that one of the camels was vicious and restive, and would not carry me safely. This was by no means agreeable intelligence, and in consequence of the delay occasioned by changing the animal, the sun was set before we fairly started.

Our little caravan consisted of twenty-eight camels, a few donkeys, a couple of goats, one of which we brought with us from Malta, and the other we had purchased at Kennè, and we carried with us tents, beds, cooking-utensils, clothes, provisions, and water, not only for the Desert, but also for the Red Sea. We had about fifteen camel-drivers, who walked by the side of their camels, two of whom constantly kept close to my Takhtrouan, which moved in the centre for safety. The camels were tied two or three together ; some stalked

TAKHTROUAN.

on before, whilst others lingered behind, and our attendants, darting in every direction, shouted, hallooed, or raised a wild and by no means unmelodious song, that sounded harmoniously as it floated upon the ambient air and broke the silence of the night. C——, mounted on a camel, rode by my side, whilst our Bedouin guide, our Ababdè Dandy as we termed him, rode sometimes in front and sometimes brought up the rear. Being furnished with a mussuk of water, the coolness of which he understood how to preserve, and a wooden bowl, his appearance was most welcome to the thirsty individuals of the party, as he most courteously distributed his favours to all. The Indian Sheik Chaund, the Portuguese cook Matiste, the Maltese Giovanni, the Ababdè, and a negro attendant, each one looking more foreign than the other, were all mounted upon camels, and I would have given something to have gone down Regent Street in grand procession, Takhtrouan and all, *exactly* as we were at this instant : I assure you I think we should have caused a great sensation, perhaps even greater than the Lord Mayor's Show. For defence, we had C——'s pistols, gun, sword, and our Ababdè Dandy, and now we were fairly entering upon the skirts of the Desert. There were still some lingering marks of vegetable life, and in the vicinity of one or two wretched-looking villages which we passed were some date-trees, and a few plants of a species of solanum, called burrambeer. We experienced several little stoppages, arising from the camels throwing off their badly-packed burdens; and once in particular, I was quite alarmed by a dreadful screaming, which was caused by our poor chickens being thrown from their elevated position on the top of a camel, and most dismal were the outcries and cackling raised. The *on-dit* was, that they made as much noise as if so many *women* were there! As it grew dark, several wild and suspicious-looking personages hung upon our rear. The Ababdè was sent to remonstrate with them, but in vain. Sheik Chaund threatened them with "a pistol," but with no effect; till at length C—— resolutely riding up to them, told them with an authoritative air, "if they did not move off, he would bring Mahomet Ali upon them." The name of Mahomet Ali was at last understood, and the substance of the threat comprehended, for after a short pause, "Mahomet Ali!" said they, and immediately decamped.

About midnight the moon rose in the east, waning towards her last quarter, when we discovered that Sheik Chaund, who had under his charge our most valuable trunks, was not with the caravan. We came to a halt and held a consultation. Conceive me in my Takhtrouan, interpreter-general to the party, surrounded by men on camels, and wild and clamorous Arabs on foot. I delivered C——'s orders to Giovanni in Italian, who explained them in Arabic to the Reis, or captain of our little band, and the answers travelled circuitously back again in the same way. Sheik Chaund was vociferated repeatedly in grand chorus; a gun was fired, and our Ababdè sent back in search of him. We were fully convinced he had fallen a victim to the Robbers of the Desert, and we thought of our suspicious-looking Arabs, till at length after considerable delay, Sheik Chaund and the Ababdè came trotting merrily up, the former having stayed behind to bring up a fallen camel.

By the light of the moon we perceived we were now in the vicinity of some buildings, and our Reis most earnestly requested permission to halt here. " What, after a journey of a few hours!" exclaimed C——. The Reis answered " this was the last place where they could get good water, and they had none for the Desert ; neither had they bread, and here they could procure some." At length C—— was prevailed upon, and we proceeded to explore the buildings to see if we could manage to take up our abode there for the night. We entered

a long and gloomy corridor, into which the
beams of the moon penetrated just sufficiently
to make a sort of darkness visible, and, uncertain who or what we might meet, we traversed
an extensive, and, as it appeared to my fears,
an almost interminable edifice. " There is
something breathing close to us," exclaimed I,
as I tremblingly caught hold of C——'s arm
for protection, my imagination conjuring up
Bedouins and Arabs, wolves, jackals, and hyænas. We paused—it was only the wind! the
night breeze sighing along the passage which
had thus alarmed me, and my terrors were soon
dispersed by the cheerful light of lamps, and
the animating sound of the voices of our attendants, who now commenced their preparation for our accommodations for the night.
By the aid of curtains and tent walls, we had
soon a comfortable inclosure made for ourselves; our couches were placed within, our
attendants lay beyond, and about three, A. M.
our little caravan was wrapt in deep repose.

On the following morning, (May 27th,) we
proceeded to examine the nature of our domicile, and found ourselves in an extensive caravansera, in the neighbourhood of the village of Bir Ambar, which had been built by
Ibrahim Pasha, for the accommodation of himself and of his Haram, when he took the field

against the Wahhabees. It was constructed
with every possible attention to the exclusion
of heat, and the admission of air. Down the
centre ran a long corridor, which divided the
building into two divisions ; on one side was a
range of small apartments, with no other light
than what was admitted by the door, and perforations, or twisted funnels, something like
chimneys, in the vaulted roofs, and before these
small apertures a wall was raised, so as to prevent even the reflection of the sun's rays entering. The Orientals justly consider darkness
and coolness as almost synonymous things, and
use every precaution to exclude the light, and
it is inconceivable how delightfully cool we
found these rooms. On the other side of
the corridor was a large open apartment,
or portico, in which we passed the night,
with troughs of water in front, and it was
very amusing to see all the camels brought
hither to drink in the course of the day. At
the farther extremity, was a large tank, and
a delightful bath, which made C—— amends
for the loss of the limpid waters of the Nile.
At the entrance of the caravansera was stationed a venerable old Arab, who had apparently
the care and superintendence of it, with a little
fire, and a coffee-pot before him, some of the
contents of which he offered to us, in the fairy

cups of Egypt. Alas, for the novice! whilst
I was admiring the simplicity, the hospitality,
the *bonhommie* of the act, out came "bucksheesh" to destroy the illusion.

Before we again started, we deemed it expedient to come to a better understanding with
our camel-drivers, in order to establish a little more regularity in our movements. Our
two interpreters, Sheik Chaund and Giovanni,
and the men, were accordingly sent for; and
C——, with all possible gravity, with pen and
ink, affecting to write down all that was said,
informed the Reis he was to be answerable for
the good behaviour of his band, and for the
safety of ourselves, and of our property; and
that they were to obey his orders in every
thing. It would have made an excellent picture; we, grandly seated at the table, delivering our orders with much pomp and assumed
dignity, in Hindoostanee and Italian, to Sheik
Chaund and Giovanni, who were gravely standing behind us, the which were transmitted in
Arabic to the Reis, and the answers travelled
back in a similar manner, the camel-drivers all
peeping, staring, wondering, and chattering, in
the mean time, in the back-ground, and arguing
with the Reis, with the utmost vehemence and
impetuosity.

Whilst the camels were loading, and C——

superintending some of the preparations for
our departure, I remained *toute seule* in one of
the small apartments I have mentioned, and an
Arab woman from the neighbouring village, seeing me alone, came to pay me a visit. She
stopped at the entrance, and made her salaam,
and then slowly advancing in a hesitating manner, as if fearful of offending me, she offered
her hand,— exclaiming, " Salamat, salamat,"
and as I gave her mine in return, " tybe, tybe,"
added she, as she raised it most gracefully to
her lips. She did *not* ask for bucksheesh, which
is worth recording; but on my *offering* her a
piastre, she accepted it with a look of surprise
and pleasure, pressed it to her lips, and retired
with another salaam. There was a courtesy,
and even an elegance in her address and deportment, which were very superior to those of
our peasants ; and from her dignified manners, I
imagine she must have been one of the principal women of the village. At the entrance of
the caravansera, I met with a young Arab woman, about ten or eleven years old, who came
up to me, with all a mother's pride, to exhibit
her child, and seemed highly gratified at the
notice I bestowed upon her dusky babe—but
she did not forget to ask for bucksheesh.

All the village turned out to witness our
departure, and before and after I was in my

Takhtrouan I was surrounded by old women, and young women, and all the children in the country, I believe, who seemed half inclined to lay violent hands upon me; they lifted up the curtains and opened the doors to gaze at me, and then set up so shrill a cry of " bucksheesh!" as almost alarmed me.

Bir Ambar, which signifies " the Well of Spices," is inhabited by the tribe of Agaazy. This was the last village we met with. And here were the last signs of cultivation, there being some of the solanum scattered about, with an immense capsule as big as a child's head, containing curious layers of seeds, of which our camels refused to eat, and which our servants told us would blister our hands. The houses are of a most singular construction; they are formed of unbaked potter's-clay, in one piece, of the shape of a bee-hive, about ten feet high and six wide, so that they resemble immense apiaries, rather than human habitations.

The sun had set before we fairly started, but the stars were brilliant beyond conception, emitting a peculiarly pure and vivid light, and amply compensating for the want of that of the moon ; the air was pleasant and agreeable, and we were now really and *boná fide* upon the Desert, traversing a wild and arid plain, slightly undulated like the waves of the sea, but firm and pleasant to walk upon, as C—— experienced, who frequently got off to take a promenade when tired of riding. We moved at the rate of two miles and a half the hour, and just as the light began to dawn we reached Legayta. Whilst our tents were pitching, which, from the total inability of procuring tent Lascars at Kennè, and from the ignorance of our attendants, took up a considerable time, I amused myself with walking about. In this spot, far as the eye could reach in every direction, was it met with a wide and extensive plain, excepting where bounded by a distant range of wild and fantastically shaped hills. The only signs of vegetable life were some solitary solanums, and one dwarf-tree of the Acacia tribe, which seemed to be the land-mark for the caravans in traversing this pathless waste. In the most distant horizon I perceived some black spots, which I at first took for stunted trees. They moved,—they advanced,—they enlarged,— they separated,—and at length camels and men were distinctly visible, slowly wending their weary way towards Legayta. Wells of water, undrinkable and bitter as soot, were what decided the movements of so many hundreds of persons. In the neighbourhood of this place were some low and wretched buildings

which were dignified by the name of Caravanseras, though certainly not equal to our pig-sties
and dog-kennels in England; however, to the
weary pilgrim they served as welcome retreats
from a burning sun, and a thermometer 105° in
the shade. Our caravan was the first that
arrived at Legayta, but in the course of an
hour I counted not less than twenty, which
arrived at the same spot, or which were advancing towards it. There seemed to be some
sort of rude order observed in their arrange-
ments; the Reis, or principal man, having
selected a favourable spot, made his camel
kneel down, the next in authority did the same
at some distance, and in the intermediate space
the others took up their position, each caravan
keeping strictly within its own limits, and not
interfering with each other; and although within the circuit of two miles there must have
been more than a thousand persons encamped
around us, only once did we hear any dis-
turbance, which proceeded from a man being
soundly beaten for stealing water. I observed a few Arab families wandering about
in the rear of the caravans, in search of
whatever might have dropped from the camels,
and one of them brought a large piece of
fire-wood to our tents, which he offered
for sale. They seemed wretchedly poor, a

couple of sticks with a ragged cloth extended across, forming their habitation, two stones and a third placed at the top constituting their kitchen, a goat and its kid their flocks. A blue shift was the attire of the women, and a ragged turban and coarse cloth round the middle that of the men.

Notwithstanding Bruce's animated, and by no means exaggerated account of this spot, we spent really a very pleasant day at Legayta. The air, though warm, was delightfully pure, and instead of the much-dreaded Samiel, a delightful North breeze blew, which agreeably attempered the intense heat of the atmosphere. From the appearance of the surrounding plain, we were almost induced to think it must have once been covered by the sea. Perhaps at the gradual subsiding of the waters of the Deluge a salt-lake may have been left, which, suddenly bursting its banks, found its way ultimately to the Red Sea; or if, as tradition states, the Nile were originally an immense lake or morass, perhaps its waters once covered this tract, and when, by forcing a way through the hills to the Mediterranean, they found a vent, this country became arid and desert, as Egypt would be at this moment, but for the fertilizing effects of that noble river.

LETTER XXVIII.

Adel Cashia.—Beautiful Nights in the Desert.—Song of the
Camel-drivers.— Caravan becomes separated.—Alarm.—
Adabiah.—Mountains of valuable Marbles.—Pleasant life
in the Desert.—Arrival at Cosseir.—Abstract of Journey
across the Desert.

AT sunset we again set out on our journey ;
the night was delightfully serene and pleasant,
and soon after we left Legayta, the undulated
plain began to swell into low and lumpy hillocks, like heaps of dust blown up by the wind,
and these gradually became shivery hills of a
brownish hue, which were intersected by innumerable tracks and roads, till they all terminated
in one grand defile, closing in, and gradually
assuming a wilder and more imposing aspect,
till we at length found ourselves completely
surrounded by mountains of a most majestic
and picturesque appearance, perfectly barren,
and without any signs of verdure or vegetation.
The sun had been some hours above the
horizon ere we reached our halting-place, Adel
Cashia, in the neighbourhood of a well, the
waters of which, though full of dust and sediment, were not ill-tasted. Our servants told us
there were a *fountain* and some *trees* six miles
off, but as we had travelled thirty-two, we

were all glad of a little repose, and we encamped in a valley which was completely surrounded by mountains of porphyry, granite,
and green marble, the shingly and stony appearance of whose surface, closely resembling
the dry beds of rivers in Italy, strongly impressed us with the idea, that it had once been
the course of a torrent. We had been gradually ascending, and the air was so peculiarly
pure and rarified, that it was evident we were
considerably elevated above the surface of the
sea. The thermometer was 105; but although
I was forced to twist an immense Cashmere
round my head to keep off the effects of the
sun, which through the canvas of our tent was
most powerful, we did not feel so relaxed and
overcome as upon the Nile.

Whilst our tents were striking in the evening for our departure, I was well amused with
watching the proceedings of some *very* humble
caravans in our neighbourhood, which probably
kept in our vicinity for safety. A coarse sail-
cloth, suspended on two sticks, formed their
sole shelter from the noontide heat. They were
now preparing their evening repast, a few
fires scattered about marked their stations and
their movements, while the fitful light the flames
emitted, imparted a gipsey cast to the scene.
An Arab woman, with two children, nearly

in a state of nature, approached me—of course I imagined for bucksheesh—but no, the inhabitants of the desert appear less rapacious when solitary, than when congregated in crowds and villages. She was in search of a little goat which had deserted her caravan for ours, and in which probably consisted all her wealth. Her husband seized the straggler, and they returned to their attempt at a tent.

Ere we again set off, day-light had vanished, and darkness set in, if darkness that could be termed, which was only a milder and a softer day. The stars were uncommonly bright, and by their friendly beams we were enabled to see objects as distinctly as by those of a full moon. The nights in the Desert were certainly transcendently beautiful, and beyond any thing I ever had a conception of before; the atmosphere was so clear, the air was so pure, that I could almost have turned Sabæan, and adored the Host of Heaven.

The camel-drivers generally sang as they marched, and their wild melodies had a very pleasing effect, falling upon the ear from the distance, or, reverberating among the rocks, awaking the sleepy echoes of the Desert. They sang in parts ; the front, the middle, and the rear of the caravan, thus keeping up a communication with each other as they wound along the valley, and cheering their camels as they stalked onwards. Occasionally the deep baying of a dog, the melancholy cry of the jackal, or the roaring of wild beasts, hoarsely resounded among the mountains, threatening death and destruction to the solitary traveller wandering through this howling wilderness.

In the middle of the night we came to a rocky pass, where some large loose fragments in the road impeded our progress, and threw our caravan into considerable confusion. There was some difficulty in passing, but the sagacious camels conveyed my Takhtrouan over in safety, picking their road, and stepping with the utmost caution among huge masses of rock. In the darkness of the defile, C—— lost sight of my litter, and imagining it to be behind, he immediately rode back with Sheik Chaund to some distance in search of me. Not meeting me, he began to be apprehensive I had encountered Pekuah's fate, and had fallen into the hands of the wandering Arabs; and he became so seriously alarmed, that dispatching his companion in one direction, he put his camel to full speed, and rode off in another by himself, forgetting the danger of losing himself in the Desert. He listened in vain for the wild chant of the camel-drivers; a death-like stillness reigned around. At this moment a wild-looking Arab emerging from a gloomy pass suddenly appeared before him. C——, who never entertained any fears for his own personal safety, now had them wound up to the highest pitch upon my account; but this proved a friendly and not a hostile apparition, and in a courteous, though somewhat authoritative manner, he pointed out the road to him. At length, after an interval of torturing suspense and anxiety, the cheering song of the camel-drivers fell once more upon C——'s ear, and to his great joy he found the Takhtrouan and its contents quite safe. Chaund was now missing, and we feared he might have lost his way among the numerous defiles of the valley, or have fallen into the hands of robbers. A gun was fired to direct his steps, and to alarm his foes. The effect was strikingly fine and grand, as the deep-toned sound burst suddenly upon the ear, startling the stillness of the night, and reverberating and re-echoing from rock to rock through the valley, till the peals gradually died away into a gentle murmur. At length after some delay, Sheik Chaund rode up, and put an end to our fears upon his account. At day-break (May 30th), we came in sight of some fantastically shaped mountains, the conical figure of which recalled the Sugar-loaves of Wicklow to my memory. In this spot, called

ARABIAH IN THE DESERT OF THE THEBAID.

Adabiah, encircled by mountains of porphyry, granite, verde antico, jasper, and green marble, of which Bruce speaks in terms of such astonishment, observing, he saw enough to build a dozen such cities as Rome, Athens, Corinth, Syracuse, Memphis, and Alexandria, did we take up our station ; and whilst our tents were pitching, I amused myself with making a sketch of the scene. At the entrance of the valley was a solitary watch-tower, of which we had seen two or three before in the Desert ; and here I could have fancied myself in Sindbad's valley of diamonds ; for though not a blade of grass was to be seen, nor any symptom either of water or vegetation, we were treading upon fragments of porphyry, jasper, alabaster, and sparkling crystal, of which the road was composed.

It is not easy to conceive the sterile grandeur of the scene, and the singularity of our position, encamped in the heart of the Desert, surrounded by wild Arabs, every moment liable to an attack from some wandering tribe, and totally dependent upon the good faith of our Ababdè guide for safety, and yet, from the novelty of all around, and the excitement incident to travelling in such uncommon regions, I may truly say, I never enjoyed myself more, despite the thermometer at 105°,

and the numerous petty inconvéniencies I was
necessarily obliged to submit to.   Certainly, no
fine lady, who could not do without her every-
day luxuries and comforts, should attempt the
Desert of the Thebaid; but I believe I was
born under a roaming star, and I must say, I
infinitely preferred this patriarchal style of life,
free and unshackled as it was, to the artificial
stupidity of civilization.   I no longer was surprised at the ardent love of the Bedouin for his
wandering life; the marvel is, how those Arabs
who were ever free to roam the pathless desert·
in liberty, could submit to the trammels of society, to the forms of a city, and to the man-
dates of an arbitrary tyrant.

Whilst at Rome, I remember often wondering where its numerous columns of porphyry
and jasper could have come from; but now I
was astonished, considering the apparently
inexhaustible quarries of these precious ma-
terials in the Desert of the Thebaid, that
more use has not been made of them by
the moderns.   Why should not the English
have an equal profusion of pillars, valuable
marbles, and verde antico, as the ancient Romans? — and why should not London be
adorned in like manner with the magnificent
cities of the ancients?   What man *has* done,
man *may* do; and as the descent from Adabiah

to the Red Sea is rapid, if it were desirable and necessary, we might procure and convey precious marbles from thence.

It was easy now to perceive from whence the Egyptians had procured the enormous masses of stones employed in the construction of their temples. These prodigious stores of marble are upon a ridge so elevated, that there is a considerable declivity to the Nile as well as to the Red Sea; and Bruce, who fifty or sixty years ago saw the remains of ancient works, and of ducts and canals, mentions a huge shaft of a pillar that was then still to be seen in the quarry. He supposes the numerous defiles and openings into the grand valley to be artificial, and not natural, caused by the labour of man, whole mountains having been cut away to preserve a slope towards the Nile as gentle as possible.

The Arabs were so alert in their movements, that this afternoon we fairly started by four P.M. There was no water in the neighbourhood, which probably expedited our departure; and this was the last night's journey to Cosseir, Dr. Johnson observes, we seldom do any thing for the last time without regret; and, as we wound along the noble and majestic mountains, I really felt quite sorry this was to be our last night in the Desert. Since I had become

s 2

inured to the rough motion of the Takhtrouan, I had been quite delighted with our nocturnal marches. The serenity of the scene, the purity of the air, the exquisite beauty of the stars, all contributed their *agérmens*, and the novelty and excitement of spending the day in the patriarchal fashion under tents in the Desert, amply compensated for the heat and inconveniencies we encountered.

The intensity of the heat was such, that, without exaggeration, water spilt upon the ground or upon a table evaporated *instantaneously*; and tea, some of which we generally preserved from our evening's repast to assuage our thirst before breakfast was prepared on the following day, literally remained quite warm during the whole night.

At midnight the defile began to widen; the mountains, gradually diminishing in height, lost their sublime and picturesque appearance, and by degrees sank into hills; we perceived ourselves rapidly descending—the air lost its purity and elasticity, and became moist and clammy. About three A.M. we passed the Well of Ambaseer, which is strongly impregnated with salt and sulphur, to which however the camels, much to the annoyance of their riders, who were not prepared for the movement, rushed with the utmost eagerness. Soon as

" the morn began to tremble o'er the sky," our caravan came to a sudden halt, and looking out, my eyes first fell upon the blue waters of the Red Sea!

We found ourselves upon a barren and extensive plain, covered with tents and caravans, outside the walls of Cosseir, at which place we had safely arrived, having completed our journey from Kennè to the Red Sea in six days and nights. We had performed it with the utmost ease, and with much gratification to ourselves. We had fortunately met with neither the robber nor the Samiel of the Desert, but in their stead with courteous Arabs, and delightful north winds, which had pleasantly attempered the heat of the atmosphere. The trifling disasters and *contre-temps* we had encountered, had been but so many adventures, attended with a little temporary annoyance and inconvenience it is true, but likewise affording a great deal of amusement; indeed I have often looked back with pleasure to my campaign in the Desert; and, when tired of the unfeelingness, selfishness, and *barbarity* of pseudo-*civilized* society, frequently have I felt disposed to exclaim—

" Fly to the Desert, oh, fly with me!"

ABSTRACT OF A JOURNEY ACROSS THE DESERT,

AT THE RATE OF
SOMETHING BETWEEN $2\frac{1}{4}$ AND $2\frac{1}{2}$ MILES PER HOUR.

First march.— May 25th.

	Hours.	Miles.
Started at 4 P. M. Reached Sheraffa at 6 P. M.	2	3

Second march.—May 26th.

Started at sunset. Reached Bir Ambar at Midnight.	6	12

Third march.—May 27th.

Started about sunset. Reached Legayta at daybreak.	10	24

Fourth march.—May 28th.

Started at Sunset. Reached Adel Cashia at 9 A. M.	12	32

Fifth march.—May 29th.

Started at 8 P. M. Reached Adabiah at 7 A. M.	11	27

Sixth march.—May 30th.

Started at 4 P. M. Reached Cosseir at Daybreak of the 31st.	10	23
	51	121

LETTER XXIX.

Cosseir.—Egyptian House.—Sun rises like a pillar of fire !
Red Sea.—Beautiful colour.—Distress from want of water.
—Locusts.—Vultures.—Moggrebyn Hadjes.—Arrival of
Franks.—Visit from the Cacheff of Cosseir.

FRESHLY and strongly blew the morning
breeze as we entered Cosseir, a small sea-port
town, at the head of a bay in the Red Sea,
where at this time were at anchor twenty or
thirty Arab Dows, ready to carry pilgrims and
grain to Mecca. A reef of coral rocks, about
six hundred yards from the shore, forms a sort
of roadstead, close to which the vessels were
stationed, none of very great size, for probably
the water here would not be deep enough for
large ships, though well calculated for small
craft, and perhaps for steam-packets. The harbour is open to the north-east and south-east
winds, but otherwise sheltered ; and to the
north of the town are numerous headlands and
little bays. To the south, a tongue of land, extending into the sea, forms the bay, and there
is an extraordinary and very high ridge of perfectly red mountains, resembling the spine of
an animal, which might well cause navigators

to bestow upon the neighbouring sea the appellation of red. To the west is a curtain of the most barren and desolate-looking hills imaginable, black in hue, with a lurid tinge over them, which seem to shut Cosseir out from the rest of the world, but through whose desert defiles we had penetrated thither. Apparently the barren plain, upon which the town now stands, was once covered by the sea, for it looks little more than a reef of curiously-coloured stones and shells, with a greenish tinge over it. No vegetation is there to be seen, and *literally* not a blade of grass, nor the least appearance of cultivation. But for the caravans of Moggrebyn Hadjes, Cosseir would probably soon dwindle into a mere village. The citadel is quite dilapidated, but there are, for an Oriental town, pretty wide streets, and tolerable bazaars, mosques, coffee-houses, &c.

We took up our abode in the house of Seedee Hoseyn, an African merchant, the whole of which we engaged during our *séjour* at Cosseir. It was cool and spacious, and when our own furniture was properly arranged, it proved really a very comfortable habitation. We entered by a gateway into an interior court, round which ran a covered portico, or verandah; above this was an open gallery, upon which all the principal rooms opened, and to

which we ascended by a tolerably wide staircase. A smaller one led to a suite of rooms,
which from their privacy and security were
evidently intended for the use of the women.
The floors and walls were composed of mud,
or perhaps of what we should call lath and
plaster, and in the latter were circular perforations, which we were uncertain whether
made to admit the air, or intended as loopholes from whence to fire upon an enemy.
On three sides of the room were platforms
elevated several inches in the Turkish fashion,
which were sad stumbling-blocks to European
feet, and the roof, which was strongly prop-
ped, was formed of rafters and matting. The
house was irregular, and somewhat in the shape
of a trapezium, situated not a stone's throw
from the sea, upon which our windows looked. Conceive my astonishment and surprise,
upon repairing thither, on first entering, to gaze
upon the exquisite beauty of the waves, and to
watch the sun which was just emerging from the
bosom of the water, to see the latter, instead of
rising in its usual circular form, assume that of
a pillar of fire! I positively doubted the evidence of my senses, and I should scarcely hope
to be believed, but that I find the ancients, and
Agatharchides in particular, have mentioned
the same phænomenon upon these coasts, where

they observed " the sun rose like a pillar of fire." Lord Valentia also noticed a similar appearance at Mocha, where he saw it set in like manner. We subsequently frequently saw it assume an elongated, but never again so completely columnar a figure. We could but think of the pillar of fire, which for forty years gave light to the Israelites in the wilderness.

The colour of the Red Sea here was of the most exquisite blue imaginable, far exceeding in beauty the boasted hue of the Mediterranean. The breakers had a peculiarly vivid and lively whiteness, which by contrast added greatly to the brilliancy of the azure main ; but, though I could have gazed for hours, it was too dazzling to permit me to do so with impunity. Through the transparent waves, a beautiful mosaic pavement, composed of corallines, shells, and coloured stones, was distinctly visible, and several curious species of sea-weed. In our rambles upon the shore we frequently collected specimens of shells, which in England would have been deemed valuable ornaments to the cabinets and drawing-rooms of collectors and virtuosi, and there was a fairy sort of crab, with the celerity and elegance of whose movements I was quite delighted, and which, with the quickness of thought, on being disturbed, would run off and attempt to hide itself in the sand.

We found the climate here not unpleasant ; the mornings and evenings were delightful, and at noon the thermometer ranged between eighty and ninety degrees, which, after one hundred and five in the Desert, was comparatively so cool, that I was frequently glad to make use of a shawl. The nights here were most lovely ; the stars shone with a brilliancy and a softness I hardly ever saw equalled, and after the heat of the day, when Vesper appeared on high in the clear blue sky, he seemed like a mild and beneficent deity. This was the season for merriment and amusement ; and accordingly tom-toms and native music were heard till day-break. This perhaps may account for the absence of *ghosts* here ; for, although from time immemorial, all our English spirits have been laid in the Red Sea, and though we were for weeks either upon it, or its shores, no phantom ever thought of paying its countrywoman a visit, to enquire what was going on in the green Isles of the West, from whence I was just arrived.

Almost all the fresh water at Cosseir was brought from Ambaseer, the well in the Desert, six miles distant, but it was so impregnated with sulphur, and smelt so offensively, that it was almost undrinkable. I never before had known what it was to be deprived of that necessary of life, and I now fully entered into the sufferings

of the Israelites, and their murmurs against
Moses, as mentioned in Holy Writ. To add
to our distress, we now first discovered that
our stock of Nile water was almost equally
bad ; and I could not easily describe to you,
how very, very much at times I longed for
a glass of clear and sparkling water fresh from
the spring.

We were, however, notwithstanding this
want of water, terribly annoyed with flies and
musquitos ; and, in one of our walks, we once
met a small flight of locusts, with their beautifully striped wings and hieroglyphically
marked foreheads. These remarkable lines
the Mahometans believe convey some mystic
meaning, and consequently regard them with
some degree of veneration. They form at
once one of the most beautiful, as well as one
of the most destructive species of the insect
tribe.

Our Arab attendants were anxious to quit
Cosseir almost immediately after their arrival, as
they considered its air and water to be prejudicial to their camels; indeed, I believe, the neighbourhood of the sea is always, in some degree,
hurtful to this ship of the Desert, but, from
the little variety we saw in the animal, as well
as vegetable kingdom, I should think Cosseir
was " neither good for man nor beast." We
saw a few migratory swallows, some plovers,

sea-gulls, and immense vultures, the which seemed sent by Providence as scavengers to an unclean and dirty people. The carrion vulture, *(vultur petenoptorus,)* was for its services installed by the ancient Egyptians in their Pantheon, and was considered by them as sacred ; and in Egypt it is still held unlawful to kill the vulture. In the paintings in the Kings' Tombs at Thebes, the Genii and Spirits are always represented with the heavy extended vulture wing, which is very unlike the butterfly wings we give to our Cupids and Psyches. These birds generally station themselves on the most elevated spot they can select, and, with their bright and sharp eyes watchfully scanning the plain beneath in search of prey, they have really a majestic and imposing appearance. We saw several thus occupied on the top of the Pyramid of Cephrenes, at Ghizà.

Cosseir was at this time extremely full, and provisions were very dear, on account of its being the height of the Hadje season. As the ships were all fully occupied by pilgrims, we had some difficulty in arranging for, and in procuring a passage to Djidda ; and C—— paid several visits to the Cacheff, to request him to expedite our departure, who told him, that at any other time he would have *obliged* the owners of the vessels to take us at a reasonable rate, but that at this moment he could not interfere, for the demand was so great. They first asked 400 dollars, then 300, and at length came down to 150; which, as Sir Hudson Lowe, who had left Cosseir but a few hours before our arrival, had been forced to give 270, we considered a very fair compromise.

Both at the Divan and in the coffee-houses, C—— frequently met several very respectable travellers from all countries, and some Hindoos, who had come from the Panjaub, and were here apparently upon mercantile adventures and speculation. Indeed, there was an endless variety of nations congregated at Cosseir, and there was the most singular contrast of features and complexions to be seen. Our host, Seedee Hoseyn, presented the jet-black features, turned-up nose, thick lips, white teeth, and good-hearted animal expression of the Negro; whilst the Chious, or *homme d'affaires* had the fine Greek outline of feature, and what Lady Morgan would term " a magnificent head," the aquiline nose, and the eye beaming with the intellect and genius of his country. Many of the Moggrebyn Hadjes appeared to have come from the very heart of Africa, and we much regretted that our inability to speak their language prevented our obtaining any information concerning a country, the interior of which appears to elude European curiosity and enterprise. We had not much cause to flatter ourselves upon our English features and complexions; for it is positively a fact, when the little dirty Arab children met us, they ran screaming away, as alarmed at the appearance of white people, as if they had seen that personage whom we delight to paint as black.

One day, as I was sitting in the verandah by myself, the Chious suddenly stood before me, and at the sight of his companion I was really as much startled, as an English lady would be, were her butler unexpectedly to introduce a Turk in full costume into her boudoir in London. I had been so long among turbans and flowing robes, that the sight of a stranger in Frank costume almost frightened me. He proved to be a Frenchman, either in disguise, or one who had seen better days, and who, we could have fancied from his appearance had been a military follower of Napoleon. He had lost his party and his way in the Desert, and having wandered to Cosseir in a half-starved state, hearing there were Franks at our house, he had come thither in hopes of finding his friends there. If I were surprised at his appearance, nothing could exceed his astonishment to meet with an English lady established, as it were, at Cosseir. " Mon Dieu ! Quel courage !" exclaimed he, on hearing I had positively crossed the Desert, shrugging his shoulders, and lifting up his hands and eyes with all the energy of his countrymen. After some refreshment, he left us in search of his companions, with whom he was fortunate enough to meet, and, on the following day, he brought them to call upon us. They were two Germans,—literary adventurers, who were travelling in these remote countries, ultimately intending to find their way into Abyssinia, of which enterprising undertaking they spoke with as much *sang-froid* as if they were arranging a trip from London to Brighton or Cheltenham. Like a true Frenchman, our first acquaintance was carrying a beautiful little poodle about with him, the which was one day stolen from him whilst asleep in the bazaar, and he applied to C—— to assist him in regaining it, who spoke to the Cacheff on the subject. The latter severely threatened the Chious with punishment if it were not *immediately* found ; and in about half an hour, to our great astonishment, the lost dog was found, brought back, and restored to its master.

In C——'s visits to the Divan of the Cacheff, he one morning exhibited his passport, which seemed to produce some sensation, and in the course of the day the call was returned in state. We were taken somewhat by surprise, and I was sitting, unveiled, at my usual occupations, when the Cacheff and his party entered the room. They were fine-looking men, with dignified and very respectful manners. The Cacheff and his principal attendant seated themselves upon our chairs and sofas quite in the European fashion, which they seemed to prefer to their own cross-legged style. The one talked to C——, whilst the other addressed his conversation to me, and asked me, through the medium of Giovanni, how I liked the country, travelling, &c.—expressed his surprise at our having come from such a distance, and at our "Belled," or country, being so far off. In fact, the Cosseir small-talk so very much resembled that of Brighton or Hastings, that had it not been for the turbans, flowing robes, and long beards of the heroes before me, I should not have perceived much difference between their observations and those of common callers in England. They seemed much pleased with an atlas which was on the table, and took coffee, which we offered them in the Oriental style, before they rose to take their leave. C—— and the Cacheff soon became upon very friendly terms, and previous to our departure C—— presented him with a pocket telescope, with which he appeared highly delighted, as it would enable him to watch the ships that entered or left the harbour. He was extremely civil to us, and rendered us every assistance in his power, and in some degree protected us from the impositions of the Arabs, who are sad extortioners.

LETTER XXX.

Embarkation on the Red Sea.—Arab Dow.—Hadjes on board.—Manners and customs.—Hadje Ships.—Yambo. Governor.—Astonishment of the Inhabitants at the sight of Franks.—Yambowys.—Reservoirs of water.—Arab architecture.—Windmills.—Tombs.—Superstitious customs. —Mar Abraham, Bishop of Jerusalem.

THE Northwest wind, though favourable for the voyage down the Red Sea, continued to blow for several days with too much violence for the timid navigators of the Red Sea to dare to venture from their port. At length, after a fortnight's *séjour* at Cosseir, it sank on the 13th of June, and we were summoned on board. The night was lovely, the sea beautifully serene, and the stars shone most brilliantly, when at 10 P. M. we first adventured upon the Red Sea, and, entering a little boat, were rowed by a crew fully answering Ali Bey's description, " black and thin as apes," to the Arab Dow, which was to convey us to Djidda. Singular, indeed, was its construction, and probably differing but little from the ships built by King Solomon 992 years before Christ, " in Ezion-geber, which is beside Eloth, on the shore of the Red Sea." It was of a large size, with one *tremendous* sail, and both the prow and the stern projected exceedingly. Heavily laden with merchandize, and with Hadjes, of which there were not fewer than three hundred on board, it was deeply immersed in the water, and as the deck was too crowded to admit of my walking across it, I was positively compelled to enter my cabin by a ladder suspended from the window.

The principal cabin, of which we were to have the exclusive use, was spacious and airy. It had five very good-sized windows in the stern, besides scuttles at the side; but we were at first dreadfully annoyed by the smell of bilge water, and we were also much incommoded with swarms of flies and musquitos.

Considering the immense number of persons in our crazy-looking vessel, the silence was astonishing, though the deck was so crowded that there *literally* was not room for the Hadjes to lie down at full-length. There were complexions of every hue, and features of every description on board. The handsome turbaned Turk; the finely-featured Greek renegado;

the wild and intelligent-looking Bedouin of the
desert; the swarthy Arab; the coal black,
woolly-headed, flat-countenanced Negro; the savage-looking Moor; the slightly-formed, dusky-
complexioned Hindoo; and our European
selves. There were also several Nubian women
and girls, who, having been taken prisoners
by Mahomet Ali's soldiers, were now sent for
sale to the Djidda slave-market: their price
was about two dollars a-head. Naked from
the waist upwards, they were much ornamented with glass-beads; their figures were finely-
formed; their head-dress and features much
resembled those in the Kings' tombs at Thebes;
they were more than ordinarily good-looking,
and their whole appearance was pleasing and
agreeable. They seemed perfectly happy, and
amused themselves with playing with their infants, and if, *par hazard,* our cabin-door were
left open, with watching my movements, apparently with much curiosity and interest.
Their fare consisted entirely of dry biscuit,
which indeed appeared to be the only food
used on board; but we frequently sent them
things from our stores, for which they always
seemed most grateful. Among them, C——
one day observed an African copying a manu-
script, in a small neat hand, which he wrote
from *right to left* with great quickness and fa-

cility, apparently undisturbed by the confusion
and Babel of languages with which he was surrounded. Some of the Hadjes put up a little
temporary awning upon deck, to protect themselves from the sun ; others lay down upon
their luggage ; but the privations and hardships necessarily undergone in the pilgrimage
to Mecca are really surprising. In a cabin in
front of ours was a Turk, who, to judge from
the respect paid to him, and the number of his
attendants, must have been a man of considerable consequence in his own country. His
manners were polished and dignified. He passed his time in reposing on his carpet, and
smoking his pipe; and though his suite occasionally betrayed their curiosity by furtively
taking a peep at me, he never looked into our
cabin, but behaved with the utmost politeness. Indeed, I think the manners of the superior Turks I have occasionally met with, are
more truly gentlemanly, and frequently preferable to those of the generality of Europeans.
There is a grandeur and almost majesty about
them, that induces one to think they are
of a high caste; and, at the same time, they
always behave with the utmost civility and
courtesy. Through the medium of Chaund
Hindee, as Sheik Chaund was termed on board,
(our other Interpreter Giovanni having left us at

Cosseir to return to Malta,) C—— and he used to have a good deal of intercourse and conversation ; and a little child belonging to himself, or to some of his party, paid daily visits to our cabin for almonds and raisins; its friends seeming as much gratified with the notice we took of it, as English parents could have been.

With a fair wind we got under weigh at 8 A. M. on the 14th of June, and sailed over the coral roadstead, the variegated surface of which was distinctly visible through the transparent waves ; and fish, eighteen inches long, were to be seen sporting among patches of white sand, and layers of green sea-weed. On the following day (June 15th), the wind was light but fair, and we stretched over to the Arabian coast. In the course of the night a poor Turk died, whose distressing groans we had distinctly heard all the preceding day ; and we saw his corpse, decently wrapt up in a linen cloth, float by our cabin windows. We were told he died of sea sickness, which was no very agreeable intelligence to those suffering at the instant under the same disorder.

On the 15th we came in sight of the Arabian coast, and we passed some islands, which from their position we imagined must be the Aurora Group. The wind freshening in the evening, the Reis made for the first creek, for it is inconceivable what timid navigators the Arabians appear to be, and we ran into a pretty little bay, with several trees and a fertile valley at the head of it. Two or three other Hadje ships, laden with pilgrims and grain, which had set sail at the same time with ourselves, kept company with us, and always came to anchor at the same spot, and frequently within a stone's throw of us, which arrangement was probably for the safety and protection of the whole. As we could distinctly see and be seen through the large stern windows, our respective movements furnished mutual amusement to all parties, for we were as much objects of curiosity to them as they were to us. Under a large awning upon the quarter-deck, the superior Turks or Moors were to be seen reposing in knots of six or seven, each smoking his pipe, or sitting cross-legged round a huge stew-pan, making their common meal from thence, every one plunging his hand in *sans cérémonie*. When the repast was concluded, water was brought by their attendants, with which they washed their faces, hands, and mouths, and salt water was not unfrequently used as a substitute for fresh. The women, in the mean time, sat near them, but half apart, like Eve, in the back ground, in full gossip with each other, or interchanging courteous

salaams and salutations with myself. When
their husbands had finished, they partook of
the remains of the meal. The female costume seemed principally to consist of the blue
cotton shift reaching to the feet, with fashionably large and loose sleeves, something in the
seduisante mode. A piece of cloth thrown over
the head was worn like a mantilla, and the face
was concealed by the mask or veil, tied up between the eyes. Those that were good-looking took care to display enough of their countenances to show that they were so, coquettishly concealing the tip of the nose and the
mouth, but leaving the contour of the head and
face distinctly visible. Some of them had even
a considerable degree of *elegance* in their dress
and appearance, and had their hair very prettily
braided down their backs. These were probably Arabs or Moors from their dress, and from
their being less immured than the Turkish
belles, of which latter we saw several occasionally emerging from the recesses of their cabins,
attired in very splendid dresses, consisting of
loose silk drawers and vests, with immense
white muslin veils gracefully thrown over the
whole figure.

After we came to anchor, which we generally did a few minutes before the other vessels
arrived, it was really an extremely pretty sight

to see them come in. A wild and not unharmonious hurrah was raised, as in full sail with the quickness of lightning they glanced past our stern windows. This was returned by our crew ; their immense sail was instantaneously lowered and furled, and silence succeeded to the pageant show, till broken by the approach of another and of another vessel. The Turkish head-dress, composed of a red skull-cap, with generally a purple tassel at the top, and immense rolls of white muslin gracefully disposed around in most becoming folds, is extremely handsome, and the decks of the Dows and Buglars had, literally speaking, very much the appearance of beds of tulips ; for being so crowded, nothing was seen of the passengers on board but their turbaned heads.

At 5 A. M. on June 17th, with a fair and steady wind, and a thermometer about 84°, we again set sail, and passed between the shore and an extensive coral reef, about two feet above water, which justified the Reis in having come to anchor on the preceding evening, with which precaution we were somewhat disposed to murmur at the moment. At about 3 P.M. a stiff breeze brought us in sight of Yambo, which our crew pronounced Zamboo, and, the sea being high, we ran down the outside of another coral reef, between which and the

main land was a backwater of the most lovely
sea-green imaginable, and though unfortunately too shallow for our vessel, presenting a
most enviable degree of serenity and calmness
within, whilst we were buffetting with rough
and boisterous waves without.

In the evening we reached Yambo, which is
in north latitude 24° 7′ 6″, and among numerous other Dows, Buglars, and vessels of every
size and description, we came to anchor in
about three fathoms of water, not two stones'
throw from the shore. The town from the
water had not an unpretty appearance. It is
situated to the north of a deep bay, running
from north-east to south-west, about a mile
and a half in depth and two miles wide; and it
is apparently far better calculated for shipping
than Cosseir, for there were several three-
masted ships here, of which we saw none there.
C ——, with the other passengers, immediately
went on shore and paid a visit to the Governor,
a respectable-looking old Turk, with a long
white beard sweeping his breast, who received
him very graciously. He was very friendly
and communicative, and told C—— the town
was under the government of Mahomet Ali,
but that its exports were very trifling, consisting merely of a few dates; that they had
seldom more than fifteen days' rain in the

YAMBO, AND MOUNTAINS IN THE VICINITY OF MEDINA

course of the year, occasionally none, and sometimes cold weather for a month together; and
that the inhabitants were chiefly Wahabbees.
He observed that Medina was far better worth
seeing than Yambo, and strongly recommended
C—— to visit it; but upon his answering,
that being a Frank and a Christian he was
not aware he might do so, the Governor appeared a little confused, and saying he did not
know he was a Frank, the which however he
might have seen by his dress, he immediately
changed the conversation.

The effects of refraction upon the sun's appearance upon this coast were really very surprising and amusing. This evening it assumed
the shape of a *mushroom* as it sank in the west!
In fact, we scarcely ever saw it set in a regularly
circular form. The thermometer whilst we were
here was about 90°.

The following day, in the afternoon, I accompanied C—— upon shore, but from the
sensation my appearance created at Yambo,
I fancy I must have been the first and only
Englishwoman that ever traversed its streets.
The Turks smoking in the coffee-houses, whose
apathy is seldom disturbed by any passing
object or event, laid down their pipes to gaze
at me; the more vivacious Arabs followed us
with looks of curiosity; the children thronged

round us, capering and dancing in ecstatic
delight; the women stopped, stood still, and
stared in mute astonishment; nay, the old
Governor himself, who was gravely smoking
in his Divan, starting with surprise, thrust his
body half out of the window at which he was
reposing, and then, with activity and curiosity
worthy an European, darting across the room,
suddenly appeared at another, to ascertain who
and what the singular personage was that had
just landed in his territories. The strictest
politeness was however observed towards us,
and when any of the children came innocently
up to us to gaze in our faces, as if to find out
what we were, some of the most respectable in
the crowd prevented them from annoying us,
and occasionally one or two, the Sindbads of the
place, who had in their day probably wandered
up to Suez or Alexandria, and there seen European women, as they drove them off with a protecting and patronising manner, significantly
but exultingly exclaimed to the bystanders, "Signora!" as much as to say "I know her name."

Yambo is a completely Arab town, very few
foreigners residing here. The Yambowys consist principally of the Bedouin tribe Djeheyne,
who dwell in the neighbourhood; they wear
the *keffie*, or green and yellow striped handkerchiefs upon their heads in the mantilla style,

of which we saw some specimens at Cosseir; a white *abba* or bernouse on their shoulders, and a vest of blue or coloured cotton under it, with a leathern girdle round their middle. They possess many ships, which navigate and trade with the different ports along the Red Sea; their provisions are almost entirely imported, but we could procure neither fruit nor vegetables of *any* kind here, and, indeed, there seemed nothing in the shops but grain of different sorts exposed for sale, the greater part of which came from Egypt and Abyssinia. There were also some tolerable attempts at pastry. The inhabitants seemed very poor, and we saw some unfortunate wretches, who were probably destitute Hadjes, literally biting the ground, as if from starvation.

The streets are very narrow, and the houses are built either of a sort of madrepore, or of rough white stone, which is full of fossils. They are low, and few are more than one story high, with flat mud roofs; as the windows do not often look into the street, they have a dull appearance. In the old buildings we saw several very curious specimens of Arabesque architecture, the round, the pointed, and the elliptic arch, though in the more modern buildings the square window appeared to have, in some degree, superseded this antique form. The Bazaar is a very poor place, and, as in Cairo, the owners sit upon stone platforms in front, under an awning, selling their goods. The coffee-houses in which the inhabitants were smoking, were merely thatched sheds supported by wooden posts.

The walls of Yambo are perhaps three miles in circumference, and enclose a great deal of waste land; they seemed at this time to be in a very dilapitated state, and bore marks of the Wahabite attacks, there being breaches through which a troop of horse might pass: if in good repair they might protect the town from incursions of cavalry, but probably not from escalade. There is no ditch, and they are flanked at intervals with square bastions and round towers, which, though in a ruined state, are exactly similar to those still to be seen in Norman castles in England. The gateways, evidently very old, present the regular Gothic arch key-stone, curious devices and arabesque tracery of those of our Cathedrals; indeed the sentences in Arabic carved in different parts closely resemble and appear like our ornamental fret-work. One of them only required ivy, for us to have imagined ourselves passing under the picturesque arched gateway of an English abbey. We went out of the Bab el Medina, or Medinah Gate, to the East, and returned by the Bab el Masri to the North of the town. An extensive sandy and arid desert presented itself to our view outside the walls, upon which no sign of vegetation was to be seen; and upon this pathless wilderness alone might be perceived in the distance, a solitary camel and its driver wending their slow and toilsome way towards Yambo. This plain, in the direction of Medina, was bounded by a singular and fantastic range of hills, apparently about ten miles distant, which from their conical figure and other circumstances struck us as evidently of volcanic production, and we subsequently found that Burckhardt mentions that this country appeared to him as if burnt with fire, and that on inquiry he had ascertained that an Earthquake, and an eruption of a Volcano, accompanied by a river of lava, had taken place in this neighbourhood in the middle of the thirteenth century.

About five minutes walk from the Medina gate are large reservoirs for water, which are excavated in the madrepore rock, twenty feet deep, thirty long, and fifteen wide, arched over. Of these, which are private property, and of which we counted seventeen, several are in ruins. We met a man with a donkey carrying mussuks of water from thence, and as we had not tasted good water since we left

the Nile, we gladly purchased some, and I do
not think I ever in my life tasted any thing
half so delicious as that which I drank *in the
hollow of my hand* (for thirsty as I was, I could
not resolve to use the man's wooden bowl,)
at the Medina gate of Yambo.   This precious
liquid is sold in measures, and as it is the
luxury as well as the necessary of life in Arabia
and other Eastern Countries, the frequent dis-
putes narrated in the Bible between the herds-
men of Isaac and Abimelech, and others, for
the possession of a well of water, seemed to us
in this thirsty land no longer unnatural.   Looking down into one of the reservoirs, I espied
a flower, positively a *flower*, one single flower
growing in solitude, and literally " wasting its
sweetness on the desert air."   The guide jump-
ed down and procured it for me, and it was,
really, the only flower, weed, or sign of vegetation we saw at Yambo.   It appeared to be a
sort of Aaron's rod.   When our goats saw it in
my hand, they flew at it most voraciously ; for,
poor things, they had not seen green meat since
they had left the fertile banks of the Nile.

In another direction we were quite startled to
see two or three windmills, exactly resembling
those we had seen erected by the Knights of St.
John, at Malta and Augusta.   I had previously
been told that the windmill came originally from

the East; but I believe, in England people are not generally aware of the Saracenic origin of this universal and very useful machine.

In the streets we saw the Mohatta, or panniers, in which the Arab ladies ride, suspended on each side of a camel. The ladies sit cross-legged on them in the Oriental fashion. We saw also the Shevria, or sofa, which is placed on the back of the camel, and in which Ali Bey travelled from Djidda to Mecca, roofed over with boughs, but the motion of which he found almost insupportable. Many of the Arab Dows, which accompanied us, had Takhtrouans suspended outside, similar in construction to that I had used in the Desert, though I saw none equal to mine, which we parted with at Cosseir to Seedee Hoseyn, for fourteen dollars, the original price having been forty-five at Cairo.

The moon, nearly at full, was throwing a silvery flood of radiance over the Bay of Yambo, whilst daylight still lingered in the west, and the night was so lovely when we re-entered our boats, that we were induced to row about a little before we returned to our prison-ship, which was a poor exchange for the pure and ambient air of heaven. The oars were pulled by an Arab child of five or six years old, and the little boy exerted himself so manfully, that he really well deserved the extra bucksheesh we bestowed on him for his labours.

The following evening we again went upon shore, and as we landed exactly under the Governor's house, all the females of his family flocked to the window to gaze at us ; however, upon C——'s looking up at them, to indulge his curiosity also, they immediately disappeared, and fled into the recesses of their Haram. We saw the Governor's stables, little better than sheds, in which were half-a-dozen horses, but none of that superior description we should have expected to have seen in an Arab town. Then passing by the windmills and some Hadje tents, we took a ramble along the sea-coast for a couple of miles, to the burial-ground, which, close to the sea, was small, and presented no tombs of magnificence. The principal one, that of one of their Peers or Saints, was in ruins. The whole scene was one of the greatest desolation, presenting a barren and desert waste, upon which grew nothing but a coarse plant, which I imagined to be a species of salicornia, which our goats refused to touch. The shore was covered with millions of shells, so minute that it required close inspection to ascertain that they were not particles of sand. There were also several of larger dimensions, but few in a perfect state, having proba-

bly been broken by the violence of the waves.
Returning through the town, we had to cross
some places so filthy, and so offensive to every
sense, that it really required some resolution to
pass ; but the Arabs seem innately and naturally a dirty race, and probably the frequent
ablutions commanded by Mahomet, were appointed by him in consequence. They appear
to be still much in the same state of simplicity,
and perhaps barbarity, as in the time of their
Prophet, whose fare consisted of dates and water, and his luxuries of honey and milk, and
when one of his successors, Omar, with a cruse
of water, set off on his red camel to conquer
the Holy Land of Palestine.

When the ill-fated Burckhardt was here in
1815, he mentions that Yambo was then deso-
lated by the plague, and he describes a curious
ceremony of a she-camel, thickly covered with
all sorts of ornaments, bells, feathers, &c. being
carried in procession through the city, and afterwards led to the burial-ground, slaughtered there,
and its flesh thrown to the vultures and dogs,
the Arabs, who are very superstitious, hoping
the plague would take refuge in the body of
the camel, and that by killing the animal they
should get rid of the contagious disorder.
Bruce, about sixty years ago, mentions something of a similar nature taking place after a

violent quarrel in the town: the belliger-
ent parties seized a camel, loaded it with reproaches, accused it of having been the cause
and origin of the dispute, and at length, putting
an end to its life, amicably settled their mis-
understanding. There seems something of the
nature of the scape-goat of the Israelites in
this singular ceremony.

Having been told there was a Christian
Sahib in one of the vessels at anchor, C——
paid him a visit, expecting to meet with a
countryman, but he found he was an Armenian
Bishop, who we subsequently ascertained was
the very Mar Abraham, whom Bishop Heber
frequently mentions in his diary, as the envoy
who was sent with visitorial powers by the
Armenian Patriarch of Ararat to the Eastern
churches in India, a suffragan dependant on
the Patriarch of Jerusalem. He was returning
from Calcutta to his diocese, in a very good
native vessel which he had entirely to himself,
and he seemed very comfortable with his rose-
wood writing-desk and poll-parrots in his cabin.
He spoke very tolerable Hindoostanee, and was
very communicative.

At the pastoral hour of 6 A. M. on the following day, did Father Abraham of Jerusalem
return C——'s visit; but unfortunately, as I
was not up, we could not ask him into our

cabin. Probably it was as well, for it would have been a singular thing for a Bishop to have clambered in at the window. C—— conversed with him from thence, and from what I could see, he appeared to be about fifty, a thin spare man, with an intelligent countenance, and with highly pleasing and recommendatory manners and address. At Yambo, the sea-port to Medina, one of the head quarters and strongholds of Mahometanism, surrounded by infidels, it was a singular place to meet with the Bishop of Jerusalem! he, ourselves, and our Portuguese cook, being probably the only Christians among several thousand Mahometans. It reminded us of the early ages of Christianity, when there were but a few followers of Christ upon earth; and though he was of the Armenian and we of the English Church, the blessed Saviour in whom we mutually believed, formed a most interesting bond of union between us.

LETTER XXXI.

Coast of the Hedjaz.—Beauty of the waters of the Red Sea.
—Coral Reefs. — Bay of Arabok. — Jaharmo.— Initiatory
rite of the Hadje. — Assumption of the Ihram.—Barren
shore.—Difficulty of return to the Arab Dow.

WE set sail again on June 20th, and in the
miseries of an Arab Dow, we learned to regret
even Yambo, poor and wretched as it was.
The atmosphere of the Red Sea was particularly
enervating and dispiriting, and though the
thermometer only ranged from 85° to 90°, yet
we felt more overcome with the heat than in
the Desert, where, though it had risen to 105°,
the air was pure and elastic. When the south
wind blew, every thing was moist and clammy,
and a sort of heated fog or vapour accompanied it, which was very heavy and oppressive.
This climate is particularly unhealthy, and a
slight scratch here will become a bad wound,
and even a common musquito bite will frequently be attended with most unpleasant consequences.

The water of the Red Sea is remarkably
clear and pellucid, and it was beautiful to see
the fish disporting in the sea-green waves, amid

gaily-coloured coral reefs, which, however, the
superstitious Arabs shun with horror and dread,
for there, do they deem, dwell evil spirits, who,
their fanciful imagination teaches them to suppose, love to lure their vessels to destruction.

The term Hadje is derived from the Hedjaz,
the Holy Land of the Mahometans, which is
a barren, unsightly, and dismal-looking coast,
with "an iron sky, and a soil of brass, where
the clouds drop no water, and the land yields
no vegetation." An occasional village and a
few date-trees are all that are ever seen to en-
liven the scene, and the recollection of the
fresh springs, luxuriant verdure, and shady
groves of my native country, frequently tormented me with the contrast they offered to
all around.

We ran down the coast for fifty miles, keeping in view a range of barren mountains, about
two or three thousand feet high, apparently a
continuation of the chain we saw at Yambo.
At 6 P. M. we came to anchor within a reef of
coral rocks, two or three miles from the coast,
and eleven or twelve in length, running parallle
with the shore. Similar reefs were out at sea,
level with its surface, and occasionally two or
three feet above the waves. The back-water
formed by them was smooth, and of the most
beautiful sea-green imaginable, four or five

fathoms deep, and the bottom, composed of sand
and corals, was distinctly visible. C———'s fishing line, not unfrequently, brought up large
pieces of the latter. If these reefs continue to
increase, they must in all probability some day
become connected with the main land, and in
process of time, the Red Sea may disappear
from the face of the globe. I believe it is ascertained that its ancient dimensions have considerably diminished in size.

With a vertical sun, on the 20th of June, did
we enter the tropics, and during the whole day
the thermometer stood at 86°. We got under
weigh at dawn, and it was with some difficulty
we kept clear from the outer reefs, from one of
which we were at one time but a few yards
distant. We were here for some time becalmed, till a favourable breeze springing up, it
carried us twenty miles beyond the first reef
into the vicinity of another about a mile
long.

At 4 P. M., accompanied by five other Dows
laden like ourselves with grain and Hadjes,
we passed through a narrow strait, into the
extensive Bay of Arabok or Rabogh, which is
about three miles wide, and perhaps nine in
circumference; and here we immediately came
to anchor close to the shore, which presented
to view, a low, level, sandy, and desert plain.

Upon this spot the first rites of the Mahometan Hadje commence. All the passengers, and we among the rest, hurried instantly on shore, and as there could not have been fewer than two thousand persons assembled, the scene of confusion that ensued is almost inconceivable, and quite indescribable. Some fell to pitching tents and temporary awnings, others to kindling fires in small holes upon the sand, whilst a band of Bedouin Arabs came down with provisions from the neighbouring village of Arabok or Rabogh, which appeared to be about four or five miles distant, and where some date-trees were visible. They offered for sale, mutton cut up in small pieces of a quarter of a pound each, wood, water, &c. all tied up in sheep-skins. The evening was damp and chilly, when in about half an hour after their landing, the pilgrims began to perform the first rite of the Hadje, termed *Jaharmo*. Stripping off their warm and gay-coloured robes and turbans, which were carefully tied up in bundles by their attendants, they plunged into the sea, where, after bathing and praying, or rather reciting certain forms of prayer, they invested themselves in the *Ihram*, which is a long piece of cloth loosely wrapt round their waists, such as is worn by the commonest Arabs. Some few threw an additional and similar piece over their shoulders, like a lady's lace-scarf. This rite is said to have been instituted by Mahomet to inculcate humility in his followers, but the sudden transition from the warm woollen garments of the Turk to the thin cotton Ihram must be very trying to the constitution, and the more we saw of the privations undergone by the pilgrims, the more were we convinced that the Hadje is no light affair, and that considerable enthusiasm and resolution must be necessary to enable them to support the hardships incident to the undertaking. Our servant, Sheik Chaund, was much importuned to turn Hadje; but fortunately for us, as we should thereby have been deprived of his services, he declined it, for, as he told his master with much *naïveté,* " He was a young man now, and did not care for such things ; some years hence, when he was an old one, he should think about the duties of his religion." The metamorphosis which took place in the appearance of the passengers, in consequence of the assumption of the Ihram, was most amusing, and even ridiculous. He who left the ship a well-dressed, majestic, and handsome-looking man, came back the bald, shivering, shaking Hadje ; and, stripped of his Turkish trappings, which certainly are most imposing and becoming, many a dignified and magnificent-looking personage was transformed, as by a magic spell, into a common-place, mean, insignificant-looking figure, seeming as if half ashamed of his appearance, and not knowing what to make of himself when divested of his flowing robes. After bathing, the Hadjes fell piously to scratching up the sand like so many dogs, and forming it into little heaps, sometimes to the number of a hundred. To judge from the disturbed state of the surface of the sand in consequence, the pilgrims must have been either great sinners or great saints. Little do our English children think, when they are making what they term " dirt pies," that they are literally only performing one of the initiatory rites of the Mahometan Hadje. The women, retiring to some little distance, apparently went through the same ceremonies, as we saw them plunging into the sea, whilst their friends kept guard over them, and waved to intruders to keep at a distance.

Although we were sadly pushed about in the crowd, which we penetrated with some difficulty, yet they all treated us with much civility and respect, notwithstanding we were the only Christians among such numbers of Mahometan devotees. At length, having effected our escape from thence, we wandered along the barren and desolate coast of the Bay of

Arabok, where the only sign of vegetation was
a coarse sort of salicornia, which from the circumstance of the goats devouring it with avid-
ity, whilst they rejected that at Yambo, we were
induced to believe must be a different species.
The shore was covered with the *débris* of large
shells, few of which were in a perfect condition,
but in such numbers, that regular hillocks, like
the Mount Testaceo in Rome, were formed by
them. It was also positively swarming with
shell-fish of every sort and description, and they
were gambolling about, and seemed to be enjoying life exceedingly. We likewise saw innumerable quantities of emmets; so that, barren as the spot appeared, it was by no means
destitute of insect life.

It was with the utmost difficulty that we
effected our return through the crowd, and
with still more that we got into the boat that
was to take us to our ship; but when in, so
many crowded after us, that I literally expected my end was to resemble that of the
Countess of Perche, the daughter of Henry I.,
who was drowned by too many pressing into
her bark. The clamour was *tremendous.* Servants flinging in the bundles of their masters'
gay garments, or searching for them in the
boat; those masters quite in consternation,
looking as if they did not know what to

think of themselves since their change of attire. The boatmen, stalking about in every direction over the heads of the passengers, and trampling under foot, the bundles so valuable in the eyes of the owners. In vain did C——, in his anxious solicitude for my safety, loudly vociferate, " Madame! Madame!" he spoke to the winds, for French is quite unknown in these countries. " Signora" was better understood, and a respectable-looking man, after he had secured accommodation for himself, did all he could to protect the poor Signora from the rude crowd.

It is singular enough that whilst French is so universally understood by Europeans, it should be of so little utility in Oriental countries. Italian, on the other hand, is of great use in Egypt and Arabia, and C—— found his Hindoostanee also very serviceable to him, as we met many Indian Hadjes and traders in the Red Sea. An African sailor here, told C—— that Mahomet Ali's government is very superior to that of the Arabs; that he suppresses robbery, murder, and injustice, whilst the latter systematically oppress their subjects, and extort money from all under their authority.

The wife of the Reis, not being able to reach her cabin, which was beneath ours, in consequence of the dense crowd upon deck, sent to request leave to be permitted to make her *entrée* into the ship through our windows. We of course granted this permission, but though C——'s curiosity induced him to take up his position where he could best see the lady without her being annoyed thereby, Gilbert Horner himself, with all his tricks and knowledge of " glamour might," obtained by *supercherie* from Michael Scott's wondrous book, did not more effectually conceal Lord Cranstoun from the eyes of the inhabitants of Branksome Hall, than did the mysterious veil impenetrably shroud the Arab dame from his view. A bundle of clothes apparently was hoisted up, pulled in at the window, pushed through the cabin, and—heigh presto!—it was gone.

No sooner were all fairly re-embarked, than the Reis and our consort vessels immediately quitted the shore, and made for deeper water and better anchorage.

LETTER XXXII.

Djidda.—House of Hoseyn Aga.—Divan.—Oriental manner of concluding a bargain.—Traditions concerning Djidda.

ALTHOUGH we were under weigh by day-break on the following morning (June 22d), yet we were becalmed for some hours. At 10 A.M. a favourable breeze at last sprang up, which by noon freshened into a strong breeze. We this day lost sight of the mountains, and kept about five or six miles from the shore, passing several coral reefs and anchoring under the lee of one at night.

The next day (June 23rd) we again fell down the coast, and at noon Djidda was the cry, and all was bustle and confusion. We anchored in the roadstead, which is formed by coral reefs, about three miles distant from the town, which from thence has a very pretty ap-pearance, with its fortifications, white edifices, and flat-topped madrepore houses. We were surprised to see so large a fleet here, for we counted no less than nineteen three-masted ves-sels, or frigates, which we were told all be-longed to the Pasha of Egypt, besides an immense number of merchantmen.

We were soon surrounded with boats ply-
ing for passengers, and the confusion became
tremendous, for all seemed anxious to leave the
Hadje ship, and to get upon shore immediately,
and every one was consequently bargaining,
bawling and screaming. We were soon in a
boat, and between rowing and sailing, in company with several others, we eventually reached the shore. As we passed, all our fellow-
passengers, and in particular our friend the
Turk, took their leave by salaaming, and sa-
luting. us most courteously; and though we
were using *green* umbrellas, no one seemed
offended at Christians making use of that
sacred colour. At Rome they say, the Roman
Catholics are less bigoted than elsewhere ; and
at Djidda, the sea-port town of Mecca, the Mussulmans certainly appeared more liberal than
elsewhere. As we advanced, amongst all the
flowing robes and turbans, with which we were
surrounded, how were we startled with the
sight of one solitary *hat!* and I really cannot
describe to you my sensations at being, in this
distant and remote region, hailed in " the accents sweet of Fatherland!" He who accosted us was an English sailor, who in these foreign countries really appeared like a *brother!*
He was equally delighted to speak to a countryman ; and we learnt from him that Sir Hud-

son Lowe, though now on the point of quitting, had not yet left Djidda, as he had been detained here for seventeen days.

Djidda is situated upon a slightly-rising ground, extending along the shore for about fifteen hundred paces, its breadth not exceeding more than half that space. It is, comparatively speaking, a modern town, and has only become of importance since the fifteenth century. The ancient half-ruined wall, which was built by Ransour el Gharry, Sultan of Egypt, affording no protection against the expected depredations and inroads of the Wahabites, a new one was erected by the inhabitants on the land side, which is strengthened, at intervals of forty or fifty paces, by watch towers and a few rusty guns, in consequence of which Djidda is considered as impregnable by the Arabs.

The streets are rather handsome, and tolerably wide for an Oriental town. The houses are well built, of white stone or madrepore, and many of them are several stories high, with flat-terraced roofs, and their windows and doorways being all arched, present many rich specimens of Arabesque architecture. We had some difficulty in landing at a sort of an attempt of a quay, and we immediately repaired to the mansion of Hoseyn Aga, the agent for

the East India Company, where Sir Hudson
Lowe was residing. His mansion very much
resembled one of the smaller Colleges in Oxford; and whoever has seen the cloisters of
Westminster Abbey, or of Lincoln Cathedral,
may have an exact idea of the interior court
of an Arab house. Indeed, the Campo Santo
at Pisa is nothing more than an Arabesque
building, upon a magnificent scale. We passed
through a heavy arched gateway into a court
surrounded by cloisters, which were supported
by handsome arches; and after ascending a staircase of Collegiate appearance, we entered an
upper apartment, where we found Hoseyn Aga
sitting in his Divan, which was exactly similar to
the immense bow windows that overhang some
of the principal entrances at Oxford. This was
slightly elevated, and a low seat ran all round,
the whole being covered with scarlet cloth.
On being invited up, we ascended two or three
steps, and took our seats on the right hand of
Hoseyn Aga. He was a remarkably fine-looking man, with an air of dignity intermingled
with *hauteur;* – handsomely clad, but the heavy
folds of his muslin turban were studiously drawn
over his right eye to conceal the loss of it; for
Mahomet Ali one day in a fit of rage pulled it
out !—yet these men are friends,—great friends,
just at present, and will remain so as long as it

may be convenient and agreeable to both parties to consider each other in that light!

Though certainly feeling myself somewhat out of my place, I was considerably amused with watching the proceedings of a Divan. Turks and Arabs came and went, themselves preferring in person their petitions and complaints to Hoseyn Aga. The superiors took seats upon the Divan, the inferiors stood or sat below the steps.

Hoseyn Aga, after signing the papers presented to him, by affixing his signet to them, flung them contemptuously towards his secretary, who was in waiting; but, as the wind generally wafted them to my feet, I believe I surprised and amused the Aga, not a little, by occasionally picking them up and handing them on. The Orientals, however polished their manners may be to their equals and superiors, seem apparently to have no idea of courtesy towards their inferiors.

The Turkish guards, the Arab attendants, the Oriental appearance of all around, struck me as so singular, that when C—— left me for a short time, while he went to pay his respects to the General, I really almost fancied myself in a dream; for there was I, sitting in Grand Divan at Djidda! probably the only English woman who ever assisted personally at one, in this, to European travellers, out-of-the-way place! However, I 'kept myself closely veiled, and the most profound respect was paid me : a lady could not have been treated with more in the most polished drawing-room in London. One of the principal Turks attempted to enter into conversation with me, and to do the honours of Djidda, though, as my knowledge of Arabic was confined to a very few phrases, his gallantry was but of little avail.

We heard here that Sir Hudson Lowe had hired a Bombay vessel to leave Djidda a fort-night earlier than usual; and as this was the best, and indeed the only opportunity that of-fered for our obtaining a passage thither, and as we were informed that at this time Djidda was very unhealthy, and had been so for some time, C—— resolved to engage the vacant cabin. The General and all his suite had been attacked with intermittent fevers, debility, loss of appetite, swellings and pains in their limbs, disorders very prevalent here. The Nachoda, Saboo ben Tayib, the Captain of the vessel, the George Cruttenden by name, was sent for, and Hoseyn Aga undertook to bring him to reasonable terms. They sat down close toge-ther, and took hold of each other's hand, un-derneath a cloth; they played with each other's fingers, looked each other full in the face, with an air at once friendly, cunning, and jocular; they spoke not one single word, but in two or three minutes the Aga, turning to C——, informed him Saboo ben Tayib would take him to Bombay for 550 dollars. I had before heard of this Oriental manner of making bargains, but I certainly never could have believed it, without the evidence of my own senses, for, the facility with which they seemed to understand each other, appeared to me, little less than miraculous.

In about a couple of hours we were summoned to dinner, which was served up in the General's apartment in the European style, with chairs and tables, knives, forks, and plates. There was excellent fish, and a profusion of every thing upon the table. Though our host, Hoseyn Aga, did not make his appearance during the meal, he afterwards came in to make his parting compliments to us before we went on board. He offered to take charge of letters for us to England, and as this was the last place from whence we should have an opportunity of writing home, most of us profited by it; but one of the party, when he was asked for his letters, saying he had none, " What !" said he, " have you no father, no mother in England ?"

Hoseyn Aga's manners were dignified. I should say there was a good deal of *haut ton* as well as *hauteur* about him. From his ap-

pearance and manners, he would any where be
taken for a gentleman. He sent his *homme
d'affaires*, Abdallah, to accompany us to the
ship, and we then all took our leave ; the General and his Aide-de-camp apparently quite delighted to get away from Djidda, where their
health had suffered considerably, and where,
from the crowded state of the town, incident
to the Mahometan Hadje, they could procure
no other accommodation than one room, and
this in Hoseyn Aga's dwelling. At other times
houses, we understood, would have been plenty,
and easily procured.

The word Djidda, I have been told, signifies
" rich ;" or, as others say, " the first of mothers."
The Mahometans say that Eve was banished
hither after her fall, and the tomb of Howa,
as they term her, is still shown two miles north
of the town, a rude structure of stone, about
four feet in length, two or three in breadth,
and as many in height. After a separation of
a hundred years, Adam rejoined her on Mount
Arafaith [near Mecca, and by the orders of the
Almighty, the angels took a tent from Paradise, called Kheyme, and pitched it for the
accommodation of our first parents, precisely
in the same spot where Seth subsequently
erected the Kaaba, and which he consecrated
to the worship of the Eternal Deity. The

body of Adam, at his death, after having been washed and purified by angels, wrapped in the winding-sheet with perfumes and aromatics by the Archangel Michael, and prayed over by Gabriel, was then deposited in Ghar 'ul Keez, the grotto of treasure on the Mountain Djebel Eb y Coubeyss. At the time of the Deluge, by the command of the Almighty, Noah took the corpse of Adam with him in the ark in a coffin, but when the flood was abated, his first care was to restore it to the grotto from whence he had taken it.

These traditions, together with the Kaaba, or wonderful black stone, which was brought to Seth by an angel, and which is in the Beit Allah, the famous mosque, or House of God, at Mecca, are, what render this country as interesting to the Mahometan Hadje, as Jerusalem was in olden time to the Crusader, and still is to the Christian Pilgrim. They account for the hills in the neighbourhood of Mecca, by saying, that when Abraham was building the Beit Allah, God ordered every mountain in the world to contribute its proportion, and the blackness of Corra Dog, a mountain in the neighbourhood of Algiers, is supposed by them to have been occasioned by its refusing to obey the injunction. The Zemzem, the sacred well of Mecca, is revered as

that which was shown to **Hagar, by the angel**
in the Wilderness, when, with her son Ishmael,
the progenitor and hero of the Arabs, she was
cast out by Abraham. It is curious to see how
much of our Sacred History the Mahometans
have mixed up with their fabulous inventions,
and to hear the names of the Patriarchs connected with these wild traditions.

LETTER XXXIII.

The George Cruttenden.—A Native Vessel.—Embarkation.—Cock-roaches.—Crew.—Natives of Hindoostan.—
Oppressive Climate.—Arrival at Hodeida.

THE night was lovely, the stars shone most
brilliantly, and daylight was even yet trembling
in the West, when we again embarked upon
the Red Sea in a little skiff rowed by wild-
looking Arabs, which was to transport us to
the George Cruttenden, which lay at anchor
some miles from the shore. This was a native
merchant ship, carrying about three hundred
tons, and navigated by Lascars, or sailors,
natives of Hindoostan.

After we reached the vessel, we were detained several hours waiting for the Nachoda,
Saboo ben Tayib, who remained on shore

transacting some business; and, as C—— was likewise absent some time giving orders about our things being transported from the Arab dow to the George Cruttenden, I began to feel very seriously alarmed for his safety, and though I did my utmost to restrain my feelings, I suppose my countenance betrayed my anxiety, for as I sat upon deck watching the last rays of daylight as they gradually disappeared, Abdallah, who spoke tolerable English, came up to me, and in a soothing manner exclaimed, " What is the matter with you ? Why look you so uneasy ? Do not be unhappy ; I will take care of you, and I will go and fetch your husband for you." I certainly could not restrain a smile at Abdallah's offered care and protection; but, as it was growing late, I was soon obliged to retire to my cabin, which was large, and of spacious dimensions, and, as the servants had not had time properly to arrange it, presented at this time a most uncomfortable and cheerless appearance. Whilst the flickering flame of the lamp cast fitful gleams of a trembling and uncertain light around, making the surrounding obscurity more dark and dismal, and whilst in solitude and gloom my fears were raised to a nervous pitch of apprehension for C—— 's safety, a violent humming and buzzing noise resounded through the cabin,

which, to my horror and consternation, was in
an instant literally filled with an army of cock-
roaches, which suddenly appeared from below.
These cock-roaches very much resembled cock-
chafers in their appearance, but considerably ex-
ceeded them in dimension, and only those who
have been on board a native merchant ship, and
have actually encountered a similar irruption,
can have any idea of its horrors. Whilst in the
Red Sea, we were constantly subject to similar
nightly visitations; and such was the disgust
they gave me, that I positively would at any
time rather encounter a snake than a swarm of
these insects. With daylight, they, however,
retreated to their holes, and C—— soon after
making his appearance, terminated my fears on
his account. He had fallen in with the Nachoda,
and had agreed to accompany him to the ship,
which had consequently detained him ; and
whilst Saboo ben Tayib was transacting his business, and saying farewell to his friends, he had
lain down in one of the Okalls in the town, and
slept there till summoned to go on board.

I must here relate an instance of Arab ho-
nesty, which, in the midst of their cunning and
extortion, deserves recording, as it is what one
would seldom meet with, even in England.
On looking over our things, C—— discovered
that a favourite gun was not forthcoming ;

and though he considered the regaining it to be quite out of the question, yet he thought it as well to endeavour to recover it. He accordingly sent Sheik Chaund to the Hadje ship to enquire for it; and there, though our cabin had been deserted, and left open to every one for nearly twenty-four hours, he discovered the gun exactly where it had been left, and in a spot too where it might have easily been seen, and taken by those in the vessel.

The crew of the George Cruttenden consisted of the Nachoda and his son, who was a fine intelligent lad, about ten or twelve years old, covered with amulets and charms, two or three mates, and about twenty-five sailors, all natives of India, so that I was once more in a new world.

Hindoostanee was spoken almost entirely on board, and C——, from his perfect knowledge of that language, became Interpreter-general to the whole party. The Indian dress consists of silk, or nankeen trowsers; a white cotton or spotted muslin vest, called an angrica, which closely fits the figure, and somewhat resembles a dressing-gown in appearance; a cumberband, or sash, composed of a handsome shawl, and a turban of a long piece of stuff, of a mixture of cotton and silk, twenty or thirty feet long, which is worn very neatly twisted round the head, in different fashions, according to the

caste of the wearer, the *tout-ensemble* being
very unlike the ample folds of the Turkish turban, and their heavy woollen garments. The
Nachoda and his principal officers were all
Mahometans. Their features were delicate and
well-formed, with an expression of countenance
cunning rather than open. Their figures were
small, light, and active; and there was something effeminate in their appearance, which was
totally dissimilar to the bold, haughty, intre-
pid look of the Turk, and to the wild, daring,
fearless air of the Arab.

The following description of the natives of
India, by Lord, in 1630, is very applicable to
their present appearance, " A people clothed in
linen garments, somewhat low descending, of a
gesture and garb, we may say, maidenly, and
well-nigh effeminate; of a countenance shy,
and somewhat estranged, yet smiling out a
glozed and somewhat bashful familiarity." The
common sailors were principally Malabar, or
Gogo men, of shorter and somewhat stouter
frames,—and there was an African, or Seedee,
the wit of the party, who was always telling
stories, laughing, and in good humour. Although the General had taken the vessel almost
exclusively for his own use, yet there were also
several poor Hadjes on board, returning to India,
who lived entirely upon the deck, and a few of

them had their wives with them. The General, his suite, and his stud, which he had increased at Djidda by the purchase of two fine horses of the famous Nedjedy breed, occupied great part of the ship, and we and our attendants the remainder.

In spite of all the hurry of the preceding day, we remained at anchor the whole of the 24th, as, on account of the narrow passage through coral reefs, by which we had to pass into the open sea, we were obliged to wait for a particular wind. On the 25th we got under weigh, but in working out, our ship ran aground; luckily it was got off without sustaining any injury, and stretching boldly out to sea, we soon lost sight of the land, and of the coral reefs in the neighbourhood of the shore. We found the atmosphere very oppressive; the thermometer being generally about 90°, and in addition to our friends the cock-roaches, who paid us nightly visits, we were troubled with musquitoes, and terribly incommoded with myriads of small ants, with which the ship was swarming, its last cargo having, unfortunately for us, been composed of sugar! They were positive nuisances, for they got into our provisions, our clothes, our hair, and their bite was so very annoying and painful, that they disturbed our rest at night.

On the 26th of June a brisk gale blew up, and
continued for some days, and on the 31st we anchored off Hodeida, three or four miles from the
shore, as from its shallowness, vessels of any size
cannot enter the bay, though it is large, extensive,
and open to all winds.   The town, from thence,
with its fortifications, castles, and white flat-roofed houses, had a very picturesque appearance.
It is about one and a half day's journey from
Beit el Fahik, or, "the house of the Sage," which
is situated in a well cultivated plain, and which
owes its name and its origin to the famous Saint
Achmet Ibn Mousa, whose sepulchre is in a
pretty little mosque near the town; and it is
about the same distance from the coffee hills,
which we saw at a distance.   Beit el Fahik is
only half a day's journey from the hills where
the plant grows, and the coffee trade attracts
thither merchants from Hedjaz, Egypt, Bar-
bary, Syria, Persia, India, and even Europe.
The roads to these hills are very bad, and inaccessible even to mules, but the scenery is said
to be delightful.   The mountains are of basalt,
and cascades falling between the apparently artificial columns, have a very picturesque effect.
At Bulgosa, the coffee plantations are upon
terraces in the form of an amphitheatre, which
are connected by flights of steps, cut in the
rock ; and the air there being fresher and cooler

than on the plain, the inhabitants have fairer complexions. The harbour of Hodeida is better than that of Loheia, which is situated to the north. That of Ghalefka, six leagues to the south, is entirely filled up, but they have there an excellent spring of water, which is ascribed to the prayers of their patron Saint, Seid Ali. At Hodeida it is also, in some degree, choked up ; before this, Zebid, five or six leagues S. S. W. of Beit el Fahik, was the principal and most commercial place in all Tehama. It still boasts of an academy, an aqueduct, and numerous mosques. It is situated near the largest and most fertile *wady* in the country, through which in rainy seasons a large river flows. Much indigo is grown in its neighbourhood, and the fields, when not ravaged with torrents, have a fertile and beautiful appearance ; coffee however seems to be the chief article of cultivation and trade ; as it is cheaper and better than elsewhere at Hodeida, from whence the hills are not two days' journey, whilst they are four from Mocha, our Nachoda stopped at the former place, in consequence, for a cargo.

It is strange that an article of such universal consumption as coffee should have been only used in modern times, as there are, I have been told, no accounts of its having been known to the ancients. When first introduced in Ethiopia it was forbidden, on account of its supposed exciting properties; the use of it, was also, for the same reason, at one time prohibited in Turkey, where it is now almost a necessary of life.

On the following day (July 1st) we went on shore, when the surf being exceedingly high, the boat beat about tremendously, and we had considerable difficulty in effecting a landing; for though the coast was covered with people, and the boat was surrounded by them, they had received general order never to assist any Fringees or Europeans: so there we continued buffeting with the waves, and beating violently for some time on the beach, till at length some Banyan traders sent their servants down to our assistance, and literally upon their heads were we carried through the surf. I was so overcome that I was obliged to sit down to recover in the gateway of the city; and, when I came to myself, I found I was surrounded by a band of indescribably wild and most savage-looking Arabs, who were eyeing me with looks of the most intense curiosity and astonishment. Whilst the gentlemen went in search of lodgings, I was deposited in the Nachoda's Duftur Khanna, or counting-house, the courts and rooms of which were filled with bales of merchandize; but as there was neither

chair nor sofa for my use, I was constrained to
lie down upon the ground, and to lay my
aching head upon a bale of coffee, as a substitute for a pillow, whilst our servant with some
difficulty procured me some lemonade, which
he brought *in a basin :* but every thing is by
comparison, and after the violent motion of the
boat, and the intense heat I had been there exposed to, these accommodations, poor as they
were, appeared delightful, from the shade and
quiet they afforded; and the soft cooing of
some sacred doves in the neighbourhood of the
house, sounded more harmoniously than any
music I ever heard, for it convinced me I was
upon land.

LETTER XXXIV.

Hodeida.—Arab House and Architecture.—Castles.—Garden of Dates.—Wild Arabs.—Coffee.—Camel's flesh.—
Hyænas.—Curiosity of Inhabitants concerning, and refusal
to accept, Arab Testament.—Dowlah's Divan.—Banyans.
—Ill-used race.

AFTER some little time, a house was discovered that was large enough to accommodate
the whole party. It belonged to one of the
principal merchants in the place, and appeared
to be one of the best in the town : but it was a

strange rambling place ; there were courts within courts, terraces upon terraces, and it seemed quite adapted for the mysterious scene of a romance.*

We entered, by a heavy arched gateway, into a court surrounded by cloisters, exactly resembling those of a college in Oxford, and these were full of bales of merchandise. From thence, a very narrow and dark staircase led to a succession of courts; at the bottom of one of them was the apartment appropriated to the General's use, where was an immense projecting window, looking upon the sea; and in the walls were several arched niches or recesses, similar to those in our cathedrals, which here seemed to serve the double purpose of tables and cupboards. At the top, near the ceiling, a heavy shelf ran all round, where were jars of sweetmeats, bottles of rose-water and perfume, and there were several awkward couches ranged

* The General might easily have had apartments procured for his own use, but he refused to avail himself of them till we were also accommodated ; and I really cannot help making use of this opportunity, to state how kind, courteous, and friendly we on every occasion invariably found Sir Hudson Lowe. When quite alone with us, he entirely lost the reserve he sometimes assumed in mixed company; and from having seen much of the world, and from his personal acquaintance with and knowledge of the political characters of the day, his conversation at such times was peculiarly amusing and entertaining.

round the room. A moveable flight of steps
led to our chamber, which was exactly on
the same plan, though on a smaller scale. All
the apartments appeared to have a sort of private court, or terrace attached to them, which
by huge folding-doors communicated with, and
formed part of the covered and upper end at
pleasure. Ours, from its furniture, appeared to
belong to the principal lady of the house ; and
there was a window which looked into a large
store-room, full of a most curious mixture of
Arab valuables, upon which " Madame" might
keep her eye constantly, without leaving her
seat.

Both here, and in other houses at Hodeida,
we were surprised at the exquisite beauty of
the carved wood-work, which was similar to,
and quite equal, if not superior, to the richest
Gothic tracery in our finest cathedrals. Much
taste and elegance were displayed in the commonest arched door and window, which latter generally projected over the streets considerably, in the same manner as in the very old
houses in London. The profusion, variety,
and ingenuity of the Arabesque ornaments and
devices were really extraordinary. From what
we saw we were fully convinced that the architecture, by us erroneously termed Gothic, derived its origin entirely and exclusively from

the heart of Arabia, and perhaps the arch should rather be termed Arabesque, or Saracenic, than Saxon or Norman; for here are still in use, and probably have been so from time immemorial, the round, the pointed, and the elliptic. Indeed, should any one, tired of the Grecian architecture, wish to revive the Gothic style in England, which some deem lost there, he should go to Hodeida, or some similar town in Arabia, to study. The General, who was equally struck with ourselves, much regretted he had no artist with him, to make sketches of the numerous interesting buildings which we saw.

The streets of Hodeida were narrow, unpaved, dirty, and overhung with the immense windows I have mentioned. The town was flanked and protected by four castles, which at a distance had very much the appearance of our old castellated mansions in England, and really looked very handsome and imposing. There were numerous thatched huts outside the walls, surrounded with dead fences, and there were also several public gardens of date-trees, which had a very Juan Fernandez appearance. The trees were at this time covered with baskets,*

* These were suspended to the branches, as we sometimes see bags on vines, to protect the grapes.

"The merry date season,
Which calls to the palm groves the young and the old."

to preserve the fruit, which was not yet ripe. In one of these public gardens which we visited, was a sort of rustic coffee-house, where, upon couches, were reposing knots of Arabs, smoking, and drinking coffee, which an old woman in attendance was preparing for them. A sofa was brought for our accommodation, and we soon became objects of general curiosity, numbers coming up to gaze at us, and others peeping through the hedge, as if alarmed at our foreign appearance. Many had magnificent dirks and creeses in their sashes, the handles of which were composed of solid silver, and were very richly embossed; these they exhibited with great pride, and were evidently much pleased with the admiration and attention we bestowed upon them.

The costume of the common women here appears to be composed of the blue cotton shift and veil; and the superior orders seem to wear the Turkish drawers, vest, turban, and veil. The men, a wild and savage-looking race, were very slightly clad, but all were well armed with javelins, spears, and creeses or daggers. We saw some with bonnets and helmets, apparently of straw, but probably of palm-leaves, as Niebuhr observes, that the " Bedouins upon

is as much a season of rejoicing in Arabia, as the harvest home in England, or the vintage in France.

the frontiers of Hedjaz and of Yemen, wear a bonnet of palm-leaves neatly plaited." We were always treated with much civility wherever we went, and sometimes the Arabs would offer me nosegays of mogrey,* though it was evidently not considered safe to wander too far from the town. One day, when we had walked to some distance, C—— sat down to make a sketch of one of the castles, and we were soon surrounded by a crowd of the wildest-looking Arabs, male and female, that you can conceive. They did not attempt to molest us, but kept at an awful distance, gazing at C—— with looks of wonder and astonishment, and even with some degree of fear, as if they thought him a magician about to throw a spell upon them. Regardless of the increasing and thickening crowd, C—— continued to draw on, till our guide testified marks of great uneasiness and alarm, and requested us to return to the town, making signs to me to keep my veil down.

The Bazaar appeared well supplied with provision, and our fare was very tolerable. We had plenty of fish, about fifty boats going out every day to sea, and returning with fish of the size and appearance of a herring; these

* A flower somewhat resembling the jessamine, with a very sweet and powerful smell.

they split down the back, and then throwing in a little salt, pack them in baskets for exportation. There was another species, about a yard long, something resembling the Niar fish of Malabar. We had also fresh dates, which when just gathered are a delightful fruit, mangoes, and other fruits and vegetables, which I had never met with before. The coffee is brought down, neatly packed in matting, from the coffee hills, which were distinctly visible from Hodeida. It was, of course, perfectly genuine and excellent; but as the whole berry, husk and all, is ground, I did not like the Arab so well as the European way of preparing it. We had very good meat, which we fancied was beef, till one day, on casual enquiry, we discovered it was *camel's* flesh which we were at the moment very composedly eating! Immediately afterwards a boy brought in some young hyænas for sale, which we took up into our arms as if they were kittens,—and very pretty little animals they were. Thus, at Hodeida, we can safely say, we had camels for dinner, and hyænas for dessert!

The poverty of the lower classes here appeared quite dreadful. Wherever we went, we were surrounded by crowds of beggars; and they stationed themselves round the door, awaiting our coming out, some literally in a state of starvation. One blind beggar used to pay us daily visits, and would pertinaciously and resolutely stand under our window, vociferating " Cowasjee — Beebee," * till we flung him something. If the Arabs in Egypt were troublesome in their applications for " bucksheesh," here they were outrageous. Whatever they saw, they made a point of asking for; and the son of our landlord, a respectable-looking young man, was as bad as any; however, when refused, he always laughed archly, without seeming the least offended ; as much as to say, " I will lose nothing for want of asking, but I see you are not such fools as to be taken in." The Arabs appear very different from the Turks ; they have none of their apathy, but a vivaciousness, astuteness, and curiosity, quite European ; at the same time, neither have they their dignified and majestic deportment.

They evinced the most intense interest in all our European novelties, and one day, as we were opening a box of books in their presence, an Arabic Testament caught their attention ; they examined it most inquisitively, and ap-

* I have been told that Cowasjee literally means " merchant," but it is the appellation almost invariably applied to Franks in Egypt and Arabia, whatever their profession may be. Beebee means " Lady," or " Madam."

peared highly pleased with its contents, at once comprehending it related to " Allah." They asked its price, where it could be procured, and seemed quite anxious to obtain a supply. They requested permission to take it home with them to peruse, but alas ! whilst we were indulging in most pleasing speculations, and fancying we might perchance be the humble instruments in the hands of Providence to introduce the Bible, and the knowledge of the Christian religion in this remote spot, scarcely had an hour elapsed ere our Testament was returned to us, evidently from no dislike or disapprobation of its contents, but probably because some of their Moollahs, or Priests, had prohibited their reading it. They, however, accepted with thankfulness and pleasure some of Mr. Jovett's Arabic spelling-books, of which he had furnished us with a supply, when at Malta. It is for the Bible and Missionary Societies to decide, but from what we saw of Arabia, I cannot but think that there is a vast field here for their exertions, if judiciously employed. There seems little bigotry, though an immense deal of selfishness, and a love of filthy lucre in the Arab character; but I, however, seriously believe that they might be, without much difficulty, converted to our holy religion, or at least weaned from the errors of their own.

Although the Dowlah never called in person, yet he sent a deputation to wait upon the gentlemen, and an immense water-melon as a present to the General. When they returned the visit, they found him sitting in his Divan, which was clean and respectable, and in the centre were the *kedras*, the largest sort of pipe in use, which were resting upon tripods. He was a little delicate-looking man, about forty years old, and had but lately come into office, for which he had given four hundred dollars to the Imaun of Sanaa, and, of course, he was making up the sum by every kind of exaction and extortion.

He received the gentlemen very courteously; expressed his surprise at their not speaking Arabic; and after the usual routine of conversation, through the medium of an interpreter, and after having been sprinkled with rose-water, they took their departure. The room was full of natives of different countries. The wild-looking Bedouin of the Desert; the more civilized Arab of the town; the slender and well-looking Abyssinian; and the coal-black Seedee, or Negro, some of whom looked perfectly astonished, and almost alarmed, at the sight of *white* men, evidently never before having seen any Fringees, or Franks.

We were informed that Mahomet Ali had

a Vakeel at this place, but that not being on terms with the present Dowlah, he had not the slightest authority here. There were twenty-five Hindoos, of that very singular caste, the Banyan, residing here for the purchase of coffee; and they complained bitterly of the heavy exactions they were subject to. They evidently preferred the Turkish to the Arab rule, and openly expressed their regret that the attention of Mahomet Ali should be turned to any other object than the subjugation of Arabia. They likewise avowed their wish that the English would take possession of the country, any government being better than that they were suffering under.

They are neither allowed to marry or to bring their wives here—to burn their dead, or to quit the place,—so that they are indeed in miserable plight. They appear very respectable merchants, but their dress and their habits are very singular. They wear a linen cloth round the middle, and an immensely large red turban, of a most singular shape, on the head. Some of them had known C—— in India, and they were quite delighted to meet him again, paying him daily visits, and always bringing with them some little offering of flowers or fruit. Their peculiar tenets prevent their depriving any thing of life, and you may imagine their consternation, upon C——'s one day asking them, forgetting whom he was addressing, what was the best thing to destroy the ants that annoyed us on board ship. He immediately corrected himself, and said he wished only to drive them into their holes, upon which they supplied us with a sort of fruit, which they said would have that effect. The Arabs are very fond of playing upon their prejudices, and a few years back, having caught, what they termed, a mermaid, by tormenting and threatening to kill it they extorted considerable sums from the humane feelings of the Banyans.

LETTER XXXV.

Tournament at Hodeida.—Visits to the Haram.—Manners and Customs of the Women.—Courteous behaviour.

THE gentlemen frequently took evening rides upon donkeys into the country, which in the Tehama appears much more fertile than in the Hedjaz, in the immediate neighbourhood of Yambo and Djidda. They one day fell in with the Dowlah, who was exercising his troops, and a sort of tournament took place, with which they were highly pleased. The cavalry, about fifty in number, mounted upon spirited blood-horses, with a somewhat jaded appearance, was composed of light active men, badly dressed, carrying long spears in their hands, and using the huge Mameluke shovel-shaped stirrup. Three or four companies of infantry, each of about twenty-five files, in two ranks, preceded the Dowlah, who kept on curveting his horse, and galloping from right to left at full speed. When he had tired one horse he mounted another, and his infantry running forward, took up their station in small detached parties of twelve or fifteen men, behind sand-banks on a rising ground, up which he furiously rode, shaking his spear, and was received, at the distance of ten or twelve paces, by the fire of the Arabs. He then turned short off, rode down the hill, and re-ascending it, was again repulsed by them. This he repeated several times ; and afterwards his whole cavalry following their leader, in single file at full gallop, shouting, shaking their weapons, and flourishing their scimetars most desperately, described a sort of circle, which at each evolution became narrower, till at last, one congregated mass was formed, and both horses and riders being exhausted with their exertions, mingled so confusedly together, that spear ultimately clashed with spear. The Dow-

lah then pulled up, and received the salutations
of the Arabs who had fired at him, by offering
his hand to each individual, who respectfully
touched his in return. They then fell into their
ranks, and two or three men, apparently the
chieftains of the party, danced a *chassée*, right
and left, flourishing drawn swords and creeses
in front of their respective companies, which
then marched off in order, to the sound of tom-
toms beating. Is not this like the chivalrous
exercises of olden time, which were practised
in Europe during the time of the Crusades?

In C——'s absence, I always remained in
my own room; but one evening, as I went upon
my terrace to enjoy the fresh sea-breeze which
was just setting in, a casement which I had never
before observed slowly opened, and a black
hand appeared waving significantly at me. Impressed with some degree of fear, I immediately
retreated, but on looking again, the waving was
repeated; and several women peeping out, beck-
oned me to them, making signs that the men
were all out of the way. Whilst I was hesitating, a Negro woman and a boy came out upon
another terrace, and vehemently importuned
me by signs to go to them. I had just been
reading Lady Mary Wortley Montague's description of a Turkish Haram — an opportunity
might never again occur of visiting an Arab

one.—After some conflict between my fears
and my curiosity, the latter conquered, and
down I went, the boy meeting me at the foot
of the stairs; and, lifting up a heavy curtain, he
introduced me into a small interior court, at
the door of which were a number of women's
slippers, and inside were about a dozen females
clothed in silk trowsers, vests closely fitting
the figure, and fastening in front, and turbans
very tastefully put on. They received me with
the utmost cordiality and delight, the principal
lady, Zaccara, as I found she was called, making
me sit down by her side, caressingly taking my
hand, presenting me with a nosegay, and, after
previously tasting it, offering me coffee, which
was brought on a silver tray, in the usual beautiful little china cups. It was, however, so perfumed that I could scarcely drink it. She did
the honours, and appeared as superior to the
others in manners and address, as an English
lady would be to her maid-servants. Her figure
was light and slender—her features pretty and
delicate—her countenance lively and intelligent,
—whilst her manners, which were peculiarly
soft and pleasing, were at the same time both
affectionate and sprightly. The other women
crowded round me with great *empressement;* by
signs we kept up a very animated conversation,
and when we could not quite comprehend each

other's meaning, we all laughed heartily. They
asked me where I came from, whether I had
many ornaments, any children, &c. exhibiting
theirs with great glee.   They were amazingly
struck with my costume, which they examined
so minutely, that I began to think I should have
had to undress to satisfy their curiosity;—but
what most amused them, was, the circumstance
of my gown fastening *behind*, which mystery
they examined over and over again, and some
broad French tucks at the bottom seemed much
to astonish them, as they could not discover
their use.   They asked me the names of every
thing I had on, and when, to please them, I
took off my cap, and let down my long hair,
Zaccara, following my example, immediately
took off her turban and showed me hers: the
Negro woman, who seemed the wit of the
party, in the mean time holding up the lace
cap upon her broad fat hand, and exhibiting
it to all around, apparently with great admiration, exclaiming " caap, caap," and also endeavouring, much to their detriment, to put on
my gloves, with which they were particularly
amused. I sat with them some time, and it was
with difficulty they consented to allow me to
leave them at last; indeed, not till I made
them understand my " Cowasjee" wanted me.
Cowasjee's claims they seemed to understand

completely, and, on my rejoining the gentlemen, if I were amused with their description
of the tournament, you may conceive how astonished they were to learn that I had been
actually visiting the Haram!

On the following morning I had an invitation, in form, to repeat my visit, and I was
conducted up a very handsome collegiate-look-
ing staircase, near which was stationed the
master of the house, apparently at his devotions, but evidently intending to have a furtive
peep at me, without my being aware of his so
doing. I was now received *in state* in the interior apartments, and all the ladies were much
more splendidly dressed than on the preceding
evening. Zaccara had on handsome striped
silk drawers, and a silk vest descending to her
feet, richly trimmed with silver lace. All
their hands and feet were dyed with henna,
and they were much surprised to see mine of
their natural colour. The furniture consisted
principally of couches ranged round the room,
upon which they invited me to sit cross-legged,
after their own mode, and seemed astonished
at my preferring our European style. On
the walls was a sentence of the Koran framed
and glazed, and in a recess was an illuminated
Koran, which they showed me. An interesting-
looking young woman, seated in a low chair,

was employed in making silver lace, the process of which she explained to me, as also its use to trim vests and turbans. My costume underwent the same minute investigation as on the yesterday, and as at this time I had on no cap, they were much struck with the manner in which my hair was dressed, and my shoes and stockings created universal astonishment. Refreshments were brought, but every thing was carefully tasted before it was offered to me,—I suppose to show no treachery was intended,—and I was again interrogated as to my ornaments, children, &c. They told me all their names, and endeavoured, but in vain, to accomplish mine.

Suddenly there was a shriek of joy, laughing and clapping of hands. They drew me quickly to the window, from whence I saw C——— walking in the streets, with one of his servants holding an umbrella over his head, surrounded by an immense concourse of people; and very foreign he certainly did look in the streets of Hodeida, with his English dress and hat. The delight of my fair, or rather of my dusky friends, was beyond description ; but it was redoubled, when they found it was *my* Cowasjee. The master of the house then came in : he treated me with the greatest deference and respect, and, bringing me a little baby with gold rings in its nose and ears, with all a father's pride he informed me it was his, and that Zaccara was its mother.

He also asked me about my children and my ornaments, the two things always apparently foremost in an Oriental imagination. My wedding-ring catching the eyes of the women, I made them partly understand its signification. but they evidently seemed to consider it as *a charm*.

Zaccara then taking my hand with a very caressing air, invited me to accompany her, and she showed me all over the house. It was completely " upstairs, downstairs, in my lady's chamber," and I saw a number of small rooms, with loopholes and windows in every direction, where they could see without being seen. They pointed out to me our Ship, the Bazaar, the Mosque, from whence the Dowlah was just returning in grand procession; and they then exhibited to me all their ornaments and trinkets. In return, I showed them such as I had about me. My friend the negro woman, poor black Zacchina as she was called, was the only one who ventured to smell to my salts, and this she did with so much eagerness, that the tears were forced into her eyes in consequence, to the great amusement of her companions.

We parted with mutual expressions of re-

gard; and though I had met with neither the
beauty of Fatima, nor the luxury of a Turkish
Haram, yet I was well pleased with the simplicity, mirth, and happiness, that apparently
reigned in the Arab one; and I should have
been churlish indeed had I not been gratified
with their friendly and artless attempts to
please me. Indeed, 1 flatter myself I made a
conquest, for a great boy of twelve or fourteen
took such a fancy to me, that he volunteered
to accompany me to " Hindy" in the " Merkab,"
or ship, and he really appeared anxious for me
to accept of his services. What should you have
thought of my Arab page? The women in
Arabia are, apparently, allowed more liberty
than in Egypt, for they seemed to be permitted
to walk out together whenever they pleased;
and once, as we were setting out for, and they
were returning from a promenade, we met in
the court. They were so carefully veiled, that
I had some difficulty to recognize my friends of
the Haram again, but they affectionately seized
my hand, and caressingly invited me to return
with them to their apartments. All the gentlemen were with me, and I cannot help thinking that the Arab ladies prolonged their interview purposely, in order to have a better view
of the Fringee Cowasjees, my companions.

The thermometer, whilst we were here,

ranged from 90° to 94°, but though the heat was intense at noon, it was pleasantly attempered in the mornings and evenings by the sea breezes, and the gentlemen found the bathing in the sea very agreeable. The dews were very heavy, but apparently innoxious; for, though C—— frequently slept on the open terrace for fresh air, he never experienced any injury from so doing.

LETTER XXXVI.

Difficult return to the ship.—Mocha.—Residency.—Imaun of Sanaa.—Predilection for English articles.—Mosque of Sheik Hadli.—Caravansera.—Abyssinian Village.—Mahometan Festival.—War dance of the Arabs.

THE surf was high and the sea very rough, when, on the afternoon of July 7th, quitting Hodeida, we again repaired to the George Cruttenden; but though we had expressly hired the boat which was to convey us thither for our own private use, we found it filled with the blind, the maimed and the halt; poor Hadjes, who hoped to obtain a passage gratis to Bombay, and whom the Nachoda allowed to come on board, it being a Mahometan charity to convey a certain number of Pilgrims home, and to feed them during the voyage. The wind

was so strong, and the waves so tremendous,
that it was with considerable difficulty our
little bark reached the ship, and this was not
effected, till one of the crew, a strange amphi-
bious-looking personage, dashing fearlessly into
the sea, by swimming and diving, at length
caught a rope flung to him by the sailors on
board, with which, after much buffeting and
contending with the waves, he at length returned to us, and knotting it to another rope,
in this rough manner was our boat hauled along
side.

At daybreak we passed some islands, and at
noon we were within sight of Mocha, and in
its roadstead, for harbour it has none, we anchored about 2 p. m. at about four miles distance from the shore.

The wind was still very powerful, the waves
high, and the surf really dreadful; but however,
we gladly caught at the opportunity of immediately going on shore in the long boat. From
its violent pitching whilst they were lowering
me into it, I was nearly precipitated into the
sea; and had not one of the party caught me
before I was consigned to the briny deep, I
verily believe I should have ended my life and
my adventures off Mocha. Although there
was a tolerable pier, running perhaps a hundred yards into the sea, yet, on account of its

roughness, we had some difficulty in effecting
a landing, and when once on terra firma, we
were instantly beset with such a host of beggars so loudly vociferating, " Beebee — Cowasjee!" that poor Beebee really felt quite alarmed.
As we passed the gates of the city, our olfactory nerves were saluted by a most inodorous
gale, proceeding from the quantities of sea-
weed, which are here thrown up by the violence of the waves, and being suffered to remain there, the intolerable stench arising from
them, when in a putrescent state, not unfrequently produces illness. The former British
factory was much incommoded thereby. The
present, to which we immediately proceeded,
is farther removed from the sea-shore, and being an excellent house for Arabia, and at this
present time fitted up in the English style, it
appeared to the way-worn wanderers extremely
comfortable. There were the heavy-arched
gateway, the interior court, narrow staircases,
projecting windows, and flat-terraced roof of
Hodeida, though the house was neither on so
large a scale, nor on so intricate a plan as our
domicile there. There were niches, or recesses,
in the walls, perforations and openings in every
direction to admit the air, a high shelf running round the room, and in some of the windows was coloured glass, or rather, I believe, a

stained transparent stone, very much resembling in appearance the painted glass in our cathedrals.

We received a most friendly and hospitable reception from the Resident, who, with his Surgeon, were the only English at Mocha. He immediately sent the latter in his schooner for the General, who had not accompanied us on shore; but the wind was so strong, and the surf so high, that it drifted away, and after many fruitless attempts, he was obliged to abandon the undertaking. The sea is so powerfully rough here, that sometimes three or four days elapse without the ships at anchor being able to communicate with the town. On the following day they were more successful, and the General came on shore. At the custom-house, though they were not so annoying as Niebuhr found them, yet they paid no attention to the Grand Signor's firman, which had hitherto been respected at every other place, and the General's things underwent the same examination with ours. The Arab government here appear to own no allegiance to the Porte, neither do they seem to have any reverence for the English. The Dowlah is an Abyssinian slave, who holds his government under the authority of the Imaun of Sanaa. The Surgeon of the Residency had just returned from thence, having been professionally sent for by the latter potentate. He was seventeen days on his journey thither, which he performed upon a donkey, accompanied by a strong guard.

The Imaun wished much to have detained Mr. ——. He appears to have a strong *penchant* for every thing European, even adopting our costume to a certain degree, and having a regular supply of hats and shoes sent to him. One day he made his appearance before his subjects in an English general's full dress uniform; but this gave such offence, that he never again ventured to make his appearance in this costume in public. The interior country of the Tehama is very hilly, and Sanaa is on such an elevation* that the climate is quite temperate, and there is every kind of European, as well as Asiatic fruit flourishing there; indeed, from the description, it seems to be almost a terrestrial paradise, and to those who have just left the Desert and the barren coast, it must really appear like the fabled gardens of Ad, which are said to be situated in these regions,

---

* It is situated on an elevated and extensive plain, surrounded by mountains, about two thousand feet high. The country is well cultivated; much wine is made by the Jews, and coffee grows in the valleys. In May, the thermometer there was about 50° in the mornings and evenings, and 75° at noon.

though only occasionally visible to the wanderer in the Wilderness. The houses are well built, some partly of marble, and they are generally glazed. The Imaun's is furnished with European articles principally. The interior of the country seems to be very unsafe, and we found cause to rejoice at having abandoned the intention we had once formed of travelling from Hodeida to Mocha by land; indeed, Mocha itself does not always appear to be quite free from the attacks and incursions of the neighbouring Arabs, for, during our temporary *séjour* there, the gates were occasionally closed to prevent their entering, and one day we were under considerable alarm for the safety of our party, who had gone to the Resident's garden-house, about two miles from the city, for the advantage of bathing, it being impossible to bathe here in the sea, on account of the rocky coast and filthy state of the shore. During their absence there was a terrible commotion, the consequences of which might have been unpleasant; the Arabs of the interior came down to seize some persons who had taken refuge in Mocha: however, they eventually retreated without doing much mischief, though they effected an *entrée*, and the gentlemen rejoined us, without having even fallen in with them.

MOCHA

Mocha, with its white chunamed, flat-terraced houses, and minarets interspersed with occasional date-trees, has rather a pretty appearance, particularly from the sea. The streets are narrow, unpaved, and overhung with projecting windows. Many of the houses are richly ornamented with highly finished cornices, fretwork and other arabesque decorations; and the mosques with their tall and elegant minarets, from whence the Muezzin calls the faithful Mussulmans to prayer, are extremely handsome, particularly that which bears the name of the famous Sheik Hadli. Through the gate which bears the same name, Christians and other unbelievers were not, till very lately, allowed to pass. I looked into the interior of one, for Fringees are not allowed to enter, and I saw but little more than a large, square, unfurnished room. A caravansera which we visited, built, I believe, by the Turks, and very much out of repair, presented to our view a large square building, with a pretty little mosque in the centre of the interior court, and unfurnished apartments all round, for the accommodation of travellers. Outside of the gates of the city was the Abyssinian village, consisting of some most extraordinary ranges of thatched, conical-shaped huts, looking like so many beehives. The Abyssinians supply Mocha with grain, wood and vegetables,* and considerable intercourse takes place between this city and Massoah on the opposite coast. Many of the Abyssinian natives are constantly to be met with in the streets of Mocha, with tall, upright and slender figures, intelligent countenances, fine features, and a peculiarly sparkling and vivacious eye ; their hair arranged, curled and dyed with the utmost care, gives a sort of foppish air to their appearance. The *mélange* of Oriental nations and costumes which we saw in Mocha was really very curious : there were, besides the Abyssinian dandies, several of our Banyan friends, with their singular turbans ; the wild-looking Bedouin of the Desert, armed *cap-à-pie* ; the more civilized Arab of the town ; the peaceful-looking Hindoo, in his silk trowsers and snow-white angrica ; and the magnificent Turk, who is, however, but rarely here to be seen, in his splendid, handsome and cumbrous attire. Here I first saw the light, the elegant, and the beautiful gazelle running about the streets, playfully attempting to butt us as we passed ; also what is termed in India the Braminee bull, with the hunch on his shoulders ; and we

---

* The Resident's table was well supplied with grapes, pomegranates, mangoes, and other fruits ; but, I believe, these were brought down from the interior.

sometimes met the Dowlah's horses exercising, among which were some of the high caste Nedjedy breed, and which, compared with our English steeds, are small, light, and active, and there were also some of the strong, heavy and ponderous Dongola species.

Although I probably was the first English woman who ever perambulated the streets of Mocha in this fearless manner, I met with no molestation; and, though at first we never went forth without a guard of Sepoys, yet subsequently C—— and I took some *tête-à-tête* walks, without any more cause for alarm, than if we had been parading the streets of Paris.

The climate of Mocha is oppressive and disspiriting, but the Surgeon told us, he did not consider it as particularly unhealthy. Owing to the deleterious effects of the water, which, though pleasant to the taste, is prejudicial to the constitution, many disorders are occasioned, particularly severe pains in the limbs, to which it is necessary to pay immediate attention. The thermometer seldom rose much above 90°, but we were all very much overcome with the heat, the atmosphere having an unpleasant moisture in it, which is very relaxing, and enervating. The evenings, however, were very pleasant, and these we used to spend upon the terraced roof of the Residency, upon which was erected a sort of light wicker-work Bungalow,

with a temporary sleeping apartment. From
the adjoining terrace we had a fine view over
the flat-roofed, white-chunamed town of Mocha,
whose houses are ornamented with fantastic
arabesque fretwork and elegant tracery; the
projecting balconies decorated with beautiful
carved woodwork, and the windows partially
glazed with stained glass, whilst the square
uniformity of the buildings is agreeably diversified with light and airy turrets. In front were
the blue waters of the Red Sea; on one side,
a dark grove of date-trees extended along the
shore; whilst on the other, beyond a wide and
barren desert, might be seen a picturesque
range of mountains.

The Banyan merchants soon found us out,
and paid us the greatest attention, frequently
calling, and bringing little offerings of Mocha
coffee and honey. When the visits were returned, the guests, before they took their leave,
were profusely sprinkled with Attargut and
rose-water, some of which, as a mark of attention, was skilfully thrown into their eyes!

The 15th of July was a great festival with
the Mahometans.* It was kept in commemo-
ration of the intended sacrifice of Isaac, or as
they say, Ishmael, whom as their progenitor
they naturally greatly venerate : the scene of
this transaction, they assert, was at Mecca instead

* The Buckree Mohurrum.

of Mount Moriah. Great splendour of attire was displayed by the inhabitants of Mocha upon this occasion. Rich and many-coloured robes were exhibited, superb vests handsomely trimmed with gold and silver, magnificent shawls, and in their turbans every one wore wreaths and nosegays of the sweet-scented Mogrey.

I saw our Nachoda Saboo ben Tayib perambulating the streets, and looking really very grand and important in a rose-coloured tunic. Upon their festivals, those Mahometans who have no fine clothes of their own, make a point of hiring them, however poor and wretched they may be at other times :— an admirable method of spreading and perpetuating the plague this, as the garments descend from generation to generation.

The women here were always closely veiled, but they seemed to enjoy as much liberty as in an European town, and in the square upon which one of our windows looked, we frequently saw them walking about, or conversing together in little knots. I believe they have the privilege of divorcing their husbands whenever they please, always retaining their marriage portion. The Arabs have a wild independence and manly frankness in their manner, which is very superior to the obsequiousness and servility of other Oriental nations. Instead of salaaming down to the ground like the Hindoos, they far more frequently offer the hand in the English fashion, and shake it heartily, quite in the true, honest, John Bull style.

We were one day witnesses to a very extraordinary and amusing spectacle—a regular war dance of the Arabs, which took place in the square opposite the Dowlah's house. A number of wild-looking natives, half-clothed, but all armed, holding in one hand a creese, a sword, or a scimitar, and in the other a raised bludgeon, moved slowly round and round, following one another in a circle, chanting a sort of recitative, to which they moved in solemn measure, with steps neither quite marching nor quite dancing, but something between both. At regular intervals, they paused, raised and clashed their weapons, simultaneously, keeping time together in a sort of grand chorus. I never saw bold, daring, savage determination, and spirited resolution so strongly and so energetically portrayed — it was one of the finest, yet wildest scenes I ever beheld — they seemed in a state of perfect enthusiasm, and fit for any bold exploit — and similar to this, perhaps, might have been the war-dances of the ancients. The rude chant was more inspiring than regular music, and I am convinced that, in this manner, the passions might be thereby raised almost to a pitch of frenzy.

LETTER XXXVII.

Straits of Bab-el-Mandeb.—Manners of the Crew and Passengers.—Monsoon.—Rough weather.—Arrival at Bombay.

On the afternoon of the 15th of July, we took leave of our kind host, and again embarked upon the rough surges of the Red Sea. We found our cabin windows closed and the dead lights up, in anticipation of the rough seas we were to encounter in the Indian Ocean. All the following day, there was "dreadful note of preparation," the cannon were taken down, and sent below, every thing on board was lashed, and the General's four horses were secured by some extra strong posts, which were put up for the purpose. The Nachoda offered us his cabin, which, though smaller than our own, from being upon deck was more airy; and of this we gladly availed ourselves, as the heat below was intolerable.

At 4 P. M. we set sail with a fair breeze, but the wind slackening at night, the Maloom or Pilot lay to, being apprehensive of passing the Straits in the night—those dreadful Straits, which, from time immemorial, have filled the heart of the wandering mariner, with fear and dismay, and which have acquired for themselves the melancholy but poetical title of Bab-el-Mandeb, or "the Gate of Tears," from the dismal end, that there too frequently awaits the ill-fated bark. The result of sad experience, and a highly fanciful imagination, lead the superstitious Arabs to believe that the Genius of the coming storm loves here to station himself, and to ensnare the unhappy voyager; or perched upon Cape Guardafui, there to enjoy the sight of the misery he has occasioned. Oh! the bathos of John Bull! Will any thing ever teach him taste and sentiment? He calls these poetically-termed Straits, by the vulgar, the ludicrous name of — THE BOBS ! ! ! Through the lesser Bob did we pass upon the morning of the 16th; a passage of about three miles wide, which is formed by the high land of the Arabian Coast, and the small desert Island of Perim; upon this, the English, at one time, endeavoured to establish a fortress, but want of water constrained them to abandon the enterprise.

The day was pleasant, and the sea, the treacherous sea continued to wear a calm and smooth aspect, whilst I, little weening. of ills to come, deemed that the Genius of the storm, out of compliment to the first Englishwoman who had passed *outwards* through "the Gate of Tears," had gallantly abstained from exacting from her his customary tribute of trouble and distress.

Alas! this pleasing, this flattering delusion was not of long continuance.

No sooner were we fairly in the Arabian Gulf, than the thermometer, which had been at 94° in the Red Sea, fell several degrees, and the light breeze freshened into a strong but steady wind. A heavy swell appeared upon the sea, and the blue heavens were obscured with clouds. To our torridized feelings, 80° of the thermometer appeared positively cool, and we all congratulated each other upon the delightful change in the atmosphere, which made it requisite to assume a warmer style of dress. Cockroaches and ants vanished from the deck, upon which it was now pleasant to spend the whole day, watching the mighty expanse of waters, and losing one's self in the delightfully wild reveries which this sublime spectacle must necessarily awaken in the coldest and most unpoetical imagination.

On the 19th, large drops of rain fell in the evening, which increasing to a heavy shower, forced us to retire to our cabins. Excepting a slight fall at Alexandria, we had not seen rain since we left Malta, and we hailed the appearance as that of an old friend, reminding us of our native country, those green isles of the west, where

"The rain it raineth every day."

2 A 2

Whilst upon deck, it was a considerable amusement to watch the proceedings of the Indian crew, which, to me, were a novel sight. Sometimes, one more devout than the rest, untying his cumberband, and spreading it upon deck, would kneel down, and go through all the mummery of the Mahometan ritual, prostrating himself, touching the ground with his forehead, and at intervals stroking his beard with the utmost gravity. In the evening, it was a fine and impressive scene, after the crew had, in a clear and sonorous voice, been called by the Muezzin to prayers, to behold them, unmindful of spectators, standing in a row, and turning their faces towards Mecca, prostrating themselves in homage, and devoutly performing their orisons.

At noon, the Nachoda and his son, the Maloom, and the principal persons on board, took their repast, which generally consisted of curry or pilau, in an immense dish, which was placed upon a carpet or mat upon deck, round which all seating themselves, each helped himself, by plunging his hand in, which, I should mention, was previously always carefully washed ; and when he had, in Homeric phrase, " satisfied the rage of hunger," or in plain English, eaten as much as he wished, he immediately arose, and going a little aside, an attendant in waiting with an ewer and basin, offered him water, with which he rinsed his mouth, and again washed his face and hands. The rest of the crew seemed to live almost entirely upon rice, which was served up in the same manner, though with less ceremony. Our Nachoda and Maloom always deferred taking an observation of the sun till after dinner, when, they said, they found their heads clearer, and themselves more competent to calculation. However, they were generally quite erroneous in their reckoning; and, it was to our kind stars we were indebted, or, I should say, to the care of Providence, for preservation in these stormy seas, rather than to their nautical skill. One day, they put two compasses close together, in order to assist each other!

One old Arab, who generally acted as steersman, and who spoke a little Italian, which he delighted to talk, took a very great interest in my welfare, and was always recommending something or other for my comfort. "Limonata" was his constant specific against every thing — and, whenever I looked paler than usual, and felt the motion of the sea unpleasant, he would attempt to console me, by telling me how many days' sail we were yet from Bombay. The pipe, or the *bury*, consisting of an unpolished cocoa-nut shell, which contained water, into which a thick reed was inserted in-

stead of the serpentine tube, termed lieh,* was
in constant use upon deck, and handed from one
to another in succession. One day whilst he
was smoking, unconsciously did I fix my eyes
thereon, upon which, imagining, I suppose, that
I was anxiously wishing for it, he immediately
offered it to me! I could but be amused with
this mark of Eastern gallantry.

The Orientals deem all Fringees to be necessarily Hakims, or physicians, and the crew were
consequently very fond of consulting the gentlemen upon their real, or fancied, disorders, and
they frequently put their medical knowledge in
practice, for their benefit. One poor man, for
whom C—— was called upon to prescribe, he
found was positively sick from vexation. He
had ventured his little all in a speculation of
merchandize, with which in the bustle of embarkation, some light-fingered thief had walked
off. C——, alas, could not " minister to a mind
diseased."

Both at noon and at night, all, but those
at the time engaged in attending to the ship,
would stretch themselves upon the deck ; and,
with the sky for their covering, and the hard
boards for their pillow, drawing their turbans
over their faces, were soon buried in slumber,

* This is similar to what is termed in India, the Hubble-
bubble.

enjoying that rest, too often sought for in vain by the European passengers.

No young lady, about to make her *debút* at her first ball, ever bestowed more care upon her ringlets, than these good people did upon their beards and mustachios ; and the patience with which they sat under the barber's hands, whilst he sought to give the latter a becoming curl, and the self-complacency with which they were constantly surveying and admiring themselves in a small pocket mirror, were really quite amusing. Let not the manly sex henceforth accuse ours of vanity, for, I verily believe, they surpass us therein, as well as in love of finery and dress.

Soon after passing the Island of Socotra, on the 21st, the sea assumed a stormy appearance, and the darkened heavens a threatening aspect. We fell in with the south-west monsoon, and, though a fair wind to take us to Bombay, for some days, it blew a regular gale, during which period the weather was so tempestuous, and the sea so rough, that the violent pitching of the vessel was most unpleasant, whilst the things breaking from their lashings, and rolling about upon deck, caused a most tremendous noise, intermingled with the awful uproar of the dashing of the waves, and the howling of the winds. The sailors could scarcely keep their footings, but " reeled to and fro like drunken men," and one of the poor Hadjes, returning from Mecca, fell a victim to the violence of the motion, which, his emaciated frame, weakened by a long course of hardships and privation, was not able to sustain.

For some days the firmament of heaven was too much obscured with clouds to make any observation, so that, after we were once fairly in the Indian Ocean, we were entirely at the mercy of the winds and waves, steering generally, and pretty much by guess, for Bombay. On the 28th, neither the Nachoda nor the Maloom, by their own acknowledgment, exactly knew where we were, when, upon sounding, a small *shell* was brought up, which evinced that we were on the bank off Bombay Harbour, and scarcely could the olive-leaf have been hailed with more transport by the inhabitants of the ark, than was this demonstration of our being near the end of our voyage, by the passengers in the George Cruttenden.

All that night we were tremendously tossed about, but on the following day,

> Lo, land! and all was well;

we had reached our wished-for haven, and about nine o'clock on the morning of the 29th of July did we cast anchor in the Harbour of Bombay.

The Island, the fort, the light-house, Colabah, with houses and barracks, intermingled with airy cocoa-nut-trees and lofty palmyras, lay outstretched before us, whilst beyond was to be seen the Continent of India; and delightful indeed did land appear to us, after so many days tossing on the Indian Ocean.

Telegraphic signs having communicated the information that Sir Hudson Lowe was on board the George Cruttenden, in a short time a government boat, with the Town Major, Lieutenant-Colonel Willis, came to receive him, and in this we all immediately proceeded to shore, congratulating ourselves, that, in a few minutes, a termination was to be put to our stormy voyage from the Straits of Bab-el-Mandeb, or " the Gate of Tears," to the Presidency of Bombay.

LETTER XXXVIII.

Landing in Bombay.—Palanquin.—Government House.—
First appearance of every thing delightful from contrast.
—Anglo-Indian Breakfast.—English Letters.—Hamauls.
—Chintz Poglie, and Road thither.

Dr. Johnson tells us that we seldom do any thing, or leave any place for the last time, without emotions of regret; but in spite of the sage moralist's observation, and at the risk of being thought very unsentimental, I must candidly acknowledge that I quitted the George Cruttenden with no sensations but those of pleasure. After so long *roughing* it among turbaned Turks and semi-civilized Arabs, the well-dressed, *hatted* gentry on the walls of the Fort of Bombay, who were watching our movements, and the cheerful appearance of several good-looking white houses, promising English comforts and accommodations, were, to such weary weather-beaten wanderers, really most agreeable objects; and after nearly a fortnight's *monsooning* on the Indian Ocean, we were right glad to land once more upon terra firma. Amid the roar of cannon, fired in honour of Sir Hudson Lowe, did we ascend the dock stairs, and here, once more did I find myself in a completely new scene, amid strange faces, and stranger garbs. A painted box, denominated a palanquin, but to my mind very much resembling a coffin in appearance, was awaiting my arrival. In this I was deposited, the Hamauls, or bearers, took it up, and the gentlemen being all accommodated with other vehicles and conveyances, off we all set to the Government House, the exterior of which is certainly not very superb, and not equal to that of many gentlemen's houses in England. The

interior, however, appeared comfortable, and
the staircase and drawing-room are handsome;
but to the feelings of those just escaped from a
little hot cabin, a rolling sea, and the torments
of ants, cockroaches, and musquitoes, the coolness of the air, the freshness and the verdure
of all around, the spacious hall, surrounded
by a noble verandah, the beautiful variety of
shrubs in the garden upon which it opened,
were positively *delightful!* At the sight of
trees, plants, and flowering shrubs, I could have
shed tears of joy; for, since we had left the
banks of the Nile, we had seen little more than
barren and desert wildernesses. It was at this
time the height of the monsoon, when vegetation in India is rank, rapid, and luxuriant.
The heavens were obscured with clouds—the
weather had the mild, pleasing, and half melancholy appearance of a *grey* day in England,
and the change and contrast which these presented to the unvarying and dazzling brilliancy
of the Egyptian and the Arabian sky, were
most grateful and refreshing to the feelings;
and after having been deprived, for such a
length of time, of the accommodation of civilized life, the English comforts and Oriental
luxuries, with which we were surrounded, were
more than ordinarily agreeable. The repast
was served up in the Anglo-Indian style, which

much resembles our *dejeunés à la fourchette.*
Different sorts of fish, some of which I had
never seen before, and which are, I believe, peculiar to Bombay,—kabaubs,—the never-failing
rice and curry, and many strange and unknown
dishes made their appearance; whilst pine-
apples, pomegranates, shaddocks, mangoes, plantains, and custard-apples, graced the board,
and seemed doubly delicious to us, from our
having been so long debarred from vegetables
and fruits of every kind. In the mean time,
the air was fanned and kept fresh and cool by
a punkah over our heads. This is an immense
framework of wood covered with cloth, which
is suspended from the ceiling in the centre of
the apartment, and kept in perpetual motion
by ropes, pulled by attendants stationed on the
outside.

A mental treat likewise awaited us, in a
packet of letters from England. It was nearly
ten months since we had left our native land,
and our movements had been so uncertain, that
we had only once heard from thence, and those
alone who have been so long separated from
their families and friends, can tell the nervous
agitation, the anxious flutter, and the almost
painfully delightful excitation, which are produced by the sight of their well-known hand-

writing, in the bosom of the wanderer in a distant country.

In tropical countries, amid groves of airy palms and wavy bananas, a letter from England will convey him, in idea, to the verdant lawns and flower-enamelled meadows of his native country, and in his mind's eye will he see the well remembered woods and glades, and in fancy will he hear the melodious notes of the blackbird and the throstle resounding through the beechen shades; the wood-pigeon breathing her soft and querulous murmurs, and the nightingale's sweetly varied note, harmoniously wafted by the gentle breeze from the distant groves, awakening the sleeping echoes around. Alas! a sad reality soon dissipates these delightful and pleasing delusions!

After duly reporting our arrival to the proper authorities, we again entered our palanquins, and proceeded to Chintz Poglie, the residence of Mr. Buchanan, one of the principal gentlemen, or, as the natives would say, one of the "Burra Sahibs" of the island, from whom we had received a most kind and friendly invitation. At Bombay, this attention is more than civil, it is real hospitality; for it is most singular that there are no hotels to which a lady could with propiety go; and, on first landing in

a foreign country, a stranger feels sadly at a
loss.   There may possibly be taverns to which
gentlemen resort, but, in India, the person that
has no friends to receive him, is much to be
pitied.

The motion of the palanquin, is, to *a griffin*,
as a person is termed for the first year of
his residence in India, somewhat unpleasant,
and gives a sensation something similar to sea
sickness ; indeed, it was long before I quite ·
liked it, and it was still longer before I became
perfectly reconciled to its use.   There is, at first,
something revolting to the feelings, in seeing
your fellow creatures employed like slaves, independent of the apparent effeminacy of thus
being carried on men's shoulders.   " They
wanted *me* to get into one of these things,"
said one of the party to me, as he handed me
in ; " as if," added he with true English independence, " as if I could not walk !"   ·

This impression, however, soon wears off,
and habit speedily reconciles individuals to
this, as well as to other customs, which were,
perhaps, at first, the most revolting to their
natures.

The Hamauls, or Palkee-bearers, are rather
a small race, but they seem wonderfully active
and strong.   In carrying the palanquin they
use a sort of long swinging trot, moving the

arm which is at liberty, up and down with a see-saw movement, occasionally shifting the pole from shoulder to shoulder, and they get on very fast, much quicker, indeed, than a man ordinarily walks.

Chintz Poglie is situated on the eastern side of the island of Bombay ; we found the road thither excellent, and on our way we had a very fine view of the magnificent harbour, studded with islands, to which the mountains on the Continent formed a bold, yet soft and beautiful back-ground.

After leaving the esplanade, or open ground which surrounds the fort of Bombay, and passing through extensive suburbs, which some persons call the Black Town, we came to enclosed pleasure-grounds, and such a constant succession of gentlemen's houses, that it reminded me of the neighbourhood of London ; but though there might be an occasional villa built somewhat in the English fashion, the generality were mere bungalows, or garden-houses, which generally consisted of a number of detached, low thatched buildings, the exterior of which resembled so many out-houses and barns. Some few had two stories, and heavy projecting roofs, like those of the Swiss, which are well calculated to keep off the sun and to carry off the rain of the monsoon ; but though the

outsides in general were very poor, the interior we found frequently fitted up with great
elegance.

Chintz Poglie was a most comfortable residence, with a noble verandah of one hundred
feet long ;—but by verandah you must not
figure to yourself the little green painted
wooden things which are patched on to the
cottage *orné* of Cheltenham and Tunbridge
Wells ; in India, they are spacious galleries,
often running all round the house, forming distinct apartments, upon which the others open,
and generally so constructed as to admit, at
pleasure, every breath of wind that blows, whilst
Venetian blinds give the power of excluding the
intensity of the noon-tide heat.   The floors are
frequently covered with the Indian mats, which
are thought so much of in England, but which
are here used for the commonest purposes.   In
the sleeping apartments, the beds are placed in
the middle of the room, and, instead of curtains,
musquito nets cover the whole, whilst windows and doors are to be seen in every direction you turn.   The houses are lighted by
lamps suspended from the ceiling, in which are
placed tumblers, or glasses, full of water, with
cocoa-nut oil and a wick swimming on the
top, and, to superintend these, is the office of a
particular set of servants, called Mussauls, who

are somewhat of an inferior grade to the Hamauls.

In the verandahs and porticoes of the houses
of those who hold high official situations, are
constantly to be seen, lounging at all hours of
the day, peons, or messengers, who, in spite of
their seeming listlessness and idleness, will
start up with the greatest activity at their
master's voice, and set off to any distance, to
execute the orders he may give them. As
our kind host held one of the very first places
in the island, that of Superintendant of the
Marine, his house was always thus beset,
and as the natives have no idea of a walk
for pleasure, I am convinced they frequently
thought me little short of insane, when they
saw me, prompted by curiosity, or wishing
for a little fresh air, issue forth to take a
stroll amid the plantations of bananas, and
cocoa-nut groves, with which the house was
surrounded ; but, in spite of the heat of these
tropical climes, I never could become sufficiently Orientalized entirely to give up walking,
which most of our countrywomen do in India,
for there was something very delightful and
pleasant in seeing the tender inhabitants of our
conservatories and hot-houses, flourishing in the
open air, or growing wild in the fields.

LETTER XXXIX.

Monsoon.—Heavy rains.—Deficiency of rain produces great
distress in India.—Tanks.—Evening drive.—Great variety
of nations and costumes at Bombay.—Vellard.—Breach
Candy.—General rendezvous of the English.

THE morning after our arrival at Bombay,
the rain fell in torrents for some hours, and
only those who have been eye-witnesses to a
monsoon, can have any idea of the impetuosity
with which it pours, in tropical countries, during that period. It appears like the bursting
of so many water-spouts, or as if the windows
of heaven were suddenly opened; and, in a few
minutes, the ground, which might have been previously perfectly dry, becomes entirely flooded.
From what I have myself seen, I can believe any
wonders of sudden inundations—of rivers over-
flowing their banks—of nullahs, or dry water
courses, instantaneously converted into rapid
and impetuous streams—but yet, that horror to
an Englishman, a rainy summer, is the greatest
blessing to a Hindoo; and a heavier calamity
cannot befall the latter, than a deficiency of
rain. His paddy, or rice-fields, would be in
consequence, not properly flooded, and, this

grain being his principal article of food, an in-
sufficiency of water invariably produces a failure of the crops, when a famine probably ensues, with its dreadful accompaniments, disease and pestilence. The Hindoos depend
upon their rice, as the Irish on their potatoes,
and the consequences are equally dreadful in
the one country as in the other, if, from any
cause, the usual quantity be not produced. I
have heard public store-houses recommended, to
be filled in plentiful seasons by Government, on
the Patriarch Joseph's plan, when, in scarcities,
a supply would always be ready, and possibly
immense revenues might thereby be raised, and
much distress averted. It is perhaps owing to
the unimproved state of agriculture, that a failure
in the crops is by no means an uncommon circumstance; and, it is said, that perhaps, on an
average, a partial one occurs once in every seven
to ten years.

During the monsoon also, the tanks, or artificial reservoirs of water, become filled, upon
which the natives principally depend for their
supply during the dry seasons. These frequently have nothing more than the appearance of large ponds in England, but occasionally they are on a very magnificent scale; and
rich natives, who wish to distinguish themselves by their benificence, either plant a tope, or

grove of mangoes, build a pagoda, or dig a tank, each of which is deemed a meritorious action.* There is one of the last at Bombay, which is very handsome; the whole of the four excavated sides are encrusted with stone, and form staircases, with terraces at intervals, which really are very agreeable promenades, and the natives are often to be seen sitting on the steps in little knots, conversing with each other after the heat of the day is over.

In the afternoon, the rain subsided, and a little before sunset, which is the hour when the Europeans take their customary drives, we issued forth to take ours. The carriages in India are constructed so as to admit, rather than to exclude the air, and the whole of the back frequently rolls up, or is distended behind in a very ugly manner. These, and other numerous precautions to keep out the heat, were sometimes so successful, that I not unfrequently found myself positively shivering with cold—but we were at this time fresh from Egypt and Arabia, where the intensity of the heat perhaps exceeds that of India, or, at least, there are not so many methods of excluding it. In India, the weather, during the monsoon, has frequently the chilly feel of a cold rainy

---

* A Guzerattee proverb says, " Plant a tree, dig a well, write a book, and go to heaven."

summer day in England, with intervals of intense sultriness ; and it is positively a fact, that for the first two or three days I was in Bombay, I should have been glad of a fire, and I was obliged to wrap myself in a large shawl to keep myself warm !

Our first drive was to Breach Candy, which is so called from the sea having formerly overflowed a part of the island there. In its neighbourhood, a vellard communicates and connects it with Love Grove, which substantial work was raised by Governor Boddam ; but, though it was the means of preventing the sea from making a breach through the whole centre of the island, the expense attendant on it, was highly disapproved by the authorities at home, who, I was told, either reprimanded the Governor severely, or removed him from his situation in consequence. In India, it is too frequently the case, that the merits and performances of an individual are not appreciated and acknowledged at the time, though, subsequently, their intrinsic worth will extort involuntary approbation and admiration. This work, which caused so much displeasure at the period of its construction, I was informed by those well calculated to judge, had eventually proved of the greatest utility, and still preserves the low lands of the island from being inundated by

the spring tides ; which, but for this, and other
works of a similar description, would destroy
all but the hills, and reduce Bombay to its former condition, for, it was once, only "a small,
rocky, barren, and pestilential island."

It being Sunday, which is with the natives
as much a holiday, perhaps I should rather say,
idle day, as with the English, they were likewise taking their evening drives and promenades.   It has been said, that Bombay is more
populous, and contains a greater variety of inhabitants, than is to be found in so small a
space in any other part of the world ; and certainly the scene which presented itself, and
which I subsequently found was of no unfre-
quent occurrence, was one of the most amusing
and singular I ever beheld.   The difference
of costumes, and equipages, reminded me of
the two or three last days of the Carnival at
Florence.   There was the grave and respectable looking Parsee, who is the descendant of
the ancient Persians, looking as consequential
and as happy as possible, in his clean white vest,
and ugly, stiff, purple cotton turban, with a
shawl thrown over his shoulders like a lady,
driving an English buggy in the English fashion.   Then followed a hackery, or common
cart of the country, creaking slowly along,
drawn by oxen, and appearing as if about to

tumble down, with a Hindoo family ; the men
half naked, but invariably with turbans on
their head ;—the women, clothed in the sarree,
or long piece of cloth or silk, which is twisted
round their persons so as to fall gracefully in
folds to the feet, like the drapery of an antique
statue, and, after forming a petticoat, it is
brought over the right shoulder, across the
bosom, and falls over the head like a veil.
This, with a small bodice fastening before or
behind, according to fancy, constitutes the
whole of their attire, and it is infinitely prettier, and far more elegant, than the Frank
female costume.

The sarree so completely covers the whole
of the person, and so effectually conceals the
figure of the wearer, that it is likewise infinitely more modest and delicate than our style of
dress, and it also possesses the advantage of
being more quickly put on ; one minute will
suffice a Hindoo belle to arrange her attire, but
they make up for the simplicity of this part of
their toilet by a profusion of ear, and nose
rings, and ornaments of every sort and description, which are frequently composed of precious stones and valuable pearls. Necklaces
of gold mohurs, or Venetian sequins, bangles
of gold and silver on their arms and ancles, and
costly rings on their toes, frequently decorate

the persons of the females of the humblest and
meanest classes, for, as there are no such things
as saving banks in India, they convert their
money into these trinkets, as the most portable
method of carrying their riches about with
them, though sometimes, in times of war, this
has given rise to most dreadful personal cruelties.

After the Hackery, would dash by an English officer in full regimentals, or a Civilian in
the light Anglo-Indian costume, on spirited
Arabs, followed perhaps by native grooms in
turbans and white cotton vests. Then would
appear a couple of Persians, carefully guiding a
pair of horses in an English curricle, attired in
long flowing robes, and graceful and becoming
turbans, with peculiarly fine features, handsome
and intelligent countenances, and dark beards
sweeping their breasts. In heavy coaches,
lighter landaulet, or singular looking Shigram-
poes, might be seen, bevies of British fair, in
Leghorn hats, silk bonnets, blond caps, and
Brussels lace veils. Feathers waving, flowers
blooming, and ribands streaming, in all the
freaks and fancies of every French and English
fashion, which may have prevailed in Europe,
during the last half dozen years. In India the
veriest *adorateur des modes*, must be content
always to be *one* year behind the belles of
London and of Paris, and, in the out stations,

at least two or three—but, however, there is no
deficiency of finery, whatever there may be of
ton, in the appearance and attire of the ladies of
Bombay. These would be driven by a coachman, and attended by footmen in Parsee, Mahometan, or Hindoo attire, whilst a Ghorawalla, or horse keeper, would run by the side
of the carriage on foot, and keep up with it
though driven at a tremendous rate, carrying
a painted chowree * in his hand, with which
he would keep the flies from annoying the
horses. In addition to these, might be seen
numerous Portuguese, whose very dark complexions and short, curly, coal-black hair, looked
more singular and more foreign in their white
cotton Frank costume than even the Asiatics
in their loosely flowing robes. There were
also Roman Catholic priests in their robes,
respectable-looking Armenians with their families, numerous half-castes in neat English
dresses, and a few Chinese, looking exactly as
if some of the figures on a China jar had
stepped forth to take an evening walk. These
were most effeminate in appearance, with a long
silky plaid of dark hair, twisted neatly round
their heads; yet their sleepy countenances, and
flat and singular features, had an air of stupid

* A switch of horse-hair, fastened to a wooden handle.

benevolence, such as may be seen in the figures
of Bhood, or Bhudda.　The wild looking Arab,
and the majestic Turk in his magnificent and
superb attire, were of rare occurrence. The
Cutchee " Burra Sahib" in a fine gilt palanquin,
with a turban a yard high, richly adorned with
gold, was also to be seen, and there was an
endless variety of Mussulmans, and Hindoos
of different castes ; the Holy Bramin, with the
sacred Zennar or cord, suspended from his
shoulder ; the Purbhoo, or writer-caste, with
their very neat turbans ; the Banyans in their
deep red, and the Bengalese with their flat ones;
the Mahrattas, the Malabarese, the Malays, and
the Boras, who are said to be Mahometanized
Jews, and who are the pedlars of the country.
In short, every religion, every caste, and every
profession, of almost every nation, from the
shores of China to the banks of the Thames.
Even in a fancy ball in London, or during the
Carnival in Italy, where every one strives to
be in a particular and original costume, it
would be impossible to meet with a greater
variety, than presented itself in this short drive,
which indeed was only what may be seen
every day in the Island of Bombay.

A particular spot at Breach Candy is the
general rendezvous of the English community,
where they meet to settle the politics of the

island, and to discuss the affairs of the day—

> " Who danced with whom, and who is like to wed,
> And who is hanged, and who is brought to bed."

And here, whilst with monsoon fury the surges of the Indian Ocean hoarsely lash the coast, or when, in a more tranquil mood, its waves gently ripple round the rocks on the shore, the English will sit for an hour at a time, talking over their neighbours, and — killing reputations. Dr. Howison says, " that were the Genius of Scandal at a loss where to establish her head quarters, he would recommend that their site should be Bombay, and that she should select her personal staff from the resident society of that island, for in no other part of the world where he has ever been, is the propensity for gossiping so unintermitting." However, I do not know after all, that the inhabitants of Bombay are more scandalously disposed than those of any other part of the world, where there is as much leisure, as little to think of, and as much less to do; and where, consequently, the affairs of others necessarily occupy the attention, and talking about them, serves as an agreeable recreation *pour passer le temps.*

LETTER XL.

Pareil, the Government House.—Menagerie.—Tiger, and Tiger adventures. — Ouran Outang. — Horticulture not much attended to at Bombay.—Similar to that of the ancient Egyptians.—Flowers and Trees.—Mango of Mazagong.—Cocoanut tree.—Bamboo.—Banana or Plantain. —Banyan.—Peepul.

PAREIL, the Government-House, and where the Governor principally resides, was once, it is said, a Jesuit's college, or convent, and the exterior has been *patched* in better taste than is generally displayed when an ancient edifice is metamorphosed into a modern residence. The drawing-room and staircase are rather handsome, but the dining-room, which is about eighty feet long, and which was once the body of an old desecrated church, is a long, ill-proportioned, and, by no means, well-furnished apartment. The grounds were rather pretty, and laid out something in the English style, though the palms and other Oriental trees proclaimed how far we were from our native land. In the menagerie was a royal tiger, stretched at his ease in his cage, but the noble prisoner looked sadly out of his place, and seemed far better calculated to range the forest, and the pathless jungle, than to be enclosed by wooden bars, within a space of twelve feet square. He was of larger dimensions than any I ever saw in England, and I could but shudder at the possibility of meeting one roaming at large, which, in the out stations, is a circumstance of by no means unusual occurrence. Tiger stories and tiger adventures constitute a leading feature in the adventures of the lovers of the marvellous in the East, and probably there are few persons who have not had the good, or bad fortune, to have had a personal rencontre with one.

A gentleman, we are acquainted with, had once the pleasure of falling into a dry nullah with one, and whilst positively lying under the paws of the ferocious animal, and of course expecting every moment to be torn to pieces, a faithful Sepoy, with a steady aim, fired at its heart and killed it, without injuring or wounding his master in the least. Another, whilst travelling at night in his palanquin, was suddenly set down by his bearers, who ran hastily away, screaming out, " baug, baug !" A tiger, a tiger ! Conceive the poor man's situation, not daring to open the doors to attempt to make his escape, yet expecting every minute to see the creature's tremendous claws making forcible *entrée*. The Hamauls, however, after taking refuge in neigh-

bouring trees, by shouts and loud cries, fortunately frightened the animal away, or their master's life must inevitably have fallen a sacrifice.
C—— himself, when on horseback at break of
day, once saw one cross the road immediately
in front of, and only a few yards from his
horse. He was warned of this perilous neigh-
bour by his poor ghorawalla falling back quite
aghast, and exclaiming in accents of horror,
" baug, baug !" The horse, however, betrayed
none of those signs of terror which it is
said instinctively to show when in the vicinity
of beasts of prey, and the tiger evincing no
wish to molest the party, went its way, and
they wended theirs. It had been watching some
flocks during the night, and just then the cry
of shepherds was heard in the neighbourhood,
and at the time of this rencontre, it was sculk-
ing off to its lair in the jungle. It is asserted
that tigers will not go out of their way to attack
travellers, unless molested by them, or instigat-
ed by hunger, but the poor natives not unfrequently fall victims to them ; and in travelling,
a tree may occasionally be seen covered with
rags, or a heap of stones, to which every pas-
senger adds a tribute, and which are the monuments marking the spot where a human being
has been destroyed.

In this collection, among other animals we

also saw a fierce-looking tiger-cat, and a porcu-
pine ; that inhabitant of the desert, an ostrich,
which was of tremendous size, and an ouran-
outang, or wild man of the woods; or as the
natives term it, "jungle ke admee ;" a most
disgusting object, and a complete caricature
of the sons of Adam ; but yet so completely
resembling one in appearance, that it really
might be easily taken for one of the Lords of
the Human race. Indeed, it is said, that in
his expedition to India, Alexander's army
meeting with a large body of these animals,
mistook them for a hostile nation, and prepared to give them battle. The ape is held sacred
by the Hindoos, and one of their principal
poems, the Ramayuna, relates the adventures
of the Monkey Hannaman, or Hunooman, who
makes a very tolerable hero, or at least hero's
companion, as he comes to the assistance of the
famous Rama at the head of an army of mon-
keys, builds a bridge from the Continent to
Ceylon, and helps him to regain his lost wife,
the fair Seita, who had been carried off by
Ravan, king of the giants, and sovereign of
that Island.

Probably the climate indisposes Europeans
from making exertions, but it is surprising that
there is not more attention paid to horticulture,
and ornamental planting by the inhabitants of

Bombay.   A few cabbages and English vegetables seem to bound their ambition.   In general,
the excuse is, that gardening, on account of
the immense quantity of water which is requisite, is very expensive.   It is difficult, however,
to believe that irrigation would be more costly
than the fuel which is used in our hot-houses
and conservatories in England, and which
however does not prevent individuals from indulging in exotic flowers and fruits.   In India,
seeds and plants are generally raised by laying
them positively under water; small trenches are
made round the roots, or the ground is laid out
in small compartments, which are surrounded
with mounds of earth, and it is the chief occupation of the cultivator, or the Mollee, as
the gardener is called, to fill these with water;
he makes a small opening to admit the stream,
and when the ground of one enclosure is completely filled and saturated, he then conducts it to
another and another, either using a hoe for the
purpose, or with his foot forming the aperture,
and reminding one of Moses' description of a
similar custom in Egypt, 1451 years before
Christ; and which, such are the unchangeable
manners of Oriental Countries, is still practised there as well as in India, though more
than three thousand years have elapsed since
the Lawgiver of the Jews flourished.

" The Land of Egypt from whence ye came out, where thou sowedst thy seed, and water-edst it with thy foot, as a garden of herbs."— Deut. chap. xi. v. 10.

The circumstance of the European inhabitants not being allowed to settle in India, must of course necessarily very much impede their either building or planting; for it is a mortifying thing to think that their labours may be all thrown away upon a stranger, whose first act may possibly be to pull down the edifices, and to root up plants which have given them so much trouble to raise, and which they have viewed with parental fondness. Among the denunciations of Divine vengeance upon the Jews for disobedience, it is expressly specified, that "They shall build a house, and not dwell therein; they shall plant a vineyard, and shall not gather the grapes thereof." This is, however, very frequently the case in India, and it would consequently be an act of folly to expend much care or money on possessions of such uncertain tenure.

In Bombay, however, where the principal civilians chiefly reside, and also those favoured few among the military who obtain staff appointments, and lucrative situations, and who probably intend to remain several years in India, it is surprising that more attention is not paid to

gardening; for in ten or twenty years, which
is a moderate calculation of time for a residence
in India, they would have a chance of seeing
trees of their own planting come to perfection.
At present, with the exception of a few individuals who have better taste, a few flowering
shrubs immediately in front of the Bungalow,
are all that are to be seen on the Island of
Bombay in general, and sometimes not even so
much.

Among those frequently cultivated in ornamental gardening in the Island of Bombay, is
the golden Mohur, which with its light acacia-
like leaves, showy blossoms, and long and airy
anthers, rising some inches above the corolla,
now of deep crimson, now of orange hue, with
golden variety, or with light yellow flowers,
surprises and delights the beholder with the
multiplicity of its colours.

The beautiful oleander, or almond - tree,
which, even in Italy, seems to be considered
as a somewhat delicate plant, here flourishes as
a common garden shrub. The magnificent hibiscus, with its deep-hued double crimson blossoms, which show so gaily amongst its green
foliage, or with its delicately white flowers, at
once astonishes by its grandeur, and pleases by
its beauty. There are also the Malabar creeper,
with its palmated leaves, and bell-shaped co-

rolla, hanging in elegant festoons, and tapestrying the walls of buildings with its delicate foliage,—the Ceylon creeper, with its beautiful blossoms of brilliant blue,—and occasionally China and other rose trees, which take the imagination to the Islands of the West.

The Gloriosa superba, and the Hoya carnosa, the inhabitants of our hot-houses, are here to be seen flourishing in open air; also the Mogrey, or the Indian jessamine, with its powerful and almost overcoming perfumes, with which the Hindoos love to adorn themselves; the men ornamenting their turbans, and the women decorating their hair therewith, or wearing chains of them as necklaces round their throats.

There are also the Indian fig, with its prickly leaves; the Palma Christi, or Ricinus communis, from which the castor oil is extracted, and whose seeds are given to female buffaloes to increase their milk; here too is the milk bush, a species of Euphorbia, of which impenetrable and impervious fences are composed.

The Neem is most peculiarly light and elegant in its appearance, somewhat resembling a young acacia or mountain ash, whilst its clusters of flowers are not dissimilar to those of the lilac, and are delightfully fragrant; as are the yellow tufts of the Bau-

bool (Acacia Arabica), from which tree a gum
is obtained, which is highly nutritious, and
which is eaten by the poorer natives as food.
Tulip trees, with their massy foliage, and
variously-coloured corollas, that with purple
and golden magnificence delight the eye, are
planted on each side of many of the public
roads, and will in time form noble avenues.
The Mango (Mangifera Indica), is not unlike
an ilex in appearance, and its leaves are of the
deepest green. The tops of this tree form a
considerable feature in Indian landscapes, and it
is considered a charity to plant them ; an act of
benevolence which is frequently performed by
the pious Hindoo. The fruit is something between a plum and an apricot, and has not unfrequently, to use Dr. Borthwick Gilchrist's
grandiloquous phrase, " a sad terebenthine
taste," which is, at first, very disagreeable.
Those who are partial to them, on first landing,
sometimes exceed in the use of them, and
prickly heat, and other disorders ensue in consequence. The mango of Mazagong, a town or
village in Bombay, is famed throughout the
East. In the reign of Shah Jehan, an abundant and fresh supply of this fruit was ensured
for his use by couriers, who were stationed between Delhi and the Mahratta coast ; and it is
said, that the parent-tree of this fine species,

from which all the others have been grafted, is, during the fruit season, honoured by a guard of Sepoys. Moore's fascinating Lalla Rookh, has given them equal celebrity in the West. Who could ever hear or eat a mango of Mazagong, without thinking of the disappointment of the learned Chamberlain Fadlaleen when the couriers failed in their duty, and when the constant supply of mangoes for the royal table, by some cruel irregularity was not forthcoming: for " to eat any mangoes but those of Mazagong, was, of course, impossible."

The tamarind is a beautiful tree, something resembling an elm, and it has all the lightness and elegance of a youthful acacia. Its fruit is of a darker colour and is drier than the West Indian ; its pods are twice as long,— and, as seen hanging upon the tree, they are not unlike those of beans in appearance. The sea-loving cocoanut-tree (Cocos nucifera,) forms a striking feature in the Island of Bombay ; and as there are numerous plantations of it, and every individual plant pays a tax to government, a considerable revenue must be thereby produced. To the natives it is invaluable, as its fruit is constantly introduced in their curries —coir cordage is manufactured from the fibrous covering of the nut, it furnishes oil for their lamps, thatch for their huts, a cloak in rainy weather, and the spirit so well known, toddy. It is curious of a morning to see this last article collected. Small steps are cut in the tree, up which the toddy-gatherer clambers quite to the top with the utmost ease, the liquor being produced by an incision made there, and it is not unpleasant in an unfermented state before sunrise. Rafters, water-pipes, fuel, and a substitute for paper, are also afforded by certain species of palms. Some people do not admire the cocoanut-tree, and perhaps on the Malabar shores, as a vessel slowly coasts up and down, it is almost tiring to see so much of it ; but the tall and airy cocoa, either singly dancing aloft in the air, or presenting, *en masse*, a continuous shade, the stems resembling the pillars of a gothic cathedral, must always be interesting, and nothing can exceed the beauty of the more youthful ones, just throwing out its branchy leaves, with a graceful and coquettish air, like a young belle in the pride of her charms, claiming, and ready to receive the homage of mankind, to her light and wavy elegance. The taller palmyra, or brab-tree, with its broad fan-shaped leaves standing on high, and crowning the exalted summits of the hills, seems proudly to aspire to reach to heaven ; but the date tree here is apparently of an inferior species, seldom bears fruit, and has not the lofty cha-

racter it assumes in Egypt and Arabia. The
areca palm, or betelnut-tree, (areca catechu)*
which is cultivated in many parts of India, but
which flourishes particularly in the Tiperah dis-
trict in Bengal, on the banks of the Megna, and
grows spontaneously on the hills in the Con-
can and North Canara, furnishes the nut, which,
mixed with betel leaf (piper betel,) and quick
lime (or chunam,) forms the composition which
the Hindoos are constantly masticating. The
bamboos, (Bambusa arundinecea,) which are, in
reality, nothing but reeds, in the space of a few
months grow to an enormous height, and have
somewhat the appearance of osiers. The famous walking-sticks are formed of the first and
smaller shoots, and the larger are employed in
the construction of buildings, and in furniture.
The plantain, or banana, with its broad and
gracefully hanging leaf, two or three yards
long, when first opened, is of the most delightfully fresh and vivid green imaginable. The
youthful foliage is wrapt up so carefully, that
as it gradually unfolds, it presents a pleasing
spectacle of the care Nature takes of her productions. But the glory of India is the
Sacred Banyan, the Indian fig-tree, Ficus

* The extract called *Cult* by the natives, *Cutch* by the
English, is obtained from the inner wood of the Acacia
Catechu.

Indica, or the Ficus Religiosa of Linnæus.
This giant of the forest, or rather forest in
itself, charitably extends its branches in every
direction, and throwing out new shoots, which
fall to the ground and there take root,
without separating from the parent tree, it
forms a continuous and a delightful. shade,
and provides a home and a shelter for the
houseless native. It is said to derive its name
of Banyan from the adoration which that caste
pays to it, who paint it daily, make offerings of
rice, and pray to it. Pennant says, it is called
the pagod tree, and tree of councils, because
idols are placed under its shade, and councils
held beneath its branches. In some places it
is believed to be the haunt of spectres, as the
ancient oaks of Wales have been of fairies.
Pillars of stone, and posts elegantly carved,
and ornamented with the most beautiful por-
celain to supply the use of mirrors, are occasionally placed under its shade.

Universal veneration is also paid all over
India to the Peepul-tree, or wild fig-tree,
(Ficus Religiosus,) which, though it has no
connection with the Banyan, is called and considered by the natives as its wife. A late
traveller mentions, that his suite, who were in
want of fire-wood, were not allowed to touch
its sacred branches, and a considerable dispute

arose between them and the natives in consequence. Spirits are supposed to delight in the
Peepul, and he was informed that an earthen
pot hanging on the tree, was brought thither
by some person whose father was dead, that
the ghost might drink! But I must have tired
you with this enumeration, and I will therefore
defer any farther account of Hindoostanee productions till another letter. Adieu!

LETTER XLI.

Vegetable productions of Bombay.—Fruits.—Rice Fields.—
Animals. — The Horse.— Buffalo. — Squirrel.— Baya or
Grosbeak.—Fire-flies and other Insects.

BOMBAY is famed all over the East for its
onions, which are certainly of a very superior
species to our western ones. They are of immense size, and so mild as to be by no means
unpleasant in taste, and they have not that very
disagreeable and almost unbearable smell that the
English onions have. The sweet potato is much
used, and the common potato, though of late introduction, is gaining ground in India, and it is
said, that the prejudice once entertained against
it by the natives is quickly passing away. The
yam (Dioscorea), and the brinjal, or egg-plant,

(Solanum Melongena,) together with the banda,
or bendy, (Hibiscus esculentus) frequently make
their appearance at table.   This last is a very
excellent and delicate vegetable ; it is a pod, or
rather capsule, three or four inches in length,
and the seeds within are quite equal to our
young peas, which they somewhat resemble.
Cardamoms (Amomum repens) and Chili pepper (Græcum Capsacum) are put down as things
of course, to eat at pleasure, with that never-
failing dish the curry.

  " Plantains, the golden and the green," are
amongst the fruits in most common use among
the natives.   I have described the tree in my
last letter ; the flower, of the class Pentandria, is
comparatively small ; the fruit is from three to
six inches long, and when the exterior skin is
stripped off, the interior presents a yellowish
white substance, very nutritive and wholesome,
something between an apricot and a pear in
taste, but perhaps superior to either ; eaten
with or without milk, it forms an excellent
breakfast for those who cannot take heavier food
in this hot country.   The custard-apple, in the
opinion of many, should rank next in delicacy.
Is is a curious-looking fruit, with a green and
rough-coated exterior ; but the interior contains
a number of dark seeds, imbedded in a cream-
like substance, very much resembling custard in

taste. The pompelmose, or shaddock, (Malus aurantia,) the sweet-lime, and the pomegranate, are very grateful and refreshing in so sultry a climate. The oranges, principally of the species which is sometimes termed mandarine, are of an inferior sort, and the grapes are not particularly good, though up the country they are remarkably fine. There are also water-melons (Angurca Citrullus), guavas (Psiduim), something like pears in appearance, and the papaw. The Jaca, or Jack-tree (Artocarpus integrifolia), is of considerable size, and the fruit is of enormous dimensions. Of its wood, very pretty furniture is made, in colour resembling satin-wood when quite new, and afterwards assuming the appearance of light mahogany.

The paddy, or rice fields, make a considerable figure at Bombay, and are of a most beautiful vivid green, but it is not considered to be wholesome to live in their vicinity. From the common hemp, the intoxicating liquor called *bang* is produced, and the Juarree (Holcus Sorghum) and Bajaree (Holcus spicatus) are used in various ways. But, I am ashamed to say, I know but little of the Indian agriculture, and I will therefore not attempt to give you information, which might prove erroneous.

The horses at Bombay are, generally speaking, Arabs, and they are peculiarly light, active,

and elegant, but so small, that the cart-horses
in England would appear like elephants in
comparison. The Braminee bull is occasionally
seen with the hunch between the shoulders,
perfectly tame, stalking about in the bazaars,
and the native carts or hackerys are invariably
drawn by oxen, of a somewhat diminutive size.*
Frequently are to be met herds of that stupid,
awkward, and uncouth animal the Buffalo,
lounging leisurely along, with its horns sometimes tightly curled up, in the smallest possible compass, like the tendrils of a vine, or extended to an immense and almost inconvenient
distance, so that the tips are nearly two yards
apart. The milk is used, and the flesh occasionally eaten, but there appears to be a prejudice against the latter, which is seldom used
at the Presidency.

The squirrels are beautifully marked with
dark stripes, and are the prettiest little animals
imaginable. They are exceedingly timid, but
yet can be tamed to a certain degree; they
used frequently to come into the room when
we were at our meals, and eat up the crumbs on
the floor; but the slightest noise or movement
would send them scampering off instantaneous-

* The oxen of Guzerat, which are occasionally brought
down to Bombay by wealthy natives, are of a different breed,
and are very large and fine.

ly to their homes. We used often to amuse ourselves by throwing nuts and cakes to them, and, when at a respectful distance, they had no objection to accept of, and to avail themselves of our proffered civilities. Pennant observes that " the brute creation in the Torrid Zone, are more at enmity with one another than in other climes," and his remark appears to be correct, for these shy, timid, little things were the most quarrelsome creatures imaginable, and would frequently pursue one another most furiously, in order to take by force the other's provisions, even when they had plenty of their own; the strongest generally proved a sad tyrant. The mus Malabarecus or Bandecoot rat is of immense size, and is very destructive, as is the musk-rat, which though smaller, leaves a disagreeable smell wherever it goes; and if perchance it pass over a bottle of wine with its cork unsealed, it acquires so unpleasant a flavour as to be undrinkable. The mongoose or ichneumon, (Viverra Ichneumon) which destroys the crocodile's eggs in Egypt, does the same to the alligator's in India; it resembles an immense lizard, and it is sometimes kept in private families for amusement.

I was particularly pleased with the Hindoostanee baya, a sort of grosbeak or sparrow, (Loxia Phillippina;) of the passerine order, and of the hang-nest tribe. The Malabarese call it Olomari, the Bengalese, Babiu, and its Sanscrit name is Berbere. This bird is of a small size, with yellowish brown plumage, yellowish head and feet, light-coloured breast and thick conical bill. It feeds on insects, is wonderfully sagacious and docile, and is easily taught to fetch and carry. The youthful lovers train the bird, and teach it by signs that it understands to pluck off thin plates of gold, called *ticas*, which the young Hindoo women wear slightly fixed between their eyes ; and as they pass through the streets, the roguish baya steals them, and brings them in triumph to his master. If a ring be dropped into a deep well, and a signal given, the baya will fly down with great celerity, and catching it before it reaches the water, bring it exultingly up to the owner ; and it is asserted, that if a house be shown it once or twice, it will, on proper signs being made, carry a note thither immediately. From this docility, it is, of course, a great favourite in Hindoostan. It suspends its curiously flask-shaped nests to the branches of cocoanut-trees, palmyras, and Indian figs, generally prefering one that overhangs a well or rivulet, perhaps on account of the superior security which is thereby ensured. It is constructed of grass

and the fibres of plants, and subdivided into
three chambers or divisions.   In the outermost
or porch, the male bird, very properly, takes his
station, and mounts guard ; in the centre, the
female hatches her eggs, which resemble pearls ;
and the inmost compartment is appropriated to
the young.   This ingenious domicile is attached
to the extremity of a slender branch, by means
of a cord half a yard long, with the entrance
downwards, in order to secure its inhabitants
from snakes and beasts of prey ; and though it of
course rocks with every breath of wind, it very
seldom sustains any injury, indeed, I only remember having seen one blown down, though
the trees close to our house were covered with
these nests.   A little tough clay, or cow's dung,
is always stuck against one side of the porch, on
which are fixed fire flies, which, it is said, are
caught, and thus imprisoned by the ingenious
baya, in order to give light to his dwelling.
But those who have no respect for traditions
and popular belief, whilst they cannot deny
that the fire flies are found thus confined,
which is an indubitable fact, yet choose to ex-
plain away this elegant device of the baya for
illuminating his airy mansion, by supposing
they are merely caught by him and placed
there for food.   Possibly the brilliancy of the

fire fly (Lampyris), is like the dazzling quali-
ties of men, which, too frequently, only serve
to hurry the owner to destruction.

It is beautiful of an evening to see the fire
flies glittering among the spreading branches of
the banyan, or sporting about the light and airy
tamarind trees, which are sometimes so covered
with them, as to appear like pyramids of light.
Whilst the stars are shining in their majesty in
the blue ethereal sky, and the planets moving
in mystic dance in the firmament above, quick
glancing in every direction below, may be seen
myriads of these luminous insects, as if seeking
to imitate the movements of the heavenly orbs,
or as if the denizens of Heaven themselves had
left their golden houses to visit this nether
sphere.

The musquitos are dreadful torments to the
new arrivals from Europe, and without a net,
sleep would be sought in vain. The flies are
also sad nuisances, and hand punkahs during
meals are frequently indispensably necessary to
drive away the swarms that incessantly attack
the food. Cockroaches are a great annoyance
to the merchants of Bombay, as they often infest their godowns or warehouses, and commit
great devastations among their goods, destroying leather articles, books, &c. most mercilessly.
In damp places, centipedes and scorpions are

not unfrequently found, but they are not of very frequent occurrence elsewhere. I only once remember to have actually seen one of the latter alive, which was crawling deliberately up C——'s dress. I at first thought it was a large spider, and I was indeed somewhat startled and alarmed, when on calling his attention to it, I found the venomous nature of the creature.

The great scourge of India, however, are the white ants, of which I have a dreadful story to tell hereafter, being, from sad experience, well calculated to bear testimony to this insect's powers of destruction, which certainly exceed all credibility, and try the patience of the sufferers from their devastations very severely; but the Indian proverb says, " Every European coming to India, learns patience if he has it not, and loses it, if he has," and mine was very severely put to the test, as I am sure you will allow, when you hear of my losses from these terrible little plagues.

LETTER XLII.

Devastation caused by Termites or White Ants.—Their extraordinary Nests, and powers of destruction.—Black Ants.—Immense size of their Nests.—Fish, Bumbelo, Pomfret, and Prawns. — Bazaar. — Jungle Fowl.—Our Poultry of Indian origin.—Turkey and Ham, never-failing dishes at Bombay.—Rage for European Articles.—Native China never used by the English.

AFTER we had left Chintz Poglie, and were established in our own house, our first care was to send for our things from the Custom House. We had sent our carriage and the greater part of our heavy articles by sea, and they had arrived at Bombay a short time previous to ourselves. What was my consternation on being informed that the greater part of them were utterly destroyed by white ants! At first I thought it was a joke, but too soon was I convinced of the dire reality of the fact. In the Custom House, many of the packages had been somewhat carelessly placed upon the ground in the godowns, the Indian term for warehouse, and the ants coming up from below, had, for some weeks, been very leisurely carrying on their devastations, without "let or molestation." Several trunks which had left England, properly packed, and full of valuable books, maps, and dresses, now presented a melancholy spectacle of shreds and rags, or a mass of dirt; for, by mastication, the white ant converts every thing into a sort of clay, which it employs in the construction of its own habitation. The East India Company would perhaps be alarmed, were they to hear that the white ants had devoured and eaten up India, which they actually had done:

> " A river and a sea,
> Were to them a dish of tea,
> And a kingdom, bread and butter."

but it was not, however, the Company's, but our property, which had thus suffered, in the shape of a fine map of the country. A curious circumstance occurred, which, in monkish days would have served for a miracle, and certainly may compete with the wonderful Mahometan one of a similar description. Among several books that were destroyed, was a Stereotype pocket Testament, and, it is a fact, that, though the cover and the whole of the margin were nibbled and injured, not one word of the sacred text had been touched. This was probably owing to something peculiar in the composition of the ink, but it certainly was singular.

The white ants are, perhaps, the most ingenious and surprising artificers in the world.

2 D 2

They invariably carry on their manœuvres under cover; and their first care seems to be, to
conceal their proceedings from the garish eye
of day. Covered communications and passages, which are, comparatively speaking, quite
equal to the fortifications at Malta, and unin-
terrupted and continuous lines of works may
be often traced, extending to immense distances.
They are regular underminers, and carry on
their labours so cleverly and secretly, that the
sufferer from their devastations has no idea of
what is going on, till he is taught by experience to be always on the *qui vive* against their
insidious attacks. One evening when we were
engaged in conversation, a strange cracking sort
of noise was heard in the room, for which, for
some time we could not account, till at length,
one of the party, whose curiosity was greatly
excited, by dint of searching, discovered it proceeded from behind one of the doors, and there
were the white ants busily at work, carrying
their labours on all round the wood-work of
the door-way. The sound arose from some of
their fortifications having given way, on having been accidentally touched. They appear
to be endued with so much sagacity and intelligence, that it is quite astonishing; and it
is really very amusing to see them at work.
If any of their covered communications are

injured or destroyed, the first white ant that comes that way, stops, considers for half a second, then immediately goes back, and in two or three minutes returns with a detachment of workmen, who fall to work and speedily repair the breaches that have been made. They seem to have a power of mastication, and they produce a sort of moist clay from their mouths, which, after a short exposure to the air, becomes dry and hard, and the spectator sees nothing but a slight thread of earth, which the novice would consider to be quite accidental, and of no consequence. Satisfied with having a shelter from curious eyes, they seldom attack the exterior of any thing, but cunningly work upon the interior; and timbers of houses, furniture, and books which are not frequently moved, may be completely destroyed, whilst their outside looks as well as ever. This was the case with our trunks, which appeared uninjured, whilst their contents were completely ruined.

Though called an ant, these termites have very little the appearance of one; they rather look like small maggots or grains of rice, and they have a queen, or female ant, like the bees, —unless this is destroyed, it is hopeless ever to attempt to get rid of them; but when this is secured, they vanish of themselves; therefore in

digging up their nests, the first object should be
to obtain possession of Her Majesty. A nest,
the progress of which we had amused ourselves
with watching for some days, was one evening
covered with winged insects, and on the following morning, a light, burning in the room, was
completely covered with them; on this being
moved they swarmed in every direction. After
settling in every part of the house, their wings,
which were about an inch long, and very much
resembled ash keys in colour and appearance,
and like gauze in substance, fell off, and were
strewed all over the floor. You may believe
that I was considerably alarmed for the safety
of our dwelling, which I expected would be
undermined and destroyed instantaneously, but
immediate precautions were taken to prevent
this impending danger, and we took care never
to indulge in such benevolent Banyan-like feelings again, as to allow the white ants undis-
turbedly to work under our roof.

As these insects will literally destroy a trunk
and its contents in one night, boxes should
never be placed upon the floor, nor even on
blocks of wood; stones and glass bottles are
the best things to put under them, but even
then they require occasional inspection, as these
indefatigable creatures will surmount even these

obstacles, and carry a communication over them to the articles above.

Wherever the black-ant abounds, it is said that the white sort disappears; for, with insects as with men, the strongest invariably wins the day, and the little destructive termites are in their turn destroyed by their black brethren. Wonderful stories are narrated of the latter, and really the size of their nests exceeds all credibility. Near Poorbunder, in Guzerat, C——— has seen in waste lands, which had been for years out of cultivation, nests of seven feet and a half high, which he ascertained by actually measuring them himself; as many in diameter, and probably more than twenty feet in circumference.* The black-ant appears

* Bishop Heber, in his Journal, mentions having seen similarly enormous ant-hills, and observes, that " the pyramids, when the comparative bulk of the insects which reared *them* is taken into the estimate, are as nothing to the works of these termites. The counterpart of one of these hills would be, if a nation should set to work to build up an artificial Snowdon, and bore it full of holes and galleries." He imagines, that the account alluded to by Lucian, as given by Ctesias, of " monstrous ants in India as large as foxes," originated in the stupendous fabrics which they rear, and which probably were supposed to have been the workmanship of a larger animal than the actual diminutive architect. There is a ridiculous story told in the East, of a box of dollars having vanished, and its disappearance being gravely attributed to its having been eaten up by the ants; upon

to be of a larger and stronger species than our common ant, and was quite different from our little tormenters in the George Cruttenden, who used to bite so dreadfully. They occasionally infest the godowns where sugar and sweet things are kept, as in England, but we never found them otherwise injurious, and they are far pleasanter inmates in a house than their treacherous, deceitful, and undermining brethren.

Bombay is well supplied with fish, and the Bumbelo is found in no other part of the world, than in its harbour. This is a sort of sand eel, which is eaten both in a fresh and dried state, and usually appears at breakfast, with a dish of rice, butter, and split pease, which, from being coloured with turmeric, is perfectly yellow, and is termed kedgaree. The Pomfret is remarkably delicate and fine upon this coast; and it was to eat the Pomfret of Bombay that the epicure Quin seriously projected a voyage to India. The prawns are remarkably fine, and are of a most magnificent size; they are called gingle by the natives, and are excellent, whether served up fresh, or eaten as a curry.

which, several files were sent from England to file their teeth ; but, though the ants had not exactly devoured, they had buried the money, which was subsequently found in their nest.

The market, or, as they would say, the Bazaar of Bombay, is very well supplied with provisions. Vegetables are brought from Salsette, now connected with Bombay by a causeway, which was begun in 1797 and was completed by the Governor, Mr. Duncan, in 1805; this, though a great convenience to the inhabitants, is considered by some persons to have injured the harbour. Butcher's-meat is not remarkably good; the mutton, unless well fed, is apt to be rather tough, but the kid is excellent. The being necessarily eaten the same day that it is killed, is probably one reason why the meat in India is not equal to our English; this is, however, of no great consequence, for, in so hot a country, to eat animal food at all is almost out of the question.

Poultry is abundant at Bombay, and, when well fed, which is equally necessary every where, the chickens are very fine. It is curious, that a bird which is now so common in England, where it has become almost naturalized, should have derived its origin from the distant country of India. Our common fowl is a native of Hindoostan, and is found in a state of nature and quite wild in the jungles of Malabar, from whence it is termed the jungle bird. The plumage of the cock is very magnificent; of a dark hue burnished with red and gold.

It is mentioned by Aristophanes, who calls it
the Persian bird, remarking that it enjoyed
that kingdom before Darius and Megabyzus,
and it was probably imported into Britain by
the Phœnicians. They were established in our
distant island in the time of Julius Cæsar, who
found them there; but he however states, that
it was not eaten by the natives, and, indeed,
that it was forbidden food. There is a very
singular species of fowl in India, the bones
of which are perfectly black; it certainly has
not a very prepossessing appearance, but the
flesh is singularly white and delicate notwithstanding.

Turkey, with its attendant ham, is a never-
failing party dish in India, and a dinner would
scarcely be deemed a dinner without one, nay,
sometimes two smoking on the board. Red-
legged partridges, quails, and snipes are occasionally seen at Bombay, but the island is too
small to furnish any quantity of game, or
amusement to the sportsman. Field sports are,
however, quite the rage at the out-stations, and
an abundance and a variety of birds are to be
found in different parts of the country. The
Chinese and the Portuguese likewise eat frogs,
which are large and numerous, and make a
tremendous noise in the swampy and marshy
parts of Bombay.

Tongues, hams, cheeses, and sweetmeats are imported from England; and it is laughable to see how much store is set by raspberry and strawberry jam; but the difficulty of obtaining an article, and the distance whence it comes, wonderfully enhance its worth. English things are considered in Bombay, to be of far more value than Indian.

What would the old dowagers of England, who doat so much on real china, say, if they were to hear that it is considered *mauvais ton* to use it in India. There, Worcester must be employed, because it is not so easily procured; and I have positively heard a very sensible lady apologizing for being so unfashionable as to have native china at her tea-table. How would the china-fanciers of Great Britain delight in the beautiful little cups in which the natives drink their coffee, but which in India, the English reject with disdain, and in the fine jars which are here used for the most ordinary purposes! However, when at Rome, one must do as they do at Rome, and no one at Bombay could venture to make use of Asiatic china, without running the risk of its being thought that he was too poor to purchase European.

LETTER XLIII.

House-rent at Bombay.—Bungalow.—Bee-hive.—Land and
Sea breezes.—Shipping and trade at Bombay.—English
Articles scarce in India.

HOUSE-rent in Bombay is somewhat high ;
two or three thousand rupees are very frequently given per annum for an unfurnished house,
of moderate size, in by no means an extensive
compound, as the enclosure or grounds in which
it stands, is termed.   This sum, on a rough
calculation, allowing two shillings to the rupee,
which is more than its actual value, though
much less than it is nominally worth, would be,
from two to three hundred pounds a year.

We arrived during the monsoon, at which
period all the families take up their abode in regular houses.   Many of such families during the
fair season, reside in temporary bungalows, and
tents pitched upon the esplanade.   From this
circumstance there was no very great variety
of vacant mansions, from which to make a
selection ; however, we had no cause to complain of that which we hired.   The exterior
was certainly not very magnificent, and looked

more like a nest of detached cottages or barns, or like an apiary, rather than a gentleman's house; "The Bee-hive," indeed, was its actual denomination.) The interior was so constructed as to resemble a suit of tents, and, handsomely fitted up, would have been extremely elegant.

Our bungalow was situated on a tongue of land, between two small bays, and, at spring-tides, our compound was surrounded on three sides, by the Indian Ocean, whilst on the fourth, rose a range of gently swelling hills, which were at this time tapestried with verdure, and topped with lofty palmyras, and wavy date-trees. It is on the western side of the Island, at the foot of Malabar hill, at the extremity of which headland is one of the Government residencies, where the Governor generally takes up his abode during the hot season. We were within a stone's throw of the sea, " the Sea of India, whose bottom is rich with pearls and ambergris, whose mountains of the coast are stored with gold and precious stones, whose gulfs breed creatures that yield ivory, and among the plants of whose shores are ebony, red wood, and the wood of Haizar, aloes, camphor, cloves, sandal wood, and all other spices, and aromatics; where parrots and peacocks are birds of the forest, and musk and civet are collected upon the lands." And it was a source of never-failing delight to gaze at the mighty expanse of water,—to mark the fitful changes of colour produced by the coming breeze, or the passing cloud—and to watch the bright waves sparkling in the sun, and petulantly dashing over the neighbouring rocks, or stealing gently and gradually on, rippling and eddying round the pebbles on the shore.

A noble verandah, projecting in front of our sitting rooms, afforded us at once a protection from the ardent rays of the sun, and presented a delightful promenade at all hours of the day, and here often, as I paced up and down, whilst listening to the hoarse resounding surges of the Indian Ocean, which lashed the walls of our compound, have I flown westward in idea, and losing myself in pleasing yet half melancholy reveries, thought down hours to minutes, in musing on our friends in England.

The land and sea breezes which alternately blow in the tropics at stated hours, delightfully attemper the ardent heat of the climate. Exposure to the former, however, which sets in at even-tide, is considered very dangerous, and fevers are frequently occasioned thereby. The latter prevails during the day, and commences about ten o'clock in the morning. This phœnomenon is produced by the rarefaction of the atmosphere over the land, by intense heat during the day, when the air over the sea, cooled by the immense body of water, rushes in from thence, and thus produces the sea breeze. The reverse takes place at night, when, it being warmer on the sea than on the land, the wind blows in the opposite direction; but, though accounted for, and produced by natural causes, it must be considered as a merciful dispensation of Providence : in a tropical country, and when oppressed with heat, it is not easy to describe with what delight the rising breeze is hailed and welcomed.

During the monsoon, native vessels never leave the harbour, but soon after cocoanut day, which this year, (1826) took place on the 17th of August, we daily saw numbers of ships, either singly or in fleets, sailing up and down the coast. They trade to all the ports between Cape Comorin and the Gulf of Cutch, and even cross the sea to Muscat and the Arabian Gulf. Many of the larger vessels, will, during the eight fair months, that is, from October to May, perform five or six trips to Surat, Demaun, Broach, Cambay, Jumboseir, and Mandavie, carrying thither the produce of Europe, Bengal, and China, and bringing back from these ports, where many of the owners reside, cotton, ghee (clarified butter,) wheat, timber, firewood, &c. The capital employed in the northen trade is said to be immense, and certainly not under 150 lacks of rupees, including cotton to double that amount. In 1820, the number of vessels of different denominations, from ten to one hundred and seventy-five ton, registered as being employed in it, is said to have amounted to 730, and the tonnage to 39,978 ; and besides these, there were several smaller boats, from two to thirty-seven ton, trading in firewood, hay, &c., whose total burthen was 6,580 tons. There are, likewise, boats even of a still less description, that make occasional trips to Bassein and Choul.

The ships from the South bring timber, pepper, cocoanuts, and corn from Malabar; rice and cotton from Canara; and hemp, pulse, firewood, and minor articles form the Southern trade. The principal export from Bombay, is cotton; but the quantity is said to fluctuate remarkably. In 1818, it amounted to 208,900 bales; in 1819, to 105,340; and in 1820, to 20,171. Before the fire at Bombay, in 1823, the bales of cotton used to be deposited on the green; but the merchants not being allowed to place them there now, they are placed upon, and occupy a part of the esplanade; the screwing the cotton is said to be very curious, 1,500 pounds being compressed into fifty feet, or one ton.

For the European market, Bombay is an excellent place to procure gums and drugs of all sorts, Mocha coffee, barilla, cornelians, agates, and Surat cotton goods. The China articles appear to be very high, and, comparatively speaking, even dearer than they would be in London; but the native merchants and retail traders are sad extortioners, and impose dreadfully on strangers, frequently asking twice as much as they will ultimately take, so that those who dislike haggling and bargaining, pay dearly for their delicacy, or perhaps I should rather say, indolence; it being a great exertion in India, to argue and battle a point with a bora or tradesman.

Since Poonah was in the hands of the English, the Bombay merchants complain that the inland commerce is entirely ruined; for, in the days of the Peishwah, immense orders used to be sent down from that court, and from those of other potentates of the interior; but now the money-getting, money-loving English, prudently keep their cash till they return to their native land. At an out-station, such as Poonah, comfort is all that a wise person would aim at;

show is out of the question, and indeed would be perfectly ridiculous.

In 1820, the same authority which has supplied me with information concerning the tonnage and cotton bales, things which you will perhaps think something out of my line, observes, that Bombay was but indifferently supplied with European luxuries and conveniences. From our own experience I can fully confirm this account, and state that, in 1826 and 1828, it certainly was not improved in this particular, for, there is scarcely a country shop in England, but would exhibit a better assortment of goods than is ordinarily to be seen at the most superior in Bombay. The English articles are generally very dear and very bad, with the exception of calicos and cambric-muslins, which may be procured at a more reasonable rate. There are but few English shopkeepers at Bombay, the retail trade there being principally in the hands of Parsees, and entirely so up the country. At one of the out-stations, where we spent a year, there were literally no English things at all, and we were obliged to employ an agent at the Presidency to furnish us with them. Indeed we generally found it cheaper to send to England at once, for what we wanted, particularly for stationery and articles of dress of every description. Leather shoes and boots, hats and cutlery, were particularly dear and bad, and we used frequently to wish that some of our distressed manufacturers would send us some of the things they were selling under prime cost at home. They talk in England of the markets in India being overstocked, but if goods are exported to the Presidencies, they certainly stay there; or, as it is sometimes stated in England, are sent back again, for they do not circulate freely through the country at present—at least not on the Bombay side—nor will they, probably, till more English settle in the interior, so as to trade and compete with the Parsees, who appear to enjoy a sort of monopoly of the inland commerce, on the western side of India.

It would be such a convenience to residents in India to be able to procure English articles with facility, that upon their account, independent of the benefit it would be of to our starving manufacturers at home, it appears almost a pity that British tradesmen should not be rather invited, than prevented from settling in the remote provinces of India.

LETTER XLIV.

Cocoanut-day at Bombay.—Native Manners not to be properly appreciated at the Presidency.—Cocoanut-day as celebrated at Poorbunder.—Indian Trade mentioned in the Bible.—Commerce perhaps intended as a means of Christianizing the World. — Trade in the Red Sea.— Coffee of Mocha.—Coffee said not to be known to the Ancients.

COCOANUT-DAY is a great festival with the Hindoos, which occurs at the full-moon, at the breaking up of the monsoon, when the sea is supposed to have become open for navigation. Upon that day, the 17th of August, about sunset, an immense number of persons collected upon the esplanade at Bombay to witness the ceremony used on the occasion; the English repaired thither as to a sort of spectacle, and all the principal natives appeared in their carriages, and in very magnificent dresses, in honour of the day, with a great profusion and display of pearls and jewels. At a certain hour, one of the principal Bramins, advancing a little way into the sea, threw a gilt cocoanut into the water, which was a signal for the multitude to follow his example, and thousands of cocoa-nuts were instantaneously seen swimming in every direction, every one being eager to make his offering.

At Bombay, however, the manners and customs of the Hindoos are not to be seen in perfection, any more than those of the inhabitants of the interior of other countries can be properly estimated at their sea-port towns, or capitals. There is such a mixture of foreigners, English, Portuguese, Chinese, Parsees, Malays, Arabs, Persians, and Armenians, that the real Hindoos are more distinguishable by the peculiarities of their costume than by any other characteristic. Indeed, those who have only visited the Presidencies, which are the limits of the Oriental travels of a great many English ladies, can have no idea of the interior, and persons who wish to see India, should visit the out-stations, or perhaps, I should rather say, the Native Courts.

At one of these, Poorbunder, on the coast of Guzerat, the chief emporium of that country and Malwa with Arabia and Persia, cocoanutday is kept with great solemnity. The Bramins pronounce a benediction over the cocoanuts, and after staining them with a vermilion paste, they deliver them to the attendant crowd, whose foreheads they likewise mark with the same paste, with a small circular spot, and stick grains of rice upon it. In the even-

ing the Rana* holds a Durbar upon the sea-
coast, sitting upon a carpet surrounded by all
his ministers and chief men, and he makes
presents of turbans to the principal merchants;
and in particular to any new one who has come
thither, which they immediately put on in his
presence. The whole shore is brilliantly illuminated with flambeaux and torches, and at
a certain hour, either when the moon is quite
at the full, or when she crosses the meridian,
the Rana rises, and followed by all his attendants, walks into the sea, into which he casts one
of the sacred cocoanuts, and immediately every
one, following his example, launches one in
also, and the waves are instantly covered with
these nuts, whilst several of the natives fearlessly plunging in, regardless of the eminent
danger of getting their heads broken by the
cocoanuts showering about them in every direction, secure as many of them as they can.
Whether this fruit, after the blessing of the
Bramins, is supposed to possess any particular
virtue I do not know;—but the natives on the
sea shore watching the full moon—the votive
offerings of fruit in honour of the change of
the seasons—and the ocean, which has for
months been vexed by storms and tempests,

* Rana is a title superior to that of Rajah, and is equiva-
lent to that of Emperor.

having now become calm and placid, and open
to navigation, altogether form a scene which
appears to me to be highly poetical and picturesque, and as described by an eye-witness,
must have been very striking.

During the monsoon, as I have before mentioned, a total stop is put to navigation of all
sort, but after this period, vessels from India,
Arabia, and Persia, from Melinda and Zan-
zibar, sail to distant countries, coasting along,
as in the days of King Solomon, whose ships,
992 years B.C. were three years going and returning from Tarshish.

" For the king's ships went to Tarshish with
the servants of Huram ; every three years once
came the ships of Tarshish, bringing gold and
silver, ivory and apes, and peacocks."

This is so exact a description of a native
voyage, and of the commodities procured in
India, that, at the risk of being thought very
presumptuous in differing from Bruce, I must
believe that King Solomon actually traded with
India, and indeed, coasting along in the country
vessels, and stopping for the different winds
and monsoons in the Red Sea, Arabian Gulf,
and Indian Ocean, it would not be easy to
make the voyage shorter even now.

The Indian trade, in all ages a source of
wealth to those by whom it has been carried

on, and which now creates so much interest in the bosoms of speculators, seems to be very distinctly mentioned in numerous places in the Bible, and I must observe, *en passant,* that the more one is in the East, the more is one astonished at the correctness of the delineations of Oriental productions, customs and countries, and with the spirited and graphical descriptions which abound in Sacred Writ.

In the 27th chapter of Ezekiel, there is a sort of regular inventory of the principal articles of the Indian trade, as carried on with Tyre, 588 years before Christ. The passages—" Many Isles were the merchandise of thine hand ; they brought thee for a present horns of ivory and ebony," would almost appear to refer to India, to the Islands of Ceylon, and of the Eastern Archipelago. " Cassia, and calamus were in thy markets ;" if these articles be, as some suppose, cinnamon and sugarcane, they are both productions of the East, as are " all spices, precious stones, and gold."

1491 years before Christ, Moses, as mentioned in the 30th chapter of Genesis, was commanded to make " an holy oil of ointment of pure myrrh, sweet cinnamon, sweet calamus and cassia," and to make a perfume of " sweet spices, stacte, onycha, and galbanum, with pure frankincense," and these all seem to be Indian articles of commerce.* But even still earlier, in the days of Joseph, 1729 years before Christ, the Ishmaelites are represented as " with their camels, bearing spicery, and balm, and myrrh, going to carry it down to Egypt," so that by caravans, or by merchant ships, the productions of India seem to have been, from the very earliest ages, transported to all parts of the civilized world.

It has been supposed that commerce is, in the hands of Providence, only one of the means by which distant nations are brought together, in order to the eventual spread of Christianity all over the face of the earth ; and it would be a pleasing idea that the coffee of Arabia, the spices of India, and the tea of China, humble plants and shrubs in themselves, but which have now become necessaries of life to all the civilized inhabitants of the world, may ultimately lead to the introduction of the knowledge of the Gospel, in the benighted countries that produce them, by inducing the Christian merchant to frequent their shores, for the purposes of trade. Surely we shall have much to answer for, if in pursuit of worldly traffic, we neglect so glorious an opportunity of serving the Lord,

* The Arabians, in whose deserts the Israelites were then wandering, to this day term the Malabar Coast, Belled-el-fol-fol, the pepper country.

and we must expect the vengeance of the
Almighty to fall upon us, if we do not our
best to convert the Gentiles from their idolatry,
when we have an opportunity, in visiting these
and other heathen countries.

The commerce in the Red Sea seems to be
principally, if not entirely carried on by the
native merchants of India. American ships
likewise trade to Mocha, following their example, and endeavouring to participate in a
branch of commerce so lucrative as the coffee
trade. The first time an American ship ever appeared in the Red Sea, was in 1803, but the great
profit of her voyage induced others to follow
her example, and they are said to have injured
the road of Mocha considerably by throwing
over their ballast ; or possibly this deterioration
may be occasioned by the sea retiring there, as
elsewhere in the Arabian Gulf. The Portuguese were the first who opened the Red Sea
to the Europeans, and the useless crusade of
Don Alphonso Albuquerque in 1513, is the
first time we ever heard of Mocha, which is
supposed not to have been in existence four
centuries ago. At the time of the disgraceful
expedition of Suliman Basha against Diu, who
commanded the fleet of the Soldan of Egypt,
Mocha is mentioned in his voyage as being merely a castle, with a Turk for its governor. It

had become the great mart of the trade between India and Egypt, when the English first visited it under Alexander Sharpey in 1609, who traded without injury; but in the following year, Sir Henry Middleton was betrayed and kept prisoner for some time. Niebuhr mentions the English being there in 1738, when the French bombarded the town, to oblige the Dowlah to pay his debts, and to reduce the duties from three to two and a half per cent.; and a short time ago, to chastise the natives for some acts of contumacy, the English sent an expedition against it, which produced several desirable concessions in our favour. The inhabitants of Mocha are not, however, quite cured of their turbulence, for not long after we left Arabia, intelligence reached Bombay of their having regularly besieged the British Residency, when the Surgeon, who behaved with much spirit, having accidentally, or intentionally, shot one of the men who were making forcible *entrée*, they vowed vengeance against him; swore they would have his life, and sent him word that his grave was dug, upon which it was deemed expedient immediately to send him to the Presidency to ensure his safety, as there was every probability that they would have taken some opportunity of putting their threat into execution. Since the clipping and

economical system has come into fashion, the
Residency at Mocha has been given up altogether, and there is now merely a native agent
employed there, as at Djidda, where the native
India merchant-ships winter; from whence it
may be inferred, that the trade in the Red
Sea is not much on the increase; and yet
it is a pity, for, as a modern writer elegantly
observes, "like the rough and russet coat of
the Persian pomegranate, which gives little
promise of the rich and crimson pulp within,
so Arabia, all forbidding as she looks, can
boast of Yemen and her sparkling springs,
of her frankincense and precious gems, her
spices and coffee berries, her luscious dates,
and the honey of the rock." Coffee is scarcely
more a necessary of life to the Arab and the
Turk, than to their Mahometan brethren in
India, and, though I confess I never discovered
its wonderful superiority, that of Mocha seems
to be considered, universally, the finest in the
world. Some, which we procured at that place,
we sent as a present to some friends in England, by whom it was highly prized, and they
have often told me it was peculiarly good,
and infinitely superior to any they could purchase in London under the name of Mocha
coffee.

It is singular, as I have before observed, that

coffee, which is now such a necessary of life in many parts of the world, should be entirely of modern introduction, and some say, that it was not known to the ancients at all, though this seems hardly credible.

END OF THE FIRST VOLUME.